Employee Share Ownership and Impacts on Organizational Value and Behavior

Sara Elouadi
Hassan II University, Casablanca, Morocco

A volume in the Advances in Business Strategy and Competitive Advantage (ABSCA) Book Series

IGI Global
PUBLISHER of TIMELY KNOWLEDGE

Published in the United States of America by
IGI Global
Business Science Reference (an imprint of IGI Global)
701 E. Chocolate Avenue
Hershey PA, USA 17033
Tel: 717-533-8845
Fax: 717-533-8661
E-mail: cust@igi-global.com
Web site: http://www.igi-global.com

Library of Congress Cataloging-in-Publication Data

Names: Elouadi, Sara, 1983- editor.
Title: Employee share ownership and impacts on organizational value and behavior / Sara Elouadi, editor.
Description: Hershey, PA : Business Science Reference, [2022] | Includes bibliographical references and index. | Summary: "This book gathered international feedback on the practice of employee share ownership and its effects on the attitudes and value of companies and its ability to alleviate the financial damage of the Covid-19 epidemic"-- Provided by publisher.
Identifiers: LCCN 2021027676 (print) | LCCN 2021027677 (ebook) | ISBN 9781799885573 (hardcover) | ISBN 9781799885580 (paperback) | ISBN 9781799885597 (ebook)
Subjects: LCSH: Employee ownership. | Organizational behavior. | COVID-19 (Disease)--Economic aspects. | Crisis management.
Classification: LCC HD5650 .E4635 2022 (print) | LCC HD5650 (ebook) | DDC 338.6/9--dc23
LC record available at https://lccn.loc.gov/2021027676
LC ebook record available at https://lccn.loc.gov/2021027677

This book is published in the IGI Global book series Advances in Business Strategy and Competitive Advantage (ABSCA) (ISSN: 2327-3429; eISSN: 2327-3437)

British Cataloguing in Publication Data
A Cataloguing in Publication record for this book is available from the British Library.

Advances in Business Strategy and Competitive Advantage (ABSCA) Book Series

ISSN:2327-3429
EISSN:2327-3437

Editor-in-Chief: Patricia Ordóñez de Pablos, Universidad de Oviedo, Spain

MISSION

Business entities are constantly seeking new ways through which to gain advantage over their competitors and strengthen their position within the business environment. With competition at an all-time high due to technological advancements allowing for competition on a global scale, firms continue to seek new ways through which to improve and strengthen their business processes, procedures, and profitability.

The **Advances in Business Strategy and Competitive Advantage (ABSCA) Book Series** is a timely series responding to the high demand for state-of-the-art research on how business strategies are created, implemented and re-designed to meet the demands of globalized competitive markets. With a focus on local and global challenges, business opportunities and the needs of society, the **ABSCA** encourages scientific discourse on doing business and managing information technologies for the creation of sustainable competitive advantage.

COVERAGE

- Co-operative Strategies
- International Business Strategy
- Strategic Alliances
- Innovation Strategy
- Economies of Scale
- Foreign Investment Decision Process
- Outsourcing
- Strategy Performance Management
- Entrepreneurship & Innovation
- Competitive Strategy

IGI Global is currently accepting manuscripts for publication within this series. To submit a proposal for a volume in this series, please contact our Acquisition Editors at Acquisitions@igi-global.com or visit: http://www.igi-global.com/publish/.

The Advances in Business Strategy and Competitive Advantage (ABSCA) Book Series (ISSN 2327-3429) is published by IGI Global, 701 E. Chocolate Avenue, Hershey, PA 17033-1240, USA, www.igi-global.com. This series is composed of titles available for purchase individually; each title is edited to be contextually exclusive from any other title within the series. For pricing and ordering information please visit http://www.igi-global.com/book-series/advances-business-strategy-competitive-advantage/73672. Postmaster: Send all address changes to above address.

Titles in this Series

For a list of additional titles in this series, please visit: http://www.igi-global.com/book-series

Handbook of Research on Emerging Business Models and the New World Economic Order
Jose Manuel Saiz-Alvarez (Catholic University of Avila, Spain, & Catholic University of Santiago de Guayaquil, Ecuador)
Business Science Reference • © 2022 • 454pp • H/C (ISBN: 9781799876892) • US $275.00

Cases on Survival and Sustainability Strategies of Social Entrepreneurs
Charles Oham (University of Greenwich, UK)
Business Science Reference • © 2022 • 305pp • H/C (ISBN: 9781799877240) • US $195.00

Digital Transformation and Internationalization Strategies in Organizations
Orkun Yildiz (Izmir Democracy University, Turkey)
Business Science Reference • © 2022 • 326pp • H/C (ISBN: 9781799881698) • US $195.00

Analyzing the Relationship Between Corporate Governance, CSR, and Sustainability
Muddassar Sarfraz (Hohai University, China) and Syed Ghulam Meran Shah (Southwestern University of Finance & Economics, China)
Business Science Reference • © 2022 • 315pp • H/C (ISBN: 9781799842347) • US $215.00

Leadership and Followership in an Organizational Change Context
Sajjad Nawaz Khan (Iqra University, Pakistan)
Business Science Reference • © 2022 • 361pp • H/C (ISBN: 9781799828075) • US $225.00

Emerging Ecosystem-Centric Business Models for Sustainable Value Creation
Xenia Ziouvelou (National Centre for Scientific Research "Demokritos", Greece & University of Southampton, UK) and Frank McGroarty (University of Southampton, UK)
Business Science Reference • © 2022 • 237pp • H/C (ISBN: 9781799848431) • US $195.00

Impact of Disruptive Technologies on the Sharing Economy
Ford Lumban Gaol (Bina Nusantara University, Jakarta, Indonesia) Natalia Filimonova (Vladimir State University, Russia) and Chandan Acharya (College of Staten Island, City University of New York, USA)
Business Science Reference • © 2021 • 269pp • H/C (ISBN: 9781799803614) • US $245.00

IGI Global
PUBLISHER of TIMELY KNOWLEDGE

701 East Chocolate Avenue, Hershey, PA 17033, USA
Tel: 717-533-8845 x100 • Fax: 717-533-8661
E-Mail: cust@igi-global.com • www.igi-global.com

Table of Contents

Detailed Table of Contents

The COVID-19 pandemic has turned the world of work upside down. It is having a dramatic effect on the employment, livelihoods, and well-being of workers and their families, as well as on businesses around the world, especially small and medium-sized enterprises. It started in China at the end of 2019, with that country's economy mainly the first to be affected. The global economy was then impacted as the virus spread. It is a bit early to estimate precisely the extent of the economic crisis on a company, but it is already certain that it is more brutal than before. Companies that have opened their capital to their employees are more likely to keep their employees than other companies that offer a significantly higher level of security to their employees (maintenance of working hours and compensation). What practical economic logic will be found in the company once employee ownership is applied? Would it be an effective way to overcome the various situations of discontent and anxiety among employees, where these feelings are already very strong?

The chapter analyses the use of employee financial participation in Lithuanian companies. The methodology of current research is based on the qualitative research method and analysis of the company's documents. In a total of 19 semi-structured individual anonymous interviews and one focus group were conducted with competent representatives of the companies – heads of human resources and finance departments of companies, heads of legal departments or top managers of law firms representing them. According to the research findings, employers set different goals for share and profit-sharing programs or measures. Among the already examined, high, long-term employee motivation dominates. It also includes aspects of employee involvement in management, strengthening loyalty, forming a sense of ownership. The Scandinavian capital corporation, which manages several companies in Lithuania and applies for a share ownership program, has succeeded in achieving its goals by strengthening employee motivation and involvement.

Family firms, in which a family controls a majority stake in the organisation, are often considered characteristically different from non-family firms. However, our understanding of employee ownership in the specific context of family firms suffers from the concerns raised by owners of several family firms about such ownership. The decision to open the capital to its employees goes beyond the question of the ownership of family business. Nevertheless, it impacts the governance of the company and raises several concerns including the transmission of information, transparency, increased formalism, and taxation. This study aims to analyze how family firms benefit from an employee ownership plan and how governance practices impact the mechanism of employee ownership plans. This study examines the financial communication of French family firms in terms of mployee ownership activities.

Business management scholars have propositioned employee share ownership as a concept bearing different perspectives. Business management practitioners have implemented the model in varying degrees suiting their organizational needs depending on the context of the organization at the particular time. Empirical research on the impact, role, and the position of employee share ownership (ESO) has produced varying results leading to far reaching conclusions as to the importance and significance of the ESO on an organization and especially at a time when a firm is undergoing through crisis. The concept of employee share ownership has led to the development of employee share ownership plans which are implemented as direct stock/share allotment, bonuses, or profit-sharing models and plans. The employer or the principal capital holder bears an exclusive discretion in making the decision of who would receive any of these options.

Section 3
Special Issues of Employee Stock Ownership Plans in Morocco

Employee share ownership (ESOP) is a highly acclaimed international incentive and motivation mechanism for employees thanks to its virtuous impact on company performance and organizational behavior. The work proposes to study the effects of this practice on the financial performance of Moroccan companies in order to assess the impact of employee participation on the creation of financial value. To this end, the authors conducted an empirical study based on two analytical methods using SPSS software. The sample is made up of 33 companies that have published and carried out at least one employee shareholding operation in Morocco since their IPO. The financial data was extracted from the accounting statements of each company for the period from 2015 to 2019. The results show that ESOP is weakly practiced by companies, and the tests do not allow to confirm of the existence of its impact on the performance of the companies studied.

The authors conducted an empirical study in the form of a questionnaire distributed to Moroccan employees. It was completed by 217 employees and relates to the year 2020. The data collected was analyzed by the method of structural equations. The authors continued the methodology of Anderson and Gerbing. The two authors proposed a two-step analysis method. This first involves performing a confirmatory analysis of the measurement model to improve its convergent validity and discriminant validity. The results of the questionnaire survey show that there is a positive and strong link between employee share ownership on the one hand and work motivation and organizational involvement on the other. Also, the tests carried out show that employee share ownership contributes significantly to reducing the departure intention.

Preface

Employee share ownership is a managerial practice developed internationally and popular with developed countries. It offers many advantages to companies, including financing by strengthening equity capital, improving the structure and financial ratios and, therefore, promotes future access to bank debt at interest rates low interest, according to several international studies.

Also, employee share ownership can be an argument for attracting and retaining the best qualified employees. And finally, employee shareholding sends a strong positive signal to the financial market as to the growth and financial health of the company likely to improve its credibility and reputation with stakeholders.

Indeed, the purchase of shares by employees is seen as a mark of confidence in its growth and sustainability. Still, it's a good idea to point out that there is not just one model for implementing ESOP, but three. The first model is deployed through the purchase of shares by employees at preferential conditions, in particular a discount on the price with or without financial aid.

This formula called Employee Share Purchase Plans (ESPP) concerns in particular large companies listed on the stock exchange. The second formula concerns stock option plans intended for employees and company directors. This is a right to purchase shares granted to employees at an advantageous exercise price fixed in advance for a given term.

This system is also applied by start-ups which present it, in particular, as a second pillar of the remuneration system in order to compensate for the risk and reward the individual performance of the founding employees. This formula is a factor in the development of start-ups, because it helps attract the best profiles and thus reinforces the attractiveness and retention of the best skills.

As such, this model can generate a real entrepreneurial dynamic likely to boost job creation and breathe new life into the international economy damaged by the epidemic. The ESOP (Employee Stock Ownership Plan) program is the third option and mainly concerns small and medium-sized companies and unlisted companies.

This American formula is undoubtedly the most appropriate for companies and employees. This is a debt buyout allowing employees to own part or all of the capital of their company without financial investment; this is the Management Buy-Out configuration of Leverage Buy-Out. This formula is very popular in the United States and concerns nearly 14 million employees. This device is proving particularly interesting for saving fragile companies in the liquidity crisis caused by the Covid-19 pandemic.

The relevance of US-style ESOP plans is linked to the fact that funding is provided by banks, and employees are not required to invest their savings in buying shares. Also, the inclusive nature of ESOP plans constitutes a factor of stability, motivation and federation of employees.

In times of economic recession, the takeover of businesses by employees is a major advantage because it saves job losses and avoids business bankruptcies by draining liquidity without resorting to state aid.

In Spain, for example, the model of sociedades laborales - companies of associated workers - is based on employee shareholding. It constitutes a rescue program for companies in difficulty, and has enabled strong job creation in all sectors of activity.

The French SCOP (Cooperative Production Company) model is a hybrid form between the company and the cooperative; management is similar to that of commercial enterprises, but capital and power are shared equitably between the associated employees. These are companies in which employees hold at least 51% of the capital, and are distinguished by the primacy given to wage compensation and long-term investment instead of capital remuneration.

The SCOPs are characterized by a democratic decision-making system based on the principle of one vote for each employee, regardless of the proportion of shares held. In Italy, the social cooperative established by Law Marcora 49/1985 aims to help workers on technical unemployment or those from companies in difficulty to join together in cooperatives in order to take over their companies and thus safeguard their jobs. This mechanism still exists and is a major instrument for promoting Italian economic growth.

The United States, a pioneer country in the development and democratization of employee share ownership, is characterized, in particular, by the scale and effectiveness of the tax incentives which facilitate the establishment and dissemination of participation plans.

For example, the Employee Retirement Income Security Act (ERISA) of 1974 is a federal law that sets minimum standards for most pension plans and provides tax benefits to all employee profit sharing and incentive schemes. The most famous formula is Employee Stock Ownership Plans (ESOP).

It is a device very similar to the French FCPE, which is funded by employers and benefits from a tax deferral until the employees retire. ESOPs provide US workers with additional income through periodic dividend payments and upon retirement, equity capital that they can sell or keep.

The second American employee shareholding scheme, less known to the general public, is called “the (401) K Plans”. It is a fund created by companies, but funded by employees who contribute a percentage of their salary.

This fund is encouraged by payments from employers capped at 6% of each employee’s salary. There are other incentive schemes in the United States, including Profit Sharing Plans (PSP), which consist of the distribution of profit shares in shares or in cash to employees and Stock Bonus Plans which consist exclusively of actions.

France ranks first in Europe in the democratization of employee share ownership, and stands out with a total number of 3.2 million employee shareholders, followed by the United Kingdom with less than two million. While the third position is occupied by Germany with nearly 700,000 employee shareholders.

These honorable results, in France, can be explained by an avant-garde legislative framework. Indeed, an old tradition of reconciliation between capital and labor has been established there since the founding ordinance of General De Gaulle in 1967.

Also, France is the only country which requires companies with more than 50 employees to set up a participation mechanism, and is distinguished by the adoption of a 100% French and unique system called the Mutual Fund of company (FCPE), which collects the sums of employee savings to invest in the purchase of shares and thus plays an intermediation role

THE CHALLENGES

The crucial interest of employee share ownership for companies and international economies makes this practice salutary and beneficial in preparing and accelerating the way out of the crisis. The Covid-19 pandemic has plunged the international economy into an unprecedented financial crisis. This is arguably the most serious crisis in human history, whether in terms of numbers or features. Thus, in the absence of activity, companies can no longer meet their costs, which has led many of them to file for bankruptcy and to lay off employees. In fact, the Corona Virus pandemic has inflicted permanent financial damage on businesses and, unfortunately, forced them to consider worst-case scenarios to mop up liquidity problems. In order to reduce the social cost of the crisis and preserve jobs, companies are called upon, more than ever, to act in solidarity with their employees by promoting employee share ownership. Now is the right time for companies to embark on the establishment and development of participation plans in order to enjoy the virtues and values of employee financial inclusion.

It is about organizing the takeover of companies in difficulty by employees by using bank debt in accordance with the American ESOP model perfectly suited to SMEs in crisis.

This virtuous system has several advantages: first, it aims to inject funds into the capital of companies weakened by the crisis. Then, it allows employees to become shareholders without committing their personal savings. And finally, the inclusive nature of ESOPs allows for better cohesion and an improvement in organizational behavior.

To promote the expansion of employee shareholding internationally, and in particular in developing countries, a triple action plan must be pursued. First, we must emphasize communication and education around the beneficial effects induced by employee shareholding by raising awareness among managers, employees and professional specifiers.

Then, the academic world is actively called upon to act in this direction by devoting more scientific research to the study of the effects of employee ownership on individual and organizational performance.

And finally the legislator must support and encourage the adoption of employee shareholding by setting up an incentive legal framework adapted to all forms of business, in particular, SMEs and very small businesses which represent a predominant share in emerging economies. Indeed, many studies highlight the positive role that tax incentives play in the development of employee share ownership. According to the latest barometer (2019) from the European Federation of Employee Share Ownership, employee savings in Europe have reached a new historic rebound mainly due to political awareness, materialized by decisions and tax breaks in favor of the employee shareholding.

In this book, we offer an in-depth study of the different aspects of international employee ownership. The first section looks at the positive effects of property in saving businesses and economies weakened by the Covid-19 crisis.

The second section brings together studies conducted internationally on the effects of employee share ownership. Finally, the third section deals with the situation of employee savings in Morocco and offers recommendations to encourage the development of employee share ownership.

ORGANIZATION OF THE BOOK

The book is organized into nine chapters. A brief description of each of the chapters follows:

Chapter 1: In this chapter, researchers analyze employee share ownership as a tool to mop up the negative repercussions of the financial crisis of Covid-19. The authors argue that far from the shocking decision of firing employees to leverage their short-term liquidity, organizations may draw other innovative options such as giving company shares to their employees to face the financial and economic crisis of Covid-19. Researchers show that employee shareholding provides the company with liquidity and generates better inclusion of employees who strengthen their link with the company.

Chapter 2: In this analysis, the authors investigate the effects of employee participation in capital and corporate governance on company performance.

The researchers try to analyze the perceptions of several internal stakeholders of the company through semi-structured individual interviews in order to grasp the meaning that the actors give to reality. The interest is to allow an exploration of phenomena that quantitative methodologies cannot capture and describe in their entirety.

Chapter 3: In this chapter, the author analyzes the practice of granting shares to employees in Lithuanian companies. The research methodology pursued is based on the qualitative research method and the analysis of company documents. A total of 19 semi-structured anonymous one-on-one interviews and a focus group were conducted with relevant business representatives - heads of corporate human resources and finance departments, heads of legal departments or senior executives of the most senior law firms representing.

Chapter 4: In this research, the authors attempt to understand the practice of employee shareholding in the very specific context of family businesses. They analyze the particularities of family businesses and provide an overview of their situation internationally and in France. The authors also explain the reasons for the reluctance of family businesses regarding employee shareholding schemes.

Chapter 5: In this study, the authors attempt to draw up an international assessment of the reasons for adopting employee share ownership plans. They analyze, among other things, the situations of India, Ghana, Kenya, Canada, European and American companies. As such, the researchers explain that there is a large difference between the laws and strategies of different countries in terms of the adoption of employee share ownership.

Chapter 6: In this chapter, the authors deal with the repercussion of the introduction of employee share ownership on financial performance of companies. They offer a review of international literature on the empirical effects of ownership on the financial value of firms. The authors present their empirical study in the context of Moroccan companies listed on the stock exchange and suggest explanations and recommendations to overcome the lack of influence of property on the financial value of Moroccan companies.

Chapter 7: In this research, the authors are interested in the attitudinal effects of employee ownership and expose the previous theoretical and empirical results and analyzes carried out on the positive behavioral changes allowed by ownership. In the context of Moroccan companies, the authors share the results of their survey on employee behavior by making comparisons between employee shareholders and non-shareholders of their company.

Chapter 8: In this analysis, the authors draw up a critical assessment of the legal and legislative situation of employee shareholding in the Moroccan context. The authors expose the strengths of the French model and offer suggestions and recommendations to improve the Moroccan legal framework.

Chapter 9: In this study the author attempts to analyze employee shareholding according to two paradigms. First the disciplinary paradigm, through the shareholder model and the partnership model. Then, the cognitive paradigm and the role of employee ownership in reducing cognitive costs.

Subsequently, the researcher shows the contribution of recent reflections related to the impact of employee shareholding on governance. Finally, the author presents the results of his empirical study conducted in the context of Moroccan companies to test the effects of ownership on corporate governance.

Introduction

Employee share ownership is a practice widely adopted by international companies because of its many virtues. Employee share ownership can be seen as an irreplaceable measure, aimed at increasing the income of employees while strengthening their link with the company.

Indeed, the only legal link that connects employees to their company is materialized by the contract of work, associating employees with capital makes it possible to solidify their relationship with the company.

From this perspective, employee share ownership is supposed to have two mutually reinforcing effects. First, it is likely to strengthen employees' confidence in their company, and secondly, it generates in return an increased development of human capital specific. However, the development of specific assets increases the dependence of employees on the company by influencing their exit costs, which makes it possible to reduce their opportunity costs.

Offering employees the opportunity to become owners of their business is a mark of recognition of the role played in creating value and enhancing their skills. In the same way, accepting to be a shareholder in your company is the translation of the desire to be associated with the future of the company. This common perception of interest generates a feeling of confidence likely to lead employees to develop their specific human capital and thus lower their opportunity costs.

According to Breton and Wintrobe (1982), trust leads to a fall in the opportunity cost of resources due to the reduction in the risk premium required, due to the relationship of confidence. Trust is, according to the two authors, an asset that employees build in order to agree to forgo short-term benefits for long-term benefits.

Similarly, Charreaux (1998) introduces the value of trust, as an element of partnership value which leads to lower opportunity costs that are willing to agree to contributors of resources because of relationships of trust.

Granting employee shares allows them to receive a share of the value they have helped create. Poulain-Rehm (2009) explains that employee shareholding plays dual role with a view to creating partnership value. He distinguishes two levels contribution of ESOPs, a formal level through the participation of employees in the representation and decision-making. And an informal level linked to the establishment of trust.

In addition, the climate of trust established by employee shareholding promotes the emergence of positive attitudes at work such as innovations and investments in specific human capital. According to Klein (1987, p. 320), being a homeowner increases loyalty, the dedication and satisfaction of working for the company.

As Tannenbaum (1983, p. 251) affirms, "property is a very attractive concept [...] being an owner values the person."

In this regard, Charreaux (1998) explains that employee share ownership is likely to generate the constitution of human capital specific to the firm by encouraging initiatives for proposals and innovations. For its part, Liebeskind (2000) highlights the role of employee share ownership for the development of human capital and employee loyalty. The two authors mobilize trust in their studies on the modes of cooperation of agents.

They point out that the formal structure alone cannot solve organizational inefficiencies, they then introduce trust as a mechanism of the informal structure that encourages cooperation.

In the same way, Dutot (2004, p. 12) explains "the loyalty of the employee to the company would correspond to the relationship of trust which unites the employee to his organization and which is expressed by his resistance to the adoption of a opportunistic behavior in the face of an external job offer."

A study by the Strategic Analysis Center (CAS 2011) shows that the social performance of companies with employee shareholding is 52% higher than that of other companies.

The report cites the trust generated by ownership as a lever for the creation of value generated.

The ESOP then allows reconciliation between work and capital in the company and reflects the extent of the trust placed by employee shareholders. Indeed, shareholders employees bear a maximum and unique risk in modern capitalism. They invest their human capital but also a significant part of their savings in the company which employs them. They thus run the risk of the cumulative loss of employment and savings.

As such, Autenne (2000) explains that by linking part of his remuneration to the fate of the company, the employee bears a risk of a downward variation in the amount of this remuneration, while being constrained by a material impossibility to diversify its work between several sectors or companies as can the other providers of capital.

Employee shareholding therefore constitutes a double contract binding the employee to his company, this relationship of trust promotes the emergence of positive attitudes towards the organization, which constitute an operationalization of trust.

Couteret (1997) highlights the productive aspect of trust and the role of positive behavior for strengthening constructive exchange, "mutual trust is based on the observation of mutual positive behavior, but it again generates such behaviors, which reinforce trust. "(Couteret 1997, p. 168).

Referring to Robinson (1996), Campoy and Neveu (2005) describe trust as a "handrail" that influences the interpretation of social behaviors in a relationship and "gives life" to the psychological contract.

Moreover, according to the authors of instrumental satisfaction, political rights and opportunities for employee shareholders' participation, provided by their dual status, condition the appearance of positive effects. Several empirical studies highlight the importance of participation in ESOP plans so that employee shareholders can develop positive attitudes at work such as satisfaction, commitment and implication.

"Employee shareholders have the opportunity to exercise active control over the decisions of the controlling coalition by creating or joining a dissident coalition. These shareholders are bring together in the form of "association" (Girard 2001, p. 130).

Employee shareholding, through the trust it reflects in the market, allows the flexibility of control constraints required by business partners such as credit.

The survey by the Ipsos Opinion institute carried out in June (1999) with a sample of employees, analyzes the motivations that encourage or would encourage employees to become shareholders of their business. The results show that 91% of employees say they have chosen share ownership employee for the confidence they have in the growth of their business.

Also, the survey carried out by the (COB-Altédia 1999), covering about 150 companies, reveals that 72% of the companies surveyed believe that employee share ownership is a positive sign given to financial communication.

Indeed, an employee shareholding policy, expressing the mutual trust of employees and leaders in the future of their business, can generate the confidence of other financial partners.

Initiated by the Foundation for Employee Ownership, a new study conducted by Rutgers University in 2020 shows the decisive impact of employee ownership in times of crisis. The results show that, companies that benefit their employees from their actions display better job stability during the Covid-19 crisis because they are 3.2 times more likely to retain their employees than other companies;

These companies offer a significantly higher level of security to their employees in terms of maintaining working hours and remuneration.

According to the same study, companies that practice employee share ownership are characterized by greater resilience in the face of the crisis and contribute to the recovery of the post-crisis economy. The survey also highlights the positive role that employee shareholders play in creating solutions for their ailing companies.

REFERENCES

Autenne, A. (2000). L'actionnariat des salariés, une perspective critique. *Revue Internationale de Droit Economique*, *14*(3), 471–498.

Breton, A., & Wintrobe, R. (1982). *The logic of bureaucratic conduct*. Cambridge University Press. doi:10.1017/CBO9780511896033

Campoy, E., & Neveu, V. (2005). *Perceptions de justice et confiance du salarié comme facteurs explicatifs des réactions individuelles à une violation du contrat psychologique. Journée de recherche « Stress, burnout et conflits de rôles*. CEROG-AGRH-IAE d'Aix-en-Provence.

Charreaux, G. (1998b). Le rôle de la confiance dans le système de gouvernance des entreprises. *Economies et Sociétés*, (8-9), 47–65.

Couteret, P. (1997). *L'impact de la confiance interpersonnelle sur l'implication organisationnelle: le cas de l'adjoint au dirigeant de petite entreprise. Actes du 8ème congrès de l'AGRH*, Montréal.

Dutot, C. (2004). *Contribution aux représentations de la fidélité des personnels à l'entreprise: Eléments de convergence et de divergence entre ouvriers et employeurs. Le cas des ouvriers de deux industries métallurgiques du Pays de Retz. Doctorat en sciences de gestion*. Université de Poitiers.

Employee Ownership Foundation. (2020). *Employee-Owned Firms in the COVID-19 Pandemic: How Majority-Owned ESOP & Other Companies Have Responded to the Covid-19 Health and Economic Crises*. Rutgers School of Management and Labor Relations.

Girard, C. (2001). Une typologie de l'activisme des actionnaires minoritaires en France. *Finance Contrôle Stratégie*, *4*(3), 123–146.

Poulain-Rehm, T. (2009). Gouvernance d'entreprise et actionnariat des salaries: Une approche conceptuelle. *Review of Finance*, *133*, 1–17.

Tannenbaum, A. (1983). Employee owned companies. In *Research in Organizational Behavior*. Academic Press.

Section 1

Employee Stock Ownership Plans and the COVID-19 Crisis

Chapter 1
Dealing With COVID-19 Through Employee Stock Ownership Plans:
Saving Money and Losing Power to Live an Extra Day

Nicolas Aubert
Aix-Marseille University, France

Miguel Cordova
https://orcid.org/0000-0002-1010-8803
Pontificia Universidad Católica del Perú, Peru

ABSTRACT

In this chapter, the authors argue that far from the shocking decision of firing employees to leverage their short-term liquidity, organizations may draw other innovative options such as giving company shares to their employees. Employee stock ownership (ESO) plans have the potential to secure financial liquidity for firms while simultaneously providing social inclusion as well as empowerment to people, relating their efforts directly to firms' performance and driving the economic system into a shared capitalism. However, while companies may be solving their financial constraints through ESO, the authors identified a trade-off related to the traditional position of hegemony of firms. They argue that the decision to share the risk through paying wages using firms' stock options derives in a progressive detriment of power and control that some organizations would not be willing to suffer.

DOI: 10.4018/978-1-7998-8557-3.ch001

"The hottest places in hell are appointed to whom, in time of moral crisis, remain neutral" Dante Alighieri (The Divine Comedy)

INTRODUCTION

Global crises are natural drivers for unexpected and difficult organizational decisions. The greater the crises' possible damages, the greater the trade-offs that organizations will have to be involved within to endure and survive. Those trade-offs would be radical while feasible for some, but likewise opening a Pandora's Box for others. Nevertheless, organizations would have the opportunity to decide and thrive, or remain neutral and die.

The World Health Organization (WHO) has declared the COVID-19 as a pandemic in mid-March 2020 (WHO, 2020), driving thousands of organizations into difficult and unforeseen challenges regarding their financial situation, supply chain disruptions, massive loss of jobs, severe drops in demand, among many other negative consequences, even including serious threats for their survival. Also, health systems' resilience around the world were challenged and most of them overwhelmed (Sagan et al., 2020). According to United Nations Conference on Trade and Development (UNCTAD, 2020), foreign direct investment (FDI) would drop down in about 30% during 2020-2021, severely affecting the international financial systems, which in turn would decrease the global annual GDP around 2% (OECD, 2020a) and 5.2% (The World Bank, 2020a), leading worldwide economy into an unprecedented recession (The World Bank, 2020; UNIDO, 2020).

The financial crisis caused by the coronavirus outbreak would drive governments and firms into difficult decisions for them to be resilient, endure, and survive. The corporations face severe trade-offs to stay alive such as firing employees to improving their liquidity. To face these unprecedented challenges and avoid massive layoffs, countries have taken extreme decisions. Soon during the crisis in 2020, the European Union launched Next Generation EU program, including a € 750 billion economic stimulus plan. The US Congress voted the Coronavirus Aid, Relief, and Economic Security (CARES) Act, which meant a $ 2 trillion economic relief package. Also, the International Monetary Fund (IMF) provided more than US$ 250 billion to its members worldwide. In addition, The World Bank provided $ 160 billion in financial assistance to developing countries, and the Latin American Development Bank injected $ 2.5 billion into this region.

To comprehensively face the consequences of the COVID-19 crisis, the public aid certainly won't be enough and radical changes from private sector will help. Moreover, effective ongoing responses as well as the proper rebuild decisions after COVID-19 would involve a multi-actor intervention, including academia, civil society, businesses, and government (Gonzalez-Perez et al., 2021; Jay, 2016). Nevertheless, how businesses reply to the financial crisis caused by the coronavirus would trace one of the most important paths to economic recovery due to their high relation to countries development potential.

We argue that an alternative to address the economic and societal issues at the same time is to turn employees into shareholders of the company they work for. Employee ownership has the potential to share the risk among the different stakeholders (mostly white collar workers) but the employees must hold participation in the management of the company as a counterpart. Since top executives in a firm seem quite related to its financial performance, it has sense sharing the risk with these wealthy enough actors in the system (Kolitz, 2020). Also, employee ownership has the potential to become an asset builder for blue collar workers, providingfree shares for them and other benefits that at the end night develop these alternatives in the local financial market. Sharing the risk and power implies a radical change in the spirit of traditional capitalism leading to shared capitalism. Kruse et al (2010) defines shared capitalism as "employment relations where the pay or wealth of workers is directly tied to workplace or firm performance. In many of these firms employees also participate in employee involvement committees or workplace teams that help management make decisions regarding the economic activities of the firm" (p. 1). Hence, the research question that we aim to address in this chapter is: How feasible could be to develop an employee ownership program in order for companies to be able to overcome the negative consequences of the COVID-19?

The financial markets would be recovered from the COVID-19 crisis but some companies would not. Just like after the 2008 crisis, non-conventional monetary policies resumed, and public money was spent to prevent bankruptcies or to help companies with liquidity problems to recover from the crisis. Among all the potential initiatives to finance, the European Federation for Employee Share Ownership calls for a public aid plan to develop employee share ownership (European Federation of Employee Shared Ownership, n.d.). There are also calls in the US to use public money to stimulate employee ownership (Mackin, 2021). This chapter reviews the literature related to employee ownership plans and uses an exploratory approach to-discuss the implications of sharing the risk within ownership firm structure, providing employee ownership alternatives to tackle the dramatic consequences of the COVID-19 crisis on their financial systems. In addition, this study provides an overview of the long-term consequences related to sharing the power while concerned providing liquidity for firms in the short-term.

CONTEXT AND BACKGROUND

As most of the contingency plans and restrictions to counter the coronavirus outbreak were focused on labor markets (Weber & Newhouse, 2021), one major consequence of the COVID-19 crisis is the loss of jobs of millions of workers around the world because of the bankruptcy of their employing companies. Firms that not were able to send their employees to work from home have faced severe consequences for their survival. In some countries, jobs that can be performed from home were less than the half (Holgersen et al., 2021). According to the International Labour Organization (ILO), in 2020 the world has lost nearly 255 million of full-time jobs, which represented four times the lose working-hours occurred in the 2009 global financial crisis (ILO, 2021). Furthermore, COVID-19 has strike harder to developing countries (Weber & Newhouse, 2021), emphasizing how geographically contingent were the pandemic effects, and consequently how contextually contingent have to be the measures for recovery as well. Moreover, firms would need the support of local governments' regulations in order to overcome insolvency issues and avoid bankruptcy (OECD, 2020b). In addition, jobs globally displacements affects not only people's regular income but its psychological health too, increasing the workloads as well as the stress levels (Teoh et al., 2021), considering that the COVID-19 has affected a job market that had an already uncertain future due to new technologies that were replacing jobs (The World Bank, 2020b).

Strict lockdown periods all over the countries have restricted the organizations' usual work flow and economic activities, carrying out dramatic problems for their operational continuity. According to Hoehn-Velasco et al. (2021), there were some firms in specific sectors that were highly impacted such as hospitality and construction, as well as workers with specific characteristics such as youngest, oldest, low-income earners, among others. Also, small and medium firms were the most affected by these lockdowns and their negative financial effects.

While losing jobs means a huge problem for countries, organizations are against the ropes as the main issue to deal with in the short term for them is the liquidity risk i.e. when a company cannot meet its short and mid-term financial obligations. To address this primary issue and according to the circumstances, companies could pay part of their employees' wage or compensate wage cut in the form of stocks. Of course, such a solution depends on the payment conditions agreed between the workers and the company. A comparable payment method exists for the shareholders when some companies with liquidity issues pay dividends to their shareholders in the form of stock dividends instead of cash. According to the National Center for Employee Ownership (*October is employee ownership month, n.d.)*, employees can buy stock directly, receive it in the form of a bonus, receive stock options, or obtain stock through a profit-sharing plan. Hence, the employees can also contribute to the aforementioned liquidity obstacle to some extent by giving up their bonuses for stocks. Such contributions can complement the public fiscal incentives and the shareholders' losses.

HOW EMPLOYEES CAN TURN INTO SHAREHOLDERS?

From a global perspective, the potential of employee ownership can be completely different from one country to another. According to the characteristics of the host country, developing employee ownership could be a challenge for two main reasons: (i) the lack of a developed capital market and (ii) the employees' financial education. Some multinational corporations had to face these two challenges when they launch their own global employee stock purchase program. For instance, The Boost plan[1] was launched by Essilor in 2017 in 57 countries with 55,000 employees in Latin America and Asia or L'Oréal with the Invest Plan in 52 countries[2]. Both companies launched their employee stock purchase plan and they both were awarded the Best French employee ownership company award in 2017 and 2018. Even though the capital market is not well developed in some countries where global companies have operations, their employee ownership plans can contribute to developing it by spreading an ownership of financial assets culture, becoming important local agents capable to diffuse the initiative through their networks (Aubert & Cordova, 2021).

The shares are usually listed on the home market of the companies. Another challenge is to increase financial education because holding a financial asset can be a very abstract concept compared to owning a house or a land for instance. For example, Blasi et al (2013) mention that, in the 19th century USA, the main source of capital was the land. They recall that the ownership culture was developed at that time when concerns about inequality led political leaders like Abraham Lincoln to sign the Homestead Act. This law allowed to sell 10% of the total area of the USA to farmers for a very small investment. In a country where capital market is not developed, investment in the employing company has to be well explained, the same way as an investment in tangible assets. Aubert and Cordova (2021) interviewed five top executives who managed employee stock purchase plans of leading companies, which have subsidiaries in different locations around the world. According to them, in some countries where stock investment does not exist, investment in the stock purchase plan was presented as buying a piece of the factory the workers were working at. Also, they deploy strong communication plans, using videos and several informative meetings, presenting the program as a long-term saving alternative plan. But financial education remains a challenge in many countries, where contextual factors seem to define the way a company implement the plan and the way employees understand it, even including where the capital markets are well developed.

A major criticism of employee ownership is that it would be too risky for employees to invest both their human capital and their savings in their company. It would be the equivalent of employees putting all their eggs in one basket. Theoretical economic models argue that investment in employee ownership is in line with the core principles of financial diversification (Aubert et al, 2009, 2018; Markowitz et al, 2010). Markowitz et al (2010) suggest that a share of the total wealth of the employees between 10 and 15% of their overall wealth may not risky and feasible. For the US where employee ownership is the most developed in the world, Kruse et al (2019) find that very few US households[3] have more than 15% of their wealth invested in company stocks. So, there is room to develop employee ownership even in the country where it is the most popular without putting employees' wealth at too much risk. How to mobilize wage income into stocks may then be adapted according to several factors related to the company and the employees' characteristics such as the demography of the workforce (executive vs non-executive with different financial constraints), and the risk and the economic sector where companies belong (some industries were more affected than others by the COVID-19 crisis).

From the employees' perspective, the appeal of gaining a share of equity as part of their overall income depends primarily on the company's prospects and on their own financial situation. For workers in companies that do recover from the crisis, receiving a share of equity as part of overall income means, by definition, that they will receive lower wages. This is because a firm that overcame the COVID-19 effects would tend to be financially weak and have depleted resources, decreasing its value in the market. Employees' interest in exchanging a proportion of their wages for equity then depends on their individual liquidity constraints—the option may suit the highest-paid workers but not the lowest paid. The latter would also increase social inequalities, even more in societies that already are suffering these kind if gaps, negatively affecting the work environment. Paying workers with equity may also influence individuals' overall wealth, and the level of risk involved will be determined by external events among other things, the same way as shares' value recovery depends on the recovery of the economic sector or industry which firms belong to. But ultimately, the employees need to trust that swapping their salary for their employer's stocks is a good strategy. According to Jessri et al (2020), employees would decide to participate in corporate venture if they perceive different incentives such as risk environment, independence, or entrepreneurial self-efficacy, besides the traditional financial incentive. Hence, by paying their regular salaries through equity shares companies would improve their short-term solvency, without incurring in massive loss of jobs. However, increasing the number of shareholders would also means distributing the power among many new participants within the firm, fragmenting the decision-making processes, and embedding these individuals with small slices of presence and participation. This new configuration of power derives from a fragmented traditional and hegemonic structure, where few were the only leaders, leaving the way to a more inclusive and diverse companies' management (Naím, 2015). According to Naím (2015), initiatives such as stock ownership plans would progressively threaten the position of hegemony of traditional firms, promoting the emergence of new actors as well as dispersing the managerial control and power.

Compensating wage cuts with stocks or requiring employees their own savings in their company stocks can be an extreme solution in many cases where employees do not earn enough to ensure their living conditions or if they do not have any savings. Granting free stocks to employees can also be a counterpart to compensate wage cuts. From this standpoint, employees accept wage cuts in exchange for shares that can be seen as a promise to benefit from the recovery. In this case, the employees do not have to cash out any money but get some rights on the future profits of the company. Another solution to finance employee stock ownership development when neither the companies nor the employees can support their cost is to rely on the end of governmental policy responses. The governments of many countries have provided funding to avoid a massive wave of bankruptcies because of liquidity or solvency problems. The mostly adopted programs by OECD countries were: Full or partial loan guarantees (29 countries), moratorium on tax payments (24 countries), new short term loans (22 countries), moratorium on financial commitments such as debt repayments, interest or lease payments (21 countries), and assistance with other significant operating expenses (20 countries) like wages. Support programs have also involved direct equity investment in SMEs in the European Union and the United States. According to the OECD Committee on Financial Markets (CMF) questionnaire, 9 countries have taken concrete steps to inject equity: Finland, Germany, Hungary, Ireland, Italy, Latvia, Lithuania, Netherlands and United Kingdom. France and Turkey were considering this option at the time of the survey. According to the IMF Policy responses to COVID-19 tracker (*Policy responses to covid19*, n.d.) many developed and developing countries[4] have directly invested in companies' equity or even nationalized some of them. Other countries could follow in the short term. According to the OECD (2020c), some governments adopted co-investment strategies involving the combination of public and private capital. Once the COVID-19 crisis is over, public assistance programs will have to be reconsidered. States could promote employee ownership either directly by transferring or selling all or part of the shares acquired to employees or indirectly by making the continuation of aid conditional on the implementation of employee share ownership plans or profit-sharing schemes. With such policies, the benefits of the recovery would also benefit to the workers and contribute to share the wealth and the voting rights attached to the shares.

ARE FIRMS WOULD BE SHARING SOMETHING ELSE BESIDES OWNERSHIP?

For employers, paying workers a share of equity as part of their income can help to improve corporate short-term liquidity; instead of cash going out in the form of salaries, companies would issue new stocks to employees. Also, firms are able to offer discounts, shares for free, and other several benefits oriented to be financially attractive as well as convenient for employees (Aubert & Cordova, 2021). This strategy has been adopted during the Great recession by companies lacking sufficient cash liquidity. In the short term, an important disadvantage of increasing the number of stocks is the dilution of earnings per share that occur when company profits are divided among more shares of its common stock. Thus, the value of each individual stock decreases accordingly. The payment of wages in equity is therefore made at the expense of shareholders' wealth precisely when they experience dividend cuts (Mooney, 2020) and sharp stock price decrease.

Another potential drawback of this equity for wage strategy is that it leaves the selection process of the employees' stock recipients at the employers' decision who could result in different power relation strategies on it (Agbontaen, 2019). In this situation, an initiative that is design as worker-oriented will turn into a disadvantage for the organizational culture as well as for inequality reduction among employees. On the other hand, leveraging employees' voice and empowerment would drive organizations to a higher level of retention, influencing their decision to stay in the firm (Samah et al, 2019), reducing firms' employee turnover rate. Hence, under financial crisis circumstances, organizations may decide not to extend to all employees this benefit, but to whom it needs to retain towards a post crisis and recovery scenario, for instance, strategic workers on key value added processes or young professionals with long-run high potential for the company.

In addition to the profit dilution of earnings per share issue that could be a real liquidity constraint for blue collar workers, some drawbacks of employee stock ownership have been documented in the academic literature. Developing employee ownership is generally a decision of the owner or the general manager of the company. Financial economics often regards employee ownership as an entrenchment strategy of management to put shares in "friendly hands" (Benartzi et al, 2007) because employees are the managers' "natural allies" against a hostile takeover (Pagano and Volpin, 2005). Another risk expected to arise with collective incentive systems like employee ownership is the freeriding or the 1/N problem. When a worker belonging to a group of N workers benefits from a collective inventive system, he gets the 1/N part of any additional effort like all his or her colleagues.

However, in the long run, most disadvantages of new share issues can be overwhelmed by the positive and very well-documented outcomes of employee stock ownership. Indeed, the increased workforce motivation of the employee owners leads to improved corporate performance, which progressively increases the value of shares. Extensive academic research of the Institute for the study of employee ownership and profit sharing at Rutgers University shows that companies can expect better performance by developing and implementing employee stock ownership programs. Most of the empirical evidence on the relation between employee ownership and performance, was reviewed by the meta-analysis of O'Boyle et al (2016). These results plead for employee ownership having positive effects higher than the above mentioned drawbacks. Empirical evidence shows that the 1/N problem can be mitigated by mutual monitoring among workers (Freeman et al, 2010).

Although employee owners voting rights work differently according to the country[5], being a shareholder usually comes with a voting right. This means that the employee owners have a voice in the decision of the company, which could transform the way how the firm perceive the management and control of its operations. In addition, there is empirical evidence that employee ownership works best coupled with worker's participation and involvement (Kruse et al, 2010). Workers' participation and involvement in decision-making may take many different forms. For instance, the European Foundation for the Improvement of Living and Working Conditions[6] (Eurofound, 2020) finds that employees working in a high-involvement organization report a high level of work engagement, are less absent from work, more likely to put in extra effort, prefer a later retirement age, and report higher levels of well-being. Also, high-involvement organization provides more opportunities for both formal and informal skill development.

On the other hand, the risk of too democratized organizations is to drive the decisions at a point where operational efficiency and diligence may suffer. According to Naím (2015), distribution of power into several small parts could drive organizational systems to unexpected inertia and dangerous delays, due to the lack of consensus, ineffective discussions, and unnecessary bureaucracy. Naím (2015) argued that this fragmentation of power is able to slowly undermine the traditional positions of power and hegemony that some companies were holding for decades. For instance, a labor strengthened by shares owning may dangerously influence into firms' payment policies, decreasing dividend payments as well as final profitability (Haw et al, 2018). These decisions would undermine firms' performance and competitiveness in the mid-term, threatening their survival in the long run. Moreover, empowered employees can achieve enough power to directly influence organizational policies and collaborate in shaping some of the rules in companies (Budjanovcanin, 2018). Thus, a proper balance of trade-offs between short and long term benefits would be under a constant conflict of interest by owners that have different expectations from firms' outcomes.

Furthermore, some organizations may promote this democratizing initiative while others may seem strongly reluctant to implement it. According to Schneider (2013), capitalism is differently deployed worldwide, emphasizing how regions such as Europe and Asia are working under a collaborative capitalism based on trust relationships and networks, the United States utilize a competitive capitalism based on free market structure, and finally Latin America has adapted a hierarchical capitalism based on deep social inequalities and traditional power relationships. Hence, the initiative of paying with shares could be positively received or not, depending on the characteristics of the organizational context (DiMaggio and Powell, 1983; Peng et al., 2009) as well as on employees' financial education and expectations. According to Useem (1984), local business elites would tend to influence on their business' environments in order to attain and keep their traditional power over time, consolidating a strongly influential upper-class in society. This business elite would extend its influence into different local society's spheres, favoring their own interests (Durand, 2018; Pettigrew, 1992), even when this individualistic behavior is against firms' financial performance and strategic objectives (Cordova, 2018). Furthermore, Cordova (2019) found that 16% of corporate network studies related to shared directors' practice had negative outcomes (referred to financial disadvantages, information asymmetry, and personal interests), while 44% of the latter refers specifically to individual interests of the business elite. Prefer individual interests rather than collective ones in the companies would prevent others to gain access to what this business elite does, and would also promote an underlying work of influence over the governments' regulatory action as well as on other organizations (Durand, 2019). According to Pfeffer (2010, p.183), there is always a cost to pay while giving power, and people and organizations have to be aware of that cost in order to decide if they are willing to pay for it. Hence, this financial alternative could be a liquidity solution for some firms, but a severe constraint for traditional power to others (Aubert & Cordova, 2020).

Finally, novel and interesting initiatives such as employee stock ownership may represent a way out of severe solvency issues for firms, but at the same time, it could be inadvertently opening long-term threats for the future of the companies. How feasible the implement of these programs as well as how prone firms could be, would largely depend on their governance structures, the characteristics of the employees, the conditions of the local context and the country's business culture.

DISCUSSION AND CONCLUSION

According to our analysis, employees can become owners as long as the conditions of the market development and their financial education allow for that, or there exist some strategic actors that facilitate this transition (Aubert & Cordova, 2021). Hence, employees could be willing to invest in their companies if they are able to identify potential benefits (Jessri et al., 2020), even when the new distribution of shares threats the firms' traditional position of power (Naím, 2015). The latter suggests, that companies have to be aware that they would not be releasing just shares, but decision-making influence and voting rights as well (Aubert & Cordova, 2020). Identifying this possible conflicting trade-off is strategically relevant for organizations' long-term plans.

Meanwhile the productive and economic systems become more complex around the world every day, global scale financial crises, such as the one caused by the COVID-19, drive organizations to make difficult and painful decisions in order to be able to continue their operations or even achieve their survival. Several disruptions on processes and generalized decreasing demand drive them to think on reducing their costs and try to increase their financial liquidity. Besides other decisions, an alternative for this is to pay employees' regular salaries using equity shares, understanding its implications in the short-term as well as in the long run.

In the short-term, this measure would increase firms' cashflow and empower employees, improving their satisfaction, assisting them to build an asset, and increasing their sense of belonging, which would reflect in the overall organizational performance. Nevertheless, it may also raise inequalities among employees, creating conflicts of interests regarding selection and retention processes. Such conflicts would also emphasize the fragmentation of civil society's faction and in turn tip the scales in favor of corporate power.

In the long-run, this decision would undermine the traditional situation of power of the organization, distributing and reallocating it into small parts, diminishing its hegemony and threatening the strategic decision-making processes with lack of diligence and agility. Furthermore, providing some sort of power to employees over the firm's competitive decisions would make them able to reshape some activities and policies, having the risk of misaligning them with firms' strategic objectives, or induce additional future risks such as labor strikes. Again, conflicts of interest would appear since major shareholders would have different long-term goals related to investment and sustainable growth, while minor shareholders would have short-term objectives such as liquidity and faster return on their investment.

Organizations would need to decide how to deal with their financial constraints, considering the implications discussed in this paper and their own capabilities and expectations to facing the crisis. Their decisions regarding this financial alternative would also be strongly shaped by the context's patterns and the interests of local business elites. Local business culture would play a strong moderating role for employee stock ownership. Which specific contextual factors as well as how they could influence in the adoption of employee ownership plans were not included in this study. Another limitation of this chapter is identifying how different organizations, according to their size, economic sector, or primary goals, would be willing to implement these kind of programs. Thus, this chapter aims to shed light about further research avenues regarding the study of these financial initiatives under different contexts and firms, in order to provide a better explanation of their effectiveness and feasibility.

REFERENCES

Abdullah, M. I., Sarfraz, M., Qun, W., & Chaudhary, M. (2019). Ownership concentration impact on firm financial performance. *Logforum*, *15*(1), 107–118. doi:10.17270/J.LOG.2019.317

Agbontaen, O. O. (2019). Workplace Diversity and Inclusion Policies: Insights from a Foreign Firm in the Nigeria Banking Sector. In Diversity within Diversity Management (pp. 239-280). Emerald Publishing Limited. doi:10.1108/S1877-636120190000021013

Aubert, N., Ben Ameur, H., Garnotel, G., & Prigent, J. L. (2018). Optimal Employee Ownership Contracts under Ambiguity Aversion. *Economic Inquiry*, *56*(1), 238–251. doi:10.1111/ecin.12478

Aubert, N., & Cordova, M. (2020). Sharing the risk at expense of power: Paying wages in equity to face the COVID-19. *Notas Académicas*. https://repositorio.pucp.edu.pe/index/handle/123456789/173261

Aubert, N., & Cordova, M. (2021). How society's constraints would undermine ESPP adaption in Latin America: The Case of Peru. In R. Zuloaga & G. Hernandez (Eds.), ESO in the Americas. Academic Press.

Aubert, N., Grand, B., Lapied, A., & Rousseau, P. (2009). Is employee ownership so senseless. *Finance*, *30*(2), 5–29. doi:10.3917/fina.302.0005

Benartzi, S., Thaler, R. H., Utkus, S. P., & Sunstein, C. R. (2007). The law and economics of company stock in 401 (k) plans. *The Journal of Law & Economics*, *50*(1), 45–79. doi:10.1086/508312

Blasi, J. R., Freeman, R. B., & Kruse, D. L. (2013). *The citizen's share: Putting ownership back into democracy*. Yale University Press.

Budjanovcanin, A. (2018). Actions speak louder than words: How employees mind the implementation gap. *International Journal of Human Resource Management*, *29*(22), 3136–3155. doi:10.1080/09585192.2018.1443959

Cordova, M. (2018). The evolution of interlocking directorates studies – A global trend perspective. *AD-Minister, 33*, 135–165. doi:10.17230/ad-minister.33.7

CordovaM. (2019). "That is OK, he is a good fellow": introducing the outcomes dichotomy for corporate networks of interlocking directorates. *RAN - Revista Academia & Negocios, 5*(1), 123-134. Retrieved from https://ssrn.com/abstract=3432045

DiMaggio, P. J., & Powell, W. W. (1983). The iron cage revisited: Institutional isomorphism and collective rationality in organizational fields. *American Sociological Review, 48*(2), 147–160. doi:10.2307/2095101

Durand, F. (2018). *Odebrecht: La empresa que capturaba gobiernos*. Fondo Editorial PUCP.

Durand, F. (2019). *La Captura del Estado en América Latina: Reflexiones Teóricas*. Fondo Editorial PUCP.

Eurofound. (2020). *How does employee involvement in decision-making benefit organisations?* European Working Conditions Survey 2015 series, Publications Office of the European Union.

European Federation of Employee Share Ownership. (n.d.). *Employee share ownership against the crisis: An employee share ownership fund to help companies*. http://www.efesonline.org/CORONA/Proposal%20-%20An%20employee%20share%20ownership%20found%20to%20help%20companies.pdf

Freeman, R. B., Kruse, D. L., & Blasi, J. R. (2010). Worker Responses to Shirking under Shared Capitalism. *Shared Capitalism at Work: Employee Ownership, Profit and Gain Sharing, and Broad-Based Stock Options*, 77.

Gonzalez-Perez, M. A., Cordova, M., Hermans, M., Nava-Aguirre, K. M., Monje-Cueto, F., Mingo, S., Tobon, S., Rodriguez, C., Salvaj, E., & Floriani, D. (2021). Crises conducting stakeholder salience: Shifts in the evolution of private universities' governance in Latin America. *Corporate Governance, 21*(6), 1194–1214. Advance online publication. doi:10.1108/CG-09-2020-0397

Haw, I., Hu, B., Wu, D., & Zhang, X. (2018). Having a Finger in the Pie: Labor Power and Corporate Payout Policy. *Financial Management, 47*(4), 993–1027. doi:10.1111/fima.12211

Hoehn-Velasco, L., Silverio-Murillo, A., & Balmori de la Miyar, J. R. (2021). The long downturn: The impact of the great lockdown on formal employment. *Journal of Economics and Business, 115*, 105983. Advance online publication. doi:10.1016/j.jeconbus.2021.105983

Holgersen, H., Jia, Z., & Svenkerud, S. (2021). Who and how many can work from home? Evidence from task descriptions. *Journal for Labour Market Research, 55*(1), 4. Advance online publication. doi:10.118612651-021-00287-z PMID:33681696

Jay, W. (2016). Civil Society's Role in a Public Health Crisis. *Issues in Science and Technology, 32*(4), 43–48.

Jessri, M., Kosmidou, V., & Ahuja, M. K. (2020). Employees' decision to participate in corporate venturing: A conjoint experiment of financial and non-financial motivations. *Journal of Business Venturing Insights, 13*, e00161. doi:10.1016/j.jbvi.2020.e00161

Kolitz, D. (2020). *Why Don't Workers Get Paid in Equity Like CEOs Do?* Giz Asks. Retrieved from https://gizmodo.com/why-don-t-regular-workers-get-paid-in-equity-like-ceos-1843749588

Kruse, D. L., Blasi, J., Weltmann, D., Kang, S., Kim, J. O., & Castellano, W. (2019). *Do Employee Share Owners Face Too Much Financial Risk?* IZA Discussion Paper No. 12303.

Kurtulus, F. A., & Kruse, D. L. (2017). *How Did Employee Ownership Firms Weather the Last Two Recessions?: Employee Ownership, Employment Stability, and Firm Survival: 1999-2011*. WE Upjohn Institute.

Mackin, C. (2021, October 6). *Toward an economic democracy*. The New Republic. Retrieved from https://newrepublic.com/article/157055/toward-economic-democracy

Markowitz, H. M., Blasi, J. R., & Kruse, D. L. (2010). Employee stock ownership and diversification. *Annals of Operations Research, 176*(1), 95–107. doi:10.100710479-009-0544-1

Mooney, A. (2020, August 22). The Great Dividend Reset: Is there a new normal for investors? *Financial Times*. Retrieved from https://www.ft.com/content/b0873571-b4f4-4c9e-aa18-318cb7589e7f

Naím, M. (2015). The End of Power. Basic Books.

O'Boyle, E. H., Patel, P. C., & Gonzalez-Mulé, E. (2016). Employee ownership and firm performance: A meta-analysis. *Human Resource Management Journal, 26*(4), 425–448. doi:10.1111/1748-8583.12115

October is employee ownership month. (n.d.). *NCEO*. Retrieved from https://www.nceo.org/

OECD. (2020a). *COVID-19 and international trade: Issues and actions.* Retrieved from https://www.oecd.org/coronavirus/policy-responses/covid-19-and-international-trade-issues-and-actions-494da2fa/

OECD. (2020b). *Supporting businesses in financial distress to avoid insolvency during the COVID-19 crisis.* https://www.oecd.org/coronavirus/policy-responses/supporting-businesses-in-financial-distress-to-avoid-insolvency-during-thecovid-19-crisis-b4154a8b/

OECD. (2020c). *COVID-19 Government Financing Support Programmes for Businesses.* www.oecd.org/finance/COVID-19-Government-Financing-Support-Programmes-for-Businesses.pdf

OECD. (2020d). *Global Financial Markets Policy Responses to COVID-19.* https://www.oecd.org/coronavirus/policy-responses/global-financial-markets-policy-responses-to-covid-19-2d98c7e0/

Pagano, M., & Volpin, P. F. (2005). Managers, workers, and corporate control. *The Journal of Finance, 60*(2), 841–868. doi:10.1111/j.1540-6261.2005.00748.x

Peng, M. W., Sun, S. L., Pinkham, B., & Chen, H. (2009). The institution-based view as a third leg for a strategy tripod. *The Academy of Management Perspectives, 23*(3), 63–81. doi:10.5465/amp.2009.43479264

Pettigrew, A. M. (1992). On studying managerial elites. *Strategic Management Journal, 13*(S2), 163–182. doi:10.1002mj.4250130911

Pfeffer, J. (2010). *Power: Why some people have it – and others don't* (1st ed.). HarperCollins Publishers.

Policy responses to covid19. (n.d.). *IMF.* Retrieved from https://www.imf.org/en/Topics/imf-and-covid19/Policy-Responses-to-COVID-19#U

Sagan, A., Thomas, S., McKee, M., Karanikolos, M., Azzopardi-Muscat, N., De La Mata, I., & Figueras, J. (2020). *COVID-19 and health systems resilience: Lessons going forwards.* World Health Organization. https://apps.who.int/iris/bitstream/handle/10665/336290/Eurohealth-26-2-20-24-eng.pdf

Samah, I. H. A., Shamsuddin, A. S., Rashid, I. M. A., & Amlus, M. H. (2019). Mediating effect of employee empowerment in the relationship between communication and retention. *International Journal of Scientific and Technology Research, 8*(12), 3457–3459. http://www.ijstr.org/final-print/dec2019/Mediating-Effect-Of-Employee-Empowerment-In-The-Relationship-Between-Communication-And-Retention-.pdf

Schneider, B. R. (2013). *Hierarchical capitalism in Latin America. Business, labor, and the challenges of equitable development* (1st ed.). Cambridge University Press. doi:10.1017/CBO9781107300446

Teoh, K. B., Cordova, M., Hor, S. N., Lim, Ch. H., Yeoh, L. K., Madhu, A., Warrier, U., Chan, J. J., Kee, D. M. H., Tan, F. E., Chia, J. X., & Chuah, Y. J. (2021). The Factors of Employee Performance: A Study of SearchNEasy. *Asia Pacific Journal of Management and Education*, *4*(1), 82–96. doi:10.32535/apjme.v4i1.1053

The World Bank. (2020a). *The Global Economic Outlook During the COVID-19 Pandemic: A Changed World.* https://www.worldbank.org/en/news/feature/2020/06/08/the-global-economic-outlook-during-the-covid-19-pandemic-a-changed-world

The World Bank. (2020b). *Tackling the impact of job displacement through public policies.* https://www.worldbank.org/en/news/feature/2020/10/20/tackling-the-impact-of-job-displacement-through-public-policies

UNCTAD. (2020). *Impact of the Covid-19 Pandemic on Global FDI and GVCs.* Global Investment Trends Monitor No. 35 (Special Issue March 2020). Geneva: UNCTAD. Retrieved from https://unctad.org/en/PublicationsLibrary/diaeiainf2020d3_en.pdf

UNIDO. (2020). *COVID-19 and the global contraction in FDI.* Retrieved from https://iap.unido.org/articles/covid-19-and-global-contraction-fdi

Useem, M. (1984). *The inner circle. Large corporations and the rise of business political activity in the U.S. and U.K.* Oxford University Press.

Weber, M., & Newhouse, D. (2021). *Developing countries introduced an unprecedented social protection and jobs policy response to mitigate the effects of the pandemic.* World Bank Blogs. https://blogs.worldbank.org/jobs/developing-countries-introduced-unprecedented-social-protection-and-jobs-policy-response

WHO. (2020). *Coronavirus disease 2019 (COVID-19).* Situation Report 51. Retrieved from https://www.who.int/docs/default-source/coronaviruse/situation-reports/20200311-sitrep-51-covid-19.pdf?sfvrsn=1ba62e57_10

ENDNOTES

1 For a video presentation of the plan: https://youtu.be/-EbWRHrOR3U. For a presentation of Essilor employee ownership plan: https://www.essilor.com/en/the-group/governance/employee-shareholding/.

2 The website of the plan is here with videos and materials in several languages: https://invest2018-loreal.com/.

3 The authors find that 15.3% of families with private-sector employees had employer stock in their portfolio, with a median value of $ 6,000 and a median percent of family net worth of 3.1%. About one in five (19.2%) of the families with employer stock exceed the 15% threshold.

4 France, Germany, India, Italy, Korea, Lithuania, Mauritius, Morocco, New Zealand (convertible bonds), Slovenia, Solomon Islands, Turkey.

5 In the US and France where employee ownership is the most developed, stocks hold in the US Employee Stock Ownership Plans (ESOPs) have no voting rights and the voting rights can be exercised indirectly in France through company savings funds.

6 The data are from the European Working Conditions Survey (EWCS) 2015, collected from a representative sample of employees across the EU Member States, Norway and the United Kingdom.

Chapter 2
Employee Ownership or How to Anticipate Financial Crises Within a Company: The Case of the Coronavirus Pandemic

Chibani Siham
Observatory of the Economic Francophoni, University of Montreal, Canada

Mohammed Elkhamlichi
Higher Institute of Maritime Studies, Morocco

ABSTRACT

The COVID-19 pandemic has turned the world of work upside down. It is having a dramatic effect on the employment, livelihoods, and well-being of workers and their families, as well as on businesses around the world, especially small and medium-sized enterprises. It started in China at the end of 2019, with that country's economy mainly the first to be affected. The global economy was then impacted as the virus spread. It is a bit early to estimate precisely the extent of the economic crisis on a company, but it is already certain that it is more brutal than before. Companies that have opened their capital to their employees are more likely to keep their employees than other companies that offer a significantly higher level of security to their employees (maintenance of working hours and compensation). What practical economic logic will be found in the company once employee ownership is applied? Would it be an effective way to overcome the various situations of discontent and anxiety among employees, where these feelings are already very strong?

DOI: 10.4018/978-1-7998-8557-3.ch002

CONTEXT AND PROBLEMATIC

The employee shareholding is considered as a world event which knows a rise in contemporary capitalism insofar as it is like an inescapable element of the regimes of growth of the principal developed countries (Aglietta & Reberioux, 2005). Thus, one Moroccan employee in two, for example, owns shares in his or her own company. In Europe, this proportion is one in five (Perotin & Robinson 2002) and in France, one employee in 10 is concerned by the phenomenon (Fas 2006). The specificity of employee share ownership is that it is supported by successive governments, but also by companies, which seem to welcome its positive effects (Kruse 2002). Thus, a broad consensus (Desbrieres 2002, p255) seems to be emerging to underline the advantages offered by employee share ownership schemes.

Regulators have notably withdrawn from the subject[1], even if their interest in the issue sometimes seems to respond to purely conjunctural imperatives[2] (Arcelor merger, "economic patriotism", for example). This enthusiasm is accompanied by a global reflection on how to build companies that are fairer in their distribution of results and on how to promote harmonious corporate development. This concern should not hide the imperative of value creation, common to all companies. Employee share ownership seems to be the ideal answer to the dual requirement of economic performance and harmonious development. This recent (re)discovery of the positive effects of employee ownership should not hide the historical and constant practice of companies in this field.

In France, for example, employee share ownership has been developing and spreading regularly[3], and has been growing in recent years. This can be seen as the effect of favourable governmental measures and of the different promotion efforts of the actors concerned (employees, managers, executives, ...) as illustrated, for example, by Wavestone, which has instituted a Free Share Allocation Plan (PAGA). This plan allows employees to become shareholders of their company under advantageous conditions by investing their participation bonus in the Wavestone Action fund. Employees are entitled to free shares two years later, provided they are still with the company and have not sold their shares in the employee shareholding fund.

This being said, employee share ownership is a performance lever: employees are proud to be shareholders of their company and it is also a way to build loyalty. However, it remains a risky investment and the company always puts forward the recommendations of the AMF to diversify its portfolio. In addition, only profit-sharing gives the right to a contribution in free shares. Beyond this contribution, employee share ownership is fiscally interesting since it is less taxed than the holding of normal shares or salary. Today, more than 50% of employees invest in the Wavestone share fund. However, employee share ownership is still a lagging type of savings in Morocco. Only large capitalizations and foreign groups, via their subsidiaries in

Morocco, stand out. An essential tool for building loyalty, employee shareholding is still not very popular in Morocco. Through this mechanism, company managers involve their employees in the financial life of the company and its results. This mechanism makes the employee a long-term shareholder of the company, while allowing to align the interests between employees, shareholders and managers.

Employee share ownership can be implemented through several schemes (savings plan, free allocation of company shares, stock options or warrants...). These different schemes have two points in common. On the one hand, the shares are offered to employees on preferential terms: either at a discount to the market price, or at the market price with an additional contribution from the employer (matching contribution). On the other hand, the shares acquired by employees are blocked for a certain period of time to encourage long-term value creation.

In Morocco, this practice remains very little developed. It is limited to large groups that offer this type of savings scheme to their employees, most often reserving capital increases for them. Recently, it is the three largest capitalizations in the market that have "invited" their employees to take part in their capital increases. The banks Banque Centrale Populaire and Attijariwafa bank, via capital increases of 2.4 billion DH and 2.21 billion DH, respectively, and Maroc Telecom, the latest example, via its recent OPV. The operator is offering 0.3% of its capital (i.e. 16.7% of the size of the operation) at a price of MAD 117.7 against MAD 125.3 for the general public.

In its information note, BCP explains, for example, that the operation has for objective "the motivation of the staff by associating it to the growth and results of BCP, and the reinforcement of the spirit of belonging of the staff members of CPM and its subsidiaries in Morocco and their mobilization around the strategic projects of the Group".

At the same time, the listing of a company on the stock market is also an opportunity to interest the company's managers and employees in its development. Over the last few years, the IPO structures carried out on the market have in most cases provided for order types dedicated exclusively to the issuer's employees. Let us quote Marsa Maroc, Total Maroc and Résidences Dar Saada for the most recent cases. These tranches represented on average In the last few years, several foreign groups with subsidiaries in Morocco have chosen to offer their Moroccan employees employee savings plans by giving them the opportunity to subscribe to shares of the parent company. In addition, in recent years, several foreign groups with subsidiaries in Morocco have chosen to allow their Moroccan employees to benefit from employee savings plans by giving them the opportunity to subscribe to shares of the parent company.

Over the first six months of 2019, 7 international groups have activated this mode of shareholding. They are Crédit Agricole, Veolia, Société Générale, Tui, Vinci, Total,

Airbus SE. The number of these offers varies, over the last 10 years, between 8 and 10 per year, with a certain recurrence of issuers who come back almost every year.

In the end, this mechanism offers the opportunity to the employee to build up a progressive savings at advantageous conditions by exposing himself to an asset that he knows better than anyone else: the share of his company.

Moroccan legislation has provided for provisions to encourage employee shareholding with the Company Savings Plan (PEE), introduced by the 2013 Finance Law. For example, the employer's contribution to the employee's savings plan is not a substitute for salary. The employer's contribution is neither considered as a salary supplement nor taxable on income, except when it exceeds 10% of the annual taxable salary.

Also, another provision of the law allows employees to invest in the capital of their company while being exempted from tax on capital gains. This tax advantage is conditioned by a ceiling on payments of MAD 600,000 and by the unavailability of the sums saved in the PEE for a minimum period of 5 years. The products generated by the portfolio must also be kept during the 5 year period. In addition, and from a conceptual point of view, employee ownership modifies, if not the structure of the firm and the behavior of its actors, at least the way it is represented. The firm is the case for the classical microeconomy, which is based on the opposition of factors of production, and for the Marxist critique, which postulates their conflictual dialectic. Employee shareholding really changes the balance of the firm by blurring the traditional boundaries that guaranteed the effectiveness and efficiency of the firm beyond any equity criteria.

One can therefore insist on the (ambiguous) consequences in terms of efficiency or put forward the integrity of such a mechanism. Employee ownership cannot be reduced to a set of incentives (e.g. fiscal for the company) and financial incentives (for the employees), where finally everybody could find his own way. It goes beyond this strict framework by inducing global consequences (financial and organizational) on the company. Employee share ownership is therefore gradually becoming an essential mechanism for profit distribution. It also allows a renewal of the space for social dialogue, notably between managers and employees, and offers a possible reconfiguration of the Capital/Labour relationship. The massive diffusion of employee shareholding leads to the question of the consequences of generalized employee shareholding on companies.

The general theme of our chapter is essentially to analyze the consequences of a generalized employee ownership on companies, in this case during the Coronavirus pandemic. What effects will employee ownership have on company performance? Can employee ownership predict a company's financial crisis, especially during the Covid pandemic19 ?

Therefore, our research deals only with generalized employee ownership, which excludes stock options from the scope of our chapter. We consider that stock options, even if they can be materialized by the holding of shares as in the framework of employee share ownership mechanisms, cannot be linked to employee ownership because of the absence of risk. Indeed, the beneficiary of stock options can know in advance his potential gain, unlike employee shareholders, who do not know it by definition. Our research problem is concerned with the effects on the firm of holding part of the employees' savings in the form of company shares and the effects on the firm of effective ownership by the employees, especially during the Covid period19. Another major consequence of employee share ownership is to give employees a "voice" (Faleye and Alii 2006) and to allow them to participate directly in the governing bodies of their company. Thus, like any shareholder, employees may be able to participate in the general meeting of shareholders and, in some cases, be represented in the governing bodies (Board of Directors, Supervisory Board). However, employee representation (and more generally, the ability of employees to influence the company) is problematic for the constitution of an efficient corporate governance, aiming at reducing the effects of the potential conflict between shareholders and managers, within the framework of a shareholder value maximization objective (Jensen and Meckling 1976; Charreaux 1997 for a presentation; Blair and Stout 1999 for a critical presentation).

In this respect, our research problem is completed by the following question: what is the impact of employee participation in the governance of their company during the Covid19 ?

Our research question[4] therefore concerns a problem that aims to examine the effects of employee participation. By "employee participation effect" we mean the consequences for the firm of the partial ownership of financial capital by its employees, whatever form (savings plan, share ownership, etc.) this ownership takes (employee share ownership in the strict sense: BEN- NER and Jones [1995]). The holding of capital leads to an effect of physical and symbolic ownership (Pierce and Alii 1991; 2001), due in particular to the weakening of the Capital/Labour opposition in the representation of the firm (Blair 1999 and 2000; Gomez 2001). The effect of employee participation then unfolds in three dimensions: the economic (financial effect of participation - right to return), the corporate governance (political effect of participation - right to control) and the corporate structure (organizational effect of participation).

We can formulate our research question definitively as follows: What are the effects of employee participation in capital and corporate governance on the performance of the company?

METHODOLOGY AND MAIN RESULTS

The objective of our study is to analyze the perceptions of several internal stakeholders of the company through individual semi-directive interviews in order to grasp the meaning that the actors give to reality. The interest is to allow an exploration of phenomena that quantitative methodologies cannot capture in their entirety.

Our epistemological reflection, of an interpretativist nature, consists in understanding the actors' reality, a reality that is essentially "perceived" (Thietart, 2014). The objective is to understand the social reality constructed by the actors and its context in order to grasp the meaning of their behaviors (Schwandt, 1994), which is adapted to our subject and to our research object of employee shareholder representatives in governance bodies. Thus, the process of creating knowledge in our research involves understanding the meaning that actors give to reality and it is a matter of understanding reality through the interpretations that these same actors make of it (Thietart, 2014). It is a matter of understanding a specific phenomenon: that of the presence of employee shareholder representatives in governance, which covers two levels (Weber's notion of Verstehen): at a first level, the individual, in his or her daily life, interprets and understands his or her own world. At a second level, as a researcher, we seek to interpret the subjective meanings underlying the behavior of the individuals we study. This requires taking into account the motivations, expectations, reasons, and beliefs of the actors on the practices by distinguishing understanding and explanation. To do so, our reasoning is oriented in an abductive perspective in that it is made of back and forth between governance theories and observations from the field.

As far as we know, the work on ESOP and its representation in governance bodies essentially uses quantitative methodologies (econometric techniques, statistical studies, etc.) which do not, however, make it possible to understand the strategies objective or subjective alliances between employee shareholders and managers. This is why we mobilize a qualitative approach in order to contribute to the reflections and the knowledge of the impact of such a representation.

This study examines several cases of international companies (6 in all) with a significant ESOP system (with a rate of over 1%). We choose to present here a case study. The latter is commonly used in different fields of social sciences, and contributes, especially in management sciences, to the knowledge of the individual, the group or the organization in an often determining structural context (Wacheux, 1996), which is particularly adapted to our study. All of them have a representative of the SA on their board of directors or supervisory board. They belong to the secondary and tertiary sectors of activity.

Before contacting the companies, we pre-tested and validated our interview guide with several employee ownership experts: FAS (Fédération Française des Actionnaires

Salariés et Anciens Salariés), FONDACT and EFES (Fédération Européenne de l'Actionnariat Salarié). The interview guide was adapted according to the interviewees and is built around employee shareholding and its representation on the board, with a central question: "Do you think that the presence of a representative of employee shareholding contributes to the improvement of the company's productivity? Do you think that this helps to overcome the problems of Covid19 ?

All the interviews were transcribed in their entirety and, from a comprehensive perspective, we proceeded to systematically code them according to the approach recommended by GIOIA et al (2013), a methodology that is among the most widely used in research based on qualitative data.

The answers provided by the interviewees partially confirm the relevance of the propositions formulated.

Our first proposition, which has two dimensions (disciplinary and partnership), is partially validated in the case of the company studied. The financial model constitutes the main backdrop to the debates on executive remuneration (Charreaux, 2004), and we note that a textile company knows how to position itself in its constraining, disciplinary function against the executive:

...] it is a role of power and it is a role of money too. ;

We are told about the CEO's compensation, we see that it is a 4.6% increase, we look at the payroll, and we see that it is a 1% increase... We are not going to say: "Oh no! We're not going to say "no, we've all worked". No! We're going to say: "for the balance of the company [...] we should...". It's the wording that needs to be different. (2)

As well as a partnership role essentially oriented towards the employees (workers), which is probably explained by his personal history:

[...] I feel a responsibility, a greater responsibility in relation to the workers [...] because I come from a family that was also working class. (2).

His view is not invalidated by the perceptions of other stakeholders. The compensation and benefits manager is absent from board discussions, which does not allow him to directly testify to the disciplinary or partnership role held by the textile company. The notion of power to influence is nuanced.

The perception of this company also negates our proposition:

Its position it is not simple [...] in relation to me, [...] that it has kept its elective mandates [...]. On certain subjects [...] when it comes, for example, to the salary of...

(the CEO) [...] she tries to take her positions, and [the employees] send her back: 'you are the representative of the first shareholder, so if there is a vote, you have to defend the interest of the shareholders [...] you can't abstain and vote against.' (3)

Its partnership role is identified as participating in the protection of the rights of stakeholders, in particular shareholders and employees (Charreaux, 2004) who, given the importance of their specific investments, are at the forefront of these stakeholders (Desbrieres, 2002). The comments of this company are significant in the sense of this manifested will to defend the interests by privileging those of the employees. Even if nothing in the speeches of the other two respondents supports our proposal.

I feel [...] a greater responsibility towards the workers"; "I feel more responsible towards the worker who earns the minimum wage and who has put in 10,000 MAD by going without (2)

The second proposition, which also has two dimensions (cognitive and behavioral) is partially validated:

The cognitive dimension leads to an analysis of the relations between managers and shareholders by considering their cognitive contribution (Charreaux, 2002): this cognitive role of the company is recognized by the person in charge of compensation and benefits (1). However, it is absent from the discourse of the employee director (3).

His level of knowledge is incomparable to that of the average employee. The level of knowledge is incomparable to that of the average employee"; "managers [...] are perhaps sometimes a little cut off from other realities (1)

Regarding the reduction of behavioral biases, the proposition is also partly validated. A company's ability to reduce behavioral biases can be understood in a complementary way with another textile company:

[...] I think there is a beginning of influence. [...] yes, it is certainly the beginning of an influence (1)

I can read, so I can inform myself. When the files arrive, I work on them. ...] I have an advantage over the others, the bosses, they don't have the time. ...] sometimes I have information that they don't always have because I have had time to inform myself. (2)

The third proposal does not seem to us to be fully validated, and proposal [P3bis] cannot be validated because there is no association representing employee shareholders within the company. However, the risk of collusion is present in the background, according to the second company:

He chooses his board members, that's clear and precise... 2. They always consider her to be one of them, since she represents the first private shareholder, and therefore she can only agree with them. (3)

But it seems to be counterbalanced by the heightened vigilance of the first company, which questions the real motivations of the CEO in all circumstances:

We stayed an hour talking [...] and he tells me "I don't do enough meetings with the directors, it would be nice if we met regularly!" ...] I say to myself why does he want to see me? To defuse? Because I asked him several problems... Is it to defuse before the board of directors? [...] . (2)

The difficulties expressed both by the first company and by the other stakeholders of this company show a need to legitimize this mandate. Indeed, the results of this work show that the textile company is seeking its place and is looking for legitimacy, especially with regard to the employees. Its mandate raises difficulties ("the step is high"). It is a new mandate, which may explain certain positioning difficulties.

It is also a "hybrid" or "ubiquitous" model of mandate, its prerogatives being the reflection of the double investment of the employee shareholders that it represents. The legislation confers this double quality on him, thus giving him normative legitimacy. Its presence also gives the company social legitimacy, but its positioning is not without certain difficulties. These difficulties are highlighted in particular by the other stakeholders, depending on its choices, which may compromise this legitimacy. Choices that may enable it to find a point of balance and its rightful place on the Board of Directors, as well as with respect to employees. The sensitive issue of directors' fees adds to the challenges of credibility and legitimacy faced by this type of director. The basis of the legitimacy of the employee director comes from his representativeness (Alanche, 2007), and the first company still has to find its own, to be integrated into the board. This mandate struggles to be as well understood and perceived as the mandate of employee representative.

In a proxemic approach, when the positioning of this director is close to the employees (or even to the workers, therefore as close as possible to the "base"), which is the case here, the risk could be confusion with the director representing the employees, and conflicts with the latter. The perception of too great a proximity to management risks revealing attempts to form alliances and thus to establish roots, in addition to maintaining the traditional divide between the strategic core and the base of the organization, the employees.

The question of employee shareholder participation in governance is still little explored, which gives our research encouraging prospects. Our objective is therefore to contribute to a better understanding of the impact of this participation. Our results call for associations and/or oppositions as well as extensions through the case studies of our sample.

DISCUSSION AND CONCLUSION

"Prevention is better than cure"[5]. This assertion, reflecting an old and widespread wisdom, is also true in the context of companies.

Employee ownership plays an important role in the post-Covid recovery19 by providing companies of all sizes with significant and sustainable resources, alone or alongside other public or private investors. Many employees or former employees have increased their savings, which are still waiting for investment opportunities. Mobilizing these savings to increase equity capital means strengthening employees' confidence in their companies and allowing them to benefit more from the value they create, by associating them with their capital.

Numerous studies[6] have already highlighted the advantages of employee shareholding in that it enables companies that introduce it to improve their performance.

What explanations can be given for this phenomenon?

Employee share ownership is a unique opportunity to bring together interests that were once thought to be antinomic by opposing labor and capital. It gives our companies the opportunity to renew their project, by the constructive confrontation of the interests of all the actors.

Employee shareholding makes it possible to achieve this objective, since it associates employees with the performance of their company by allowing them to benefit from financial, social and tax advantages that constitute a significant complement to their remuneration, provided that their shares remain blocked for a minimum number of years[7]. It is also by this means that it will be possible to make the interests of employees and shareholders converge, since the profits distributed to the latter are very often in conflict with the increase in labor costs. On the contrary, employee shareholding[8] makes it possible to provide additional compensation without the need to increase salaries.

Finally, stock market outperformance can be explained by the fact that the capitalization subscribed by employees constitutes a strong signal to investors since it constitutes "a credible capital core". Indeed, the employee shareholding mechanism encourages employee shareholders to hold their shares for a minimum of five years. This nucleus participates in part in an "anti-hostile takeover" strategy in many companies. For example, Société Générale was able to escape the BNP offensive, and Essilor shows that the employee shareholding developed within the company serves as a potential bulwark against any threat of a takeover.

Indeed, the right of shareholders to participate in collective decisions is a principle of public order, and even, to a certain extent, one could speak of an absolute public order, insofar as any clause in the articles of association could not derogate from it. Thus, to include employees in the constitution of the capital would expressly open up access to the company's decision-making spheres. Shareholding confers rights on employees, who become contributors of capital, to protect themselves against possible risks by guaranteeing them indirect control through access to certain information and legal recourse in the event of a dispute over the information. Employee shareholders can also have direct control over decisions by participating in shareholders' meetings, or even by exercising voting rights on boards of directors as employee shareholders

This type of shareholding has the effect of limiting hostile or friendly takeover bids on the financial and stock markets[9]. At a time when the massive entry The capital of public companies is more volatile because of the presence of foreign investors, but employee ownership can give it a high degree of stability, which in turn gives companies a margin of independence from the pressure of foreign funds.

Employee shareholders can play a central role in the independence of their company from predatory strategies. This function of employee ownership is much more apparent in other countries where this form of capital ownership is itself more widespread.

The virtues of employee ownership are well documented: it allows both to consolidate equity and to ensure the financial performance of the company[10]. In addition, this shareholding has a certain stability and, as we have noted above, it can therefore constitute an effective tool for resisting undesirable takeover bids.

However, is agency theory the only explanation for the outperformance of companies with high employee ownership? It seems that other arguments, this time of a more psycho-sociological nature, can explain the phenomenon.

Thus, a detailed analysis of the influence of employee ownership on value creation requires a distinction to be made between, on the one hand, the question of managerial and non-managerial employee ownership, and, on the other hand, the question of the change in governance, which is evolving from a shareholder perspective to a partnership perspective. In the perspective of shareholder governance, it is mainly the ownership of employee-managers that finds conceptual justification thanks to the theory of agency. This theory focuses on the divergence of interests and the asymmetry of information between the different actors of the company, in particular the shareholders and the managers. The resulting agency costs are supposed to be reduced, in particular, by associating managers with the capital and management of the firm. Holmström (1979), noting that managers have considerable latitude to define an investment policy that would not maximize the value of the firm because of the information asymmetry that characterizes their relations with shareholders, suggests using one or more measures of organizational performance as an estimate of the unobservable actions of managers, and to link part of their compensation to this performance, with any information being added to the performance evaluation model and to the compensation contract to the extent that it has marginal information content on the executive's behavior. Jensen and Meclking (1976), for their part, show a positive correlation between the property rights owned by the managers, i.e. their shareholding, and the value of the firm. However, the shift from a monistic to a plural conception of the firm does not fail to underline the limits of this analytical framework and to raise the question of an increased recognition of the preponderant role of specific human capital. Indeed, while the agency model focuses on the relationship between shareholders and managers, while giving a secondary place to the other stakeholders of the firm, current developments underline the diversity of interests at stake, within the framework of a stakeholder theory (Freeman, 1984; Hill and Jones, 1992; Clarkson, 1995). An increasing number of authors are expressing the desire for a balance between the interests of the firm's various stakeholders, i.e. all those who incur a risk in relation to the products of its activities, whether primary (employees, creditors, customers, suppliers, government) or secondary (pressure groups and the media), and those of the contributors of capital, so that value can be appreciated more broadly through a plural vision of the firm. Thus, the objective would no longer be to maximize shareholder value, but rather the total or global value of the firm (Fama, 1978; Blair, 1996). However, the conception of the firm as a place for maximizing the value of the firm for all its stakeholders, despite its important analytical contribution, remains rather vague, not to mention its operationality (Hirigoyen and Caby, 1998). One of the main difficulties lies in the problems linked to the definition of a specific objective function for the company, which can be a source of managerial opportunism (Jensen, 2001). Faced with this difficulty, authors such as Hirigoyen and Caby (1998) explore similar conceptual approaches, based on the notion of specific assets (Williamson, 1985). The idea is that the development of the firm relies on two particular resources, the capital provided by the shareholders and the skills provided by the employees, the firm constituting a combination of specific capital and labour (Aoki, 1984) or a node of specific investments (Rajan and Zingales, 1998). While the role of shareholders is, under these conditions, to choose the most efficient coalition of employees (Rajan and Zingales, 1998), Blair (1997) distinguishes two types of risk borne by specific human capital: first, that the rent and quasi-rents generated by human capital are expropriated ex post by the firm's other stakeholders; second, that its current value fluctuates in the future, either because the skills would no longer be useful to the firm, or because the firm would no longer generate sufficient rents. Under these conditions, it is important that the overall risk be reduced or at least remunerated, because the risk is that the specific capital will disappear, which would penalize all the stakeholders. The remuneration of risk leads to employees being considered as residual creditors, like shareholders, with value being created for their benefit if the wages received are higher than their opportunity cost (Parrat, 1999). Blair (1997) proposes to remunerate risk through employee share ownership, whereby the remuneration of employees through company shares can provide a mechanism to encourage and protect investments in specific human capital. The idea is that employee share ownership gives employees certain control rights and simultaneously aligns the interests of employees and external equity holders. The positioning of employee ownership in the perspective of partnership governance is therefore justified.

However, the results obtained must be considered in the light of the limitations that taint the scope of the study, and suggest that further studies be carried out. The conduct of the research was strongly constrained by difficulties in accessing data. In order to obtain more convincing results, it would be appropriate to constitute a sample composed of two subsets: a subset comprising companies with a marked employee ownership policy and a subset comprising companies without employee ownership, which would imply knowing precisely the composition of the ownership structure of the companies considered. In this perspective, the method of matching two sub-samples of strictly equal size could be implemented, which would make it possible to respond to the criticism of the inequality in the size of the current sample between firms meeting the IAS criteria and the others. It would also be appropriate to broaden the temporal scope of the investigation. An analysis conducted over a single three-year period inherently limits the scope of the results, especially since the second part of the period under consideration was characterized by a fall in equity markets, which may have affected the distribution of the value created at that time. Further analysis using the 2004 and 2005 data provided by the FAS should help to overcome this shortcoming. In addition, future research should focus on qualitative approaches, which, by soliciting the opinions of employee shareholders and assessing their attitudes and behaviors - vectors of organizational performance - would allow for a better understanding of the organizational context and costs of implementing employee share ownership policy, and to put it into perspective with respect to the company's overall social policy. One of the unresolved questions is how to characterize the causal relationship between employee ownership policy and performance: is the former a cause or a consequence of the latter? Do companies encourage their employees to participate in their capital in order to improve their performance, or is satisfactory performance a prerequisite for the implementation of an employee share ownership scheme? Beyond that, it would be appropriate to consider the possible improvement of corporate governance through the combination of shareholder and employee status, by assessing the opportunity for employees to be also shareholders of their company, and in particular by understanding the consequences of this lesser diversification on the management of their human and financial capital. While employee ownership offers promising prospects for development within companies, it also opens up equally promising avenues of research.

REFERENCES

Acharya, V., Myers, S. C., & Rajan, R. G. (2011). The internal governance of firms. *The Journal of Finance*, *66*(3), 689–720. doi:10.1111/j.1540-6261.2011.01649.x

Aglietta & Reberioux. (2004). *Dérives du capitalisme financier*. Albin Michel.

Alanche. (2007). Un salarié au conseil d'administration de Renault. *Alternatives économiques*, 264.

Aoki. (1984). *The Cooperative Game Theory of the Firm*. Oxford University Press.

Barney, J. (1991). Firm resources and sustained competitive advantage. *Journal of Management*, *17*(1), 99–120. doi:10.1177/014920639101700108

Ben-Ner, A., & Jones, D. C. (1995). Employee participation, ownership and productivity: A theoretical framework. *Industrial Relations*, *34*(4), 532–554. doi:10.1111/j.1468-232X.1995.tb00387.x

Bruder. (2008). L'actionnariat salarié, avantages financiers, représentation démocratique des actionnaires salariés au sein des instances dirigeantes. Aumage.

Chaput. (1986). Droit de la prévention et du règlement amiable des difficultés des entreprises. *PUF, 2*.

Dares. (2004). ACEMO-PIPA survey. *Premières Synthèses, 38*(2).

Mabileau, R. (2004). *L'évolution des modes de rémunérations dans l'entreprise*. Thèse Bibliothèque Universitaire de Nantes.

Reeves. (2007). *Companies work, happiness and employee ownership*. www.richard-reeves.com/pages/books/coco_companies/synopsis.asp

Trewhitt, L. (2000). Employee Buyouts and Employee Involvement: A Case Study Investigation of Employee Attitudes. *Industrial Relations Journal*, *31*(5), 437–453. doi:10.1111/1468-2338.00175

Van Dyne, L., & Pierce, J. L. (2004). Psychological ownership and feelings of possession: Three fields studies predicting employee attitudes and organizational citizenship behavior. *Journal of Organizational Behavior*, *25*(4), 439–459. doi:10.1002/job.249

ENDNOTES

1 As shown by the abundant political reflection on employee share ownership: Chérioux (1999), Balligand-De Foucault (2000), Cornut-Gentille-Godfrain (2005) reports; 2005 Finance Law, Contrat France 2005; Edouard Balladur's tribune, Les Echos, July 19, 2004, Dominique de Villepin's intervention, September 1, 2005, Ollier's deputy's proposal, November 8, 2005; draft bill for the development of employee participation and shareholding (2006); Act n° 2006- 1770 of December 30, 2006 for the development of employee participation and shareholding.

2 Pell-mell, it was seen as a way to counter takeovers, to reward employees with a very attractive tax regime (free share allocations), to boost growth through consumption (early release of "Sarkozy" shares), etc.

3 The increase in the number of employee shareholders in France is as follows: 700,000 in 1998; 900,000 in 1999; 1.2 million in 2000; 2 million in 2001; 2.3 million in 2002 and probably around 3 million in 2006 (source: FAS guides). The spread of employee share ownership schemes is gradual. 0.5% of companies with 0 to 9 employees had a collective employee share ownership scheme in 2002, this figure rising to 19.1% for companies with more than 1,000 employees (source: DARES, ACEMO-PIPA survey in Premières Synthèses, September 2004, n°38.2).

4 In the context of our research, we consider the effect of direct or indirect employee ownership on the company's performance without distinction. The literature analyzing the employee ownership-performance link does not make this distinction (Pierce and Rodgers 2004; Blair and Alii 2000; Faleye and Alii 2006). Consequently, we have made the methodological choice to operationalize our "employee ownership" variable, in particular through the share of capital held by employee shareholders. However, in our conclusion, we will discuss the respective effect of direct and indirect employee ownership.

5 "Prevention means first and foremost making managers aware of the current situation and the evolution of the company. It is then to set up possibilities of alert, or even of amicable settlement of emerging difficulties when the

unfavourable evolution is confirmed" Chaput, Yves, Droit de la prévention et du règlement amiable des difficultés des entreprises, PUF, 1986, n° 2.

6 Ben-Ner, A. & D. Jones, Employee participation, ownership and productivity: a theoretical framework, Industrial relations, vol. 34, no 4, 1995, p. 532 et S ; Richard REEVES COCO companies work, happiness and employee ownership, www.richard-reeves.com/pages/books/coco_companies/synopsis.asp, février 2007, pp. 7. 2.

7 For a more precise definition of this mechanism, see Bruder, A., L'actionnariat salarié, avantages financiers, représentation démocratique des actionnaires salariés au sein des instances dirigeantes, éd. Aumage, February 2008.

8 On the question of alternative modes of remuneration, see for example: R. Mabileau, L'évolution des modes de rémunérations dans l'entreprise, Thèse Bibliothèque Universitaire de Nantes, 2004.

9 It must be admitted that this is an undeniable reinforcement of the powers of employees, who have not only the powers of labour law, but also those of company law. Thus, one must recall the very important role played by the employee shareholders of Société Générale at the time of the defense against the hostile takeover bid launched in 1999 by its competitor, BNP. V. " La puissance éphémère des employés de la Société générale ", Le Monde, June 14, 2000, quoted by André SOBCZAK, Réseaux de sociétés et codes de conduite: un nouveau modèle de régulation des relations de travail pour les entreprises européennes le déclin, la décadence des instruments traditionnels d'expression des salaries, thesis, European University Institute, Florence, 2001, p.114.

10 Auzero, Gilles, Actions de préférence et actionnariat salarié, Bulletin Joly Sociétés, 01 November 2006 n° 11, P. 1288.

Section 2
Employee Stock Ownership Plans in International Studies

Chapter 3
The Use of Employee Financial Participation in Lithuanian Companies

Jaroslav Dvorak
Klaipeda University, Lithuania

Remigijus Civinskas
Vytautas Magnus University, Lithuania

ABSTRACT

The chapter analyses the use of employee financial participation in Lithuanian companies. The methodology of current research is based on the qualitative research method and analysis of the company's documents. In a total of 19 semi-structured individual anonymous interviews and one focus group were conducted with competent representatives of the companies – heads of human resources and finance departments of companies, heads of legal departments or top managers of law firms representing them. According to the research findings, employers set different goals for share and profit-sharing programs or measures. Among the already examined, high, long-term employee motivation dominates. It also includes aspects of employee involvement in management, strengthening loyalty, forming a sense of ownership. The Scandinavian capital corporation, which manages several companies in Lithuania and applies for a share ownership program, has succeeded in achieving its goals by strengthening employee motivation and involvement.

DOI: 10.4018/978-1-7998-8557-3.ch003

INTRODUCTION

Employee financial participation (in two forms - sharing profits or property with employees) is a noticeable social phenomenon in a large number of Western European companies (Kim, Patel, 2017). In Lithuania, this phenomenon is not so bright, especially if it is associated with long-term employee share programs (Civinskas, Dvorak, 2017; Civinskas, Dvorak, 2019). In Lithuania, this phenomenon is usually related to one scheme - a stock option or an employee option transaction. This is due to one of the main issues in the labor market over the last five years, i. e. the desire to retain qualified and experienced employees in the companies, to motivate them to work productively, to achieve good results and to remain loyal to the company.

In general, academics, business experts and policy makers agree that this form of employee participation in corporate governance benefits not only employees but also companies. The concept of employee ownership is based on the idea of the employee owner (Aubert, Kern, et al. 2017; Whitfield, Pendleton, et al. 2017). Employees, as owners, can receive higher dividend income at a time when the company is profitable. Thus, the income received by employees motivates them depending on the company's performance (Lowitzsch, Dunsch, et. al. 2017). True, there are internal factors and organizational circumstances that lead to these schemes not being effective.

The issue of employee financial participation has received considerable attention over the last few decades. In essence, it has become the basis for interdisciplinary approaches. Employee financial participation is examined not only by economists (Bryson, Freeman, Lucifora et al. 2013; Miller, 2012; Ugarkovic, 2008; Wolff, 2012) human resource management specialists (Poutsma, Kaarsemaker, 2015; Poutsma, Ligthart, Kaarsemaker, 2017; Elouadi, 2020; Uribetxebarria et. al., 2020), but also by researchers in the field of public policy (Lowitzsch, 2009; Case, Quarrey, 2019; Weltmann, 2019) and business ethics (Kruse, Freeman, Blasi, 2010; Reynolds, 2014). One of the most noticeable directions of research is related to the involvement of employees in order to motivate, ensure loyalty or likewise. Perhaps most prominent in the academic field is approach to labor relations. Interoperability between employees and employers is understood as involvement in decision-making related to a company's financial performance. More specifically, employee involvement schemes, usually set up by employers, anticipate that the company's performance will be relevant to them. In addition, employees can combine personal and company performance.

In the academic field, there is a popular research topic, which establishes the relationship between employee ownership and the efficiency of the company's operations (Kim, Patel, 2017). Part of the empirical studies found out the links (they are not necessarily strong in all variables) between firm performance (employee productivity, financial performance, personnel management stability) and employee financial participation (Whitfield, Pendleton, et al. 2017; Kurtulus, Kruse, 2018; Richter, Schrader, 2017; Kang, Kim, 2019). According to other research, companies are negatively affected for a number of reasons: employee shareholders are guided by narrow interests and the pursuit of benefits, investment in research and development is reduced, risks are not properly managed, and etc. (Faleye, Mehrotra, Morck, 2006; Aubert, Kern, Hollandts, 2017). The "dark part" of employee ownership is usually seen at a time when employees are pursuing purely personal interests for personal gain (Guedri, Hollandts, 2008; Srivastava, Bhatia, 2020). In addition, research findings often emphasize that application of enabling the share to employee is a very complex phenomenon, making it really difficult to distinguish the unambiguous benefits.

A specific research direction is the interaction of employee ownership with investment attraction (this is usually relevant for so-called start-ups). Venture capital investors are often interested in effective employee incentives (Geczy, Jeffers, Musto, et al. 2016).

Employee financial participation (both in the form of profit sharing and employee share sharing) has gradually increased over several decades (2014 comparative study data) (Lowitzsch, Hashi, 2014). The development of employee ownership is also confirmed by the report of the Federation of Employee Ownership conducted in 2016 (Mathieu, 2017). It reveals that the phenomenon of employee stock ownership is growing in many countries. There are currently around 8 million employees in Europe holding shares in the companies in which they work (mostly, i.e. around 3 million, in France). On the other hand, this trend is not observed in all countries. For example, in Lithuania, as in some other Baltic countries, the number of employees holding shares has decreased. Employees acquire shares in companies during the privatization of state or municipal companies (1990s), after which the transfer of ownership begins.

The aim of the research is to investigate employee financial participation forms used by Lithuanian companies. This study seeks to answer the following research questions: a) How and why do employers choose to apply employee financial participation practices? b) What factors limit the initiation and development of employee financial participation programs?

Research Methods

Two methods were used to analyze the topic of employee financial participation: 1) the method of logical analysis when examining the internal documents of companies; 2) qualitative research method using group and individual interview forms.

Qualitative Research

In total of 19 semi-structured individual anonymous interviews and one focus group were conducted. The in-depth interview was chosen because of the relevant collection of some data (on the application of employee share and profit-sharing programs, their content, etc.) and the importance in analyzing the opinions of the informants. This approach can be effective in encouraging informants to demonstrate in detail their views and experiences regarding employee financial participation. In addition, this approach reveals practices of employee participation programs and individual plans, effects on employee involvement in corporate governance, motivation, and loyalty. Interviews with informants helped to reveal other issues - awareness of employees and businesses, financial participation and its application practices.

Interview sample size was based on specific characteristics of research (Conceptual model of Janice M. Morse) - research questions (the narrow scope of, the smaller sample size needed), the nature of the topic (the more "noticeable", the smaller sample size) and the quality of the data (the richer the data, the smaller). The comparatively small case sample size in this article was therefore compensated by intensity of data. The very in-depth interviews with managers and decision makers per business sector assured the quality of information.

Several criteria were used to sample the respondents. First, the interviews were aimed at competent representatives of the companies - heads of human resources and finance departments of companies, heads of legal departments or top managers of law firms representing them. Second, respondents were selected based on four criteria. Due to the relevance of the topic, interviews were conducted with 1) representatives of finance (banks, investment funds, insurance companies, etc.) and 2) representatives of start-up companies. 3) Companies applying employee share plans or profit-sharing schemes were also selected. 4) Multinational corporations whose so-called parent companies apply employee share schemes are also included in the qualitative researcg (regardless of whether they transfer their schemes to subsidiaries in Lithuania). The selection of respodents also took into account the information found that companies apply employee share schemes or employee profit sharing schemes. In addition, the facts about the philosophy of social responsibility and the application of management measures, the philosophy of sustainable business of companies are considered to be an important indicator of companies' innovation in the field of employee involvement. Unfortunately, it has not been possible to select all companies that apply broad employee share programs (shares are distributed not only to executives or managers). It should be noted that such practices are not recorded or otherwise collected. The sample also took into account the size of the enterprises, including representatives of both large and medium-sized enterprises, small and micro-enterprises.

The duration of individual interviews ranges from 20 minutes to an hour. The interviews were conducted in 2019 by phone or by meeting with respondents. The interviews were anonymized as requested by most of the participants. They explained that they could share information a little more openly anonymously.

Limitations of Qualitative Research

Respondents (especially those representing limited liability joint stock companies) were not always able to disclose details of employee financial participation programs in companies. Such a restriction was explained by a company secret. Another limitation was related to the limited understanding of employee financial participation. For example, most respondents were well aware of one method of employee profit-sharing (usually variable-rate programs, in which salary supplements are allocated from companies 'annual profits and paid in cash or stock options), while others were less well known. The biggest obstacle to qualitative research became the availability of some respondents (top managers of companies, finance and HR managers).

THEORETICAL FOUNDATION

To analyze the facts gathered in more detail the principal – agent theory and stakeholders' theory were used. These theories are most often applied when integrating them in research that analyzes employee financial participation in order to elucidate the phenomenon of employee ownership and examine the performance of the agent.

Stakeholders' Theory

The stakeholders' theory explains that organizations are responsible for meeting the interests of different stakeholders (customers, employees, business partners, authorities, local communities, etc.) (Freeman, Harrison, Wicks, et al. 2010). The stakeholders' governance is a combination of three components: good corporate governance (protecting the interests of shareholders), effective stakeholder relations (protecting their interests, including the employees), and protecting the environment (Freeman, 1984; Freeman, Harrison, Wicks, Parmar, et. al. 2010). Employees are important stakeholders for companies. For this reason, business owners (major shareholders) seek to reconcile the interests of employees and the company (Elouadi, Noamene, Chaher, 2016). The ownership of employees, for example through the transfer of shares in a company, is a way in which those interests can be reconciled. Theorists discuss how appropriate can be used the ways and techniques of employee financial participation that to make employees or others the relevant stakeholders.

Many scientists who have used this theoretical approach have confirmed positive results (Lamberg, Savage, Pajunen, 2003; Zattoni, 2011; Thompson, McWilliams, et. al. 2014). This aproach also allows to analyze the interests of other stakeholders - employee representatives (trade unions, works councils), the government - and their compatibility with the interests of the company. True, some have seen some shortcomings in the choice of inappropriate schemes, excessive application, and misalignment harmonization of incentives etc. (Brandes, Dharwadkar, Lemesis, 2003; Damiani, 2009). Finally, this theory has limitations in explaining the organizational contexts of employee financial participation and corporate governance. Nor does it explain the circumstances and factors in which an employee's behavior changes. This theory is best complemented by agency theory.

Agency Theory

This approach is also called the principal-agent theory. The developers of this theory believe that organizations incur significant costs in separating the rights and control of owners (Fama, Jensen, 1983). The problem of the agent (employee or employees) arises when his and the principal (business owners') goals are incompatible. In this case, the cost of monitoring employees for the owner due to moral risks (personal interest, limited rationality, unwillingness to take risks) increases significantly. The problem is exacerbated by certain conditions. For example, monitoring of employee behavior becomes complicated for the principal at a time when the hierarchy of structures in organizations is being reduced. In this case, the involvement of employees through financial means enables them to be directed to the company's performance. In this way, they become agents of the company as the principal. In this case, the links between employee salaries and the company's performance reconcile the interests of the principal and the agent. Critics (Wagner, Parker, Christiansen, 2003; Kroumova, Sesil, 2006) of this theory note that employee financial participation may not be a sufficiently effective incentive. In addition, as already mentioned, a significant number of empirical studies do not show a link between the application of financial participation schemes and the performance of the company. On the other hand, this theory is important in analyzing the allocation of firm ownership to executives. Researchers and practitioners are debating whether the "rewarding" of managers (integration into variable remuneration systems) with shares properly shapes their behavior. For example, some researchers argue that stock options (as an incentive system) reduce the willingness of executives to make risky decisions (Jaffee, Freeman, 2000; Martin, Gomez-Mejia, Wiseman, 2013; Baixauli-Soler, Belda-Ruiz, Sanchez-Marin, 2015; Sahakiants, Festing, 2019). True, followers of the classical agency theory made opposite assumptions.

MANAGEMENT STOCK OPTION AND THEIR USE

Stock options (sometimes referred to as "management stock options" or "managerial persons stock options") for executives and professionals working with high-risk solutions (mostly in the banking and financial sectors) are used quite often in Lithuanian companies. Usually, large multinational corporations do this. They usually relocate their "executive stock option" programs without special adaptation. "Executive Options" programs are also implemented by several Lithuanian capital companies in Lithuania, which also have extensive schemes. In doing so, they seek to encourage and direct leaders as well-functioning agents (Rimas, 2010). Executives are also often subject to share allocation plans initiated by major shareholders. The aim of executive stock option programs or instruments not only to encourage executives as agents, but also to reconcile the interests of shareholders and senior (less frequently and middle-level) executives, and to address risk aversion issues. As discussed in the theoretical section, agency theory explains that managers, when acting as agents, are encouraged to make risky decisions (Jensen, Meckling, 1976). This is driven by the belief that risky decisions will have a positive effect (reducing their opportunism and selfishness, such as investing in unprofitable projects, employing "their own" people, etc.) and their share ownership (linked to stock options or other forms of share ownership). In this case, it is assumed that managers, unlike shareholders, are more likely to avoid risky decisions (Eisenhardt, 1989). However, this statement (giving ownership of shares to managers encourages risky decisions) has been questioned. Researchers relying on other theories (e.g., applying the behavioral agent model theory) explain that stock ownership does not change the behavior of managers. This was also substantiated by the findings of empirical research. In many cases, the issuance of stock options has been shown to encourage risk-averse behavior and adversely affect managerial decisions (Sanders, Hambrick, 2007; Martin, Gomez-Mejia, Wiseman, 2013). The scientific debate has led to the agreement that the ownership of shares creates the effects of "mixed gamble". This means that giving stock options to managers can be beneficial and non-beneficial, i. y. In situations of uncertainty, proxies can act both in the interests of shareholders (more risky decisions are made) and selfishly (risk is avoided). Of course, one or the other action can lead to positive or negative decisions. Empirical research only substantiates that stock option mechanisms influence managerial behavior (Lim, Mccann, 2013; Zona, 2016; Triki, Ureche-Rangau, 2012). The scientific discussion and research results discussed together show that executive stock options do not necessarily create well-functioning systems management incentive and behavioral guidance (or alignment with shareholder interests) systems. This is probably one of the reasons why "executive stock options" are not as widespread as they could be. A qualitative study revealed that share ownership as the effectiveness of the incentive is often discussed in companies operating in Lithuania. Representatives of companies exercising "executive stock options" and taking part in the current research generally considered them an appropriate incentive. On the other hand, several respondents questioned the effectiveness of this measure. The best-reserved approach to these programs was revealed in a discussion in a Scandinavian capital company. There has been a lot of discussion in the company's remuneration committee about whether it is worthwhile to expand the "executive stock option program," which currently applies to a very narrow number of senior executives. During the interview, generalizing the discussion about its expansion, the respondent noticed that:

Hard to say, really hard to say. That very slippery thing with those stocks is. We also have a ... [mention the name of the program] program. But it is only for the whole top, top management. This is already an instrument that is being dropped from ... [name of corporation] from the group. We only have the freedom to choose the specific employees who will be promoted by the shares. They acquire the rights to receive the shares after three years, as with the deferral. Managers receive shares for free. Yes, we have those stock options too. Behold. Another is relevant to us now. We are currently working to modernize the payroll and benefit systems. That's how we keep striving, looking for new ways to motivate ... This is our annual supplement as well, - under discussion. About those promotions. This is what we discussed about extending the said program to other executives. But you know, maybe we're still ready to introduce it. This can be unattractive (interview with INF12).

This interview reveals that the company did not dare to apply the extended long-term incentive program to executives (it only applies to a few hundred employees across the corporation) for several reasons: 1) potential inadmissibility; 2) effective promotion of other parts and benefits of the variable remuneration system; 3) in this company, middle level managers do not face high-risk solutions. It should be noted that this program is based on a performance-vested scheme. Specifically, shares are granted on condition that the company stated objectives are met[1].

AB Linas Agro Group proposed a slightly different plan for granting employee shares[2]. The company sought to involve "employees and members of the bodies of the company in the company's capital" through the share option plan (AB Linas Group Agro, 2018). This plan for the allocation of shares in the company was to act as an additional incentive. The rules for the issuance of shares approved in 2018 stipulate that the shares are granted to employees who have served for at least 20 years. On June 1, 2018, by the decision of the General Meeting of Shareholders, option agreements were concluded with the employees of AB Linas Agro Group and its subsidiaries. These employees will acquire the right to shares after at least three years in accordance with the procedure established in the option agreements[3].

The shares are granted free of charge. Current research clarified that the shares were granted mainly to executives[4]. This stock option agreement was like a reward for merit for executives and other employees. The stock option plan was not directly linked to profit distribution as discussed earlier. However, the operations of the companies belonging to the group were profitable in 2018[5]. It is important to note that this stock option plan also provided for modified deferral periods of 3, 4 and 5 years. Apparently, such a deferral clause in stock options could have kept certain employees in the group for longer. The cases discussed reveal several things. Foreign capital companies transfer "executive stock option" programs to subsidiaries operating in Lithuania, even if they do not have extensive programs. These stock option programs seek to align the interests and leadership behaviors of executives by aligning them with the interests of shareholders and achieving greater performance. Similar programs are applied in their subsidiaries by such corporations as ASA Orkla (Management option program), AB Swedbank Group (Individual Program 2019, IP 2019) AB SEB Group (Restricted Share Program 2019).

SHARE DONATION PROGRAMES AND THEIR EFFECTIVENESS

As already discussed in the previous chapters, sometimes the CEOs of Lithuanian open or closed joint-stock companies donate or sell shares at symbolic prices. According to representatives of law firms, it can be predicted that this was a popular practice[6]. The choice of such a scheme is particularly attractive when the company has one or more shareholders (and if there are several, there is a consensus between them). Confidence and an organizational culture that responds to shareholder values are also very important in this place. This was confirmed by several interview data (interviews with INF13; INF14). In fact, in Lithuania, these share gift or sale agreements (usually for a symbolic price) are applied not only by open but also by closed type companies. It is important to note that in practice there are two ways of transferring shares according to the goals of companies: 1) giving shares to employees (mostly deserving ones) by consolidating the company's values (for the purpose of strengthening organizational culture) and increasing motivation; 2) sharing the business with deserving employees (usually managers).

The analysis of the qualitative study, as discussed in the previous section, revealed that share donations aim to embed culture (share donations are linked to the embedding of cultural values, the style of key shareholders and, at the same time, managers and serve as a tool). Interestingly, the informant reflected on the choices between the three schemes: shareholders donating shares, the company donating shares, and shareholder options.

We donated shares. These were personal shares. [...] We have been considering and are still considering stock options. In our case, it was the donation of shares as such. We thought about an extension. We talked at length here with Taxes (informally means Taxation Inspectorate). If we donate shares every year, the Taxes, then they'll interpret the content for something completely different. In that sense, it will be understood as a labour relationship. So, we had to ..., we took a one-off move and stopped. Then options. Options, that's what we've discussed a lot with lawyers. And not only discussed, but ready to do options options. But the options .... Now I won't say exactly. We are stuck now, and we have been stuck for years. Indeed, everything hangs because of the uncertainty of how they will be taxed when they are accepted. The State Taxation Inspectorate has not clearly formed a vision of how we will tax options here in Lithuania (interview INF14).

This quote from the interview reveals that for the informant (he himself is one of the two main shareholders), the donation of shares was the most acceptable for the purpose (this is an understandable one-off measure. It is associated with the anniversary of the company's activities, a group of highly deserving employees, great trust in them. Thus, the grant of shares was a form of gratitude). On the other hand, the owners of the company also thought about the possible continuity of this measure. Clearly, the most important factor in choosing this scheme is the favorable tax environment. Interestingly, the tax uncertainties prevented the company from approving the stock option program, although it was prepared for it.

The sale of the shares to employee at a symbolic price is another scheme often applied by companies. Otherwise, it's one way to share the business with employees who deserve it and are significant to the continuity of the business. This is illustrated by the case of one company. In 2019, the director and main shareholder of UAB Ad Rem Transport transferred one third of the shares to two company executives. This seems to have been driven not only by the drive to retain executives, but also by the company's culture (Stamkauskienė, 2018; Miknevičius, 2019).

In summary, the schemes in question are alternatives to stock options and may be acceptable in some cases, depending on the objectives of the companies. As already analyzed, they are usually practically associated with the transfer of a part of the business to exceptional executives or the motivation of deserving employees, the strengthening of the organizational culture. Their main drawback is related to the restrictions on continued application due to uncertainties in the tax environment.

STOCK OPTION PROGRAMS FOR START-UPS

Qualitative research reveals that start-up companies in Lithuania usually apply or are preparing to apply stock option programs[7]. The limitations of the qualitative research did not allow to reveal the variety of applied schemes, but helped to detect the features of the dominant ones. This was due to the fact that the informant, who is well versed in the application of options in the start-up ecosystem, shared his generalizing insights. He revealed the content elements of the share ownership program applied in the company and compared them with those applied in other startups.

At the beginning of the presentation, the informant noticed that their company has an extensive program (applicable to all employees, not exclusive programmers, systems analysts, software architects, etc.). It was driven by the personal attitudes and business philosophy of executives:

Executives, we decide it ourselves. We decided to give options to absolutely everyone (since 2013) when we started working more seriously. That philosophy came from the owners themselves and that philosophy is maintained to this day. That decision was very simple and unambiguous. We never doubted this decision. I think we will continue to apply this. This is the business philosophy. If you think, the people you hire don't create value and don't need to be given options, then why hire those people at all? The people who work for us, according to our philosophy, all create value. Unambiguously, they all create value by holding different positions and working in different fields. Clearly, it can be explained that a strong and experienced programmer creates more value than an administrator does. Objectively, remuneration based on merit can be made through the amounts of options distributed. But the administrator also creates a lot of invisible value, so he can also aim to get a large number of options.

The informant revealed that in companies, the preparation of programs usually depends on the attitudes and goals of the company's managers. He also emphasized that hedge fund managers, who bring models of applicable options with the proposed investment, may also have some influence. He noted that start-up companies setting up branches in Lithuania can also bring ideas and programs for the application of employee stock options. The company under investigation has been exercising the stock option program for seven years. The deferral period for the acquisition of options in this company is as long as ten years. This is indeed atypical. The informant emphasizes this and notes in comparison that the start-ups in the USA and Lithuania apply different moments of acquisition of stock options:

We have stock options for ten years. However, our practice should not be seen as an example, as it is quite unique. We make a decision that is more motivating for employees. The bottom line is that options don't need to be redeemed very abruptly. It usually takes months to years in the US. The periods are quite short. [...] Two to three year periods is a really good option.

The stock option repurchase mechanism seems most complicated to the informant. This is particularly relevant for limited joint-stock companies that apply similar schemes. The scheme must provide for and coordinate the repurchase of stock options so that employees can actually sell the stocks they purchase (Kahle, 2002). Certainly, the value of employee stocks, he believes, could rise sharply after corporate sales.

[...] Until the employees can't have those options in cash, there is no such big exit. Until it's one, two, three, then the system, those options won't work and they won't be so heavily valued. [...] Listed companies are already ready. Having reached such a level that they are able to list their shares successfully and the stock exchange trades those shares. This is usually not the early stage of a company's development. These are companies that have reached a fairly good level in sales. Profitable companies. In this case, a completely different dynamic prevails. In listed companies, when an employee comes and receives shares, she does not expect (or expects much less) that the value of his shares will grow exponentially. In the startup, a small technology company that is just starting out can grow 20 to 50 times from the start. Everyone has such an expectation that it will grow very strongly. This is because doubling the value of shares in a listed company is a very big achievement.

The informant pointed out that one of the largest start-ups, JSC Vinted[8], had bought out stocks from its employees several times. It should be noted that it is possible that this company applies extensive schemes (Baltrušaitytė, 2015). It should be noted that these stock option programs are initiated not only by start-ups who have reached a sufficiently high level of maturity, but also by small companies. For example, according the representative of internationally operating company "DappRadar" the decision to exercise share options depends on:

The idea of offering employees preferential purchase of company stocks is simple. Lithuania is rising and developing, so we offer our employees another reason to stay and work here. In addition, we have a long-term business strategy in this country. We want to invest in our employees and that they get value from their hard work. In addition, we want to attract the most outstanding talents in our field (CVbankas.lt, 2019).

On the other hand, the information provided shows that this company is still in the process of clarifying the effectiveness of this motivation and incentive measure and plans to finalize it in 2020. The implementation of such a program is encouraged by one of the company's representatives with experience in participating in similar programs.

A qualitative study revealed that start-up companies in Lithuania usually apply or are preparing to apply stock option programs. Some start-ups use broad schemes, and some opt for narrower ones. This is determined by the business philosophy, the attitudes of the founders and the established culture. Atypical schemes apply to start-ups. Hedge fund managers are also influenced by the models of options applied with the proposed investment. Start-up companies establishing branches in Lithuania are also significant for the takeover of the models.

CONCLUSION

In Lithuania, the policy of support for employee financial participation was launched five years ago. Its aim was to extend existing regulation to the needs of businesses. Also, by changing the existing tax regulation, a more favorable tax environment for the application of share options was created (amendments to the Laws on Personal Income Tax and State Social Insurance). The results of this policy have not been effective enough. First of all, the legal regulation is quite confusing and constantly changing. The taxation of employee shares and the practical application of tax incentives remained unclear.

Employers set different goals for share and profit-sharing programs or measures. Among the already examined, high, long-term employee motivation dominates. It also includes aspects of employee involvement in management, strengthening loyalty, forming a sense of ownership. Qualitative research data revealed that stock option programs are less likely to attract investment from venture capital funds or reduce staff costs. Several informants mentioned that their company's stock option program wants to reconcile interests between the company's shareholders, management and employees. Thus, the investigation showed that the allocation of employee shares (shares granted to companies and major shareholders) was used by several companies as a measure of a cultural nature. In conclusion, it is banal to note that proper goal setting and efforts to achieve them are only one side of the coin. Indeed, employee share or profit-sharing programs and measures may be ineffective because it will not be in the best interests of the employees and the incentive will not be properly selected. All of them in this case will be another "written off" as a failed staff development measure.

Analysis of the qualitative study data revealed that the objectives of employees as agents and employers as clients do not coincide or are likely to coincide (companies that have introduced employee stock option programs). This was confirmed by making reservations on the basis of the fact that stock option schemes have recently been launched, which makes it difficult to assess their effectiveness. The goals and interests of employers are compatible only if bonuses are paid to employees when the company makes a profit or achieves the set financial goals. The study tried to explain the reasons, which leads to an incompatibility of the goals of the clients (employers) and agents (employees).

However, not everything can be painted in shades of black. The Scandinavian capital corporation, which manages several companies in Lithuania and applies a share ownership program, has succeeded in achieving its goals by strengthening employee motivation and involvement. This was due to a combination of factors: 1) the reliability of the corporation and the increasing value of the shares; 2) longevity of the stock option program; 2) dividends are paid annually; 3) liquidity and reliability of shares. Clearly, the employees acquired shares in the parent company, which reduced their ability to act as agents of the companies. As the study revealed, this was more effective in ensuring remuneration bonuses for employees from profits.

The inconsistency of goals is also evident in the case of start-ups. Some employees (as the case of one company reveals) do not believe in the success of the company and refuse to participate in stock option programs. On the other hand, even successful and long-standing stock option companies face difficulties in motivating employees. It is difficult for them to explain all the benefits that employees derive from receiving shares. Employees question the ability to sell shares in a successful company because they don't see examples of good practice or so-called success stories. This summary of opinions suggests that the interests of employers as customers and employees are almost incompatible, often conflicting. This is primarily related to employee share ownership. Giving gingerbread through employee share ownership forms is not very attractive.

REFERENCES

Aubert, N., Kern, A., & Hollandts, X. (2017). Employee stock ownership and the cost of capital. *Research in International Business and Finance*, *41*, 67–78. doi:10.1016/j.ribaf.2017.04.007

Aubert, N., Kern, A., & Hollandts, X. (2017). Employee stock ownership and the cost of capital. *Research in International Business and Finance*, *41*, 67–78. doi:10.1016/j.ribaf.2017.04.007

Baixauli-Soler, J. S., Belda-Ruiz, M., & Sanchez-Marin, G. (2015). Executive stock options, gender diversity in the top management team, and firm risk taking. *Journal of Business Research*, *68*(2), 451–463. doi:10.1016/j.jbusres.2014.06.003

Baltrušaitytė, M. (2015). Jeigu jiems pavyks – įkvėps tūkstančius. *Valstybė*. https://www.delfi.lt/verslas/verslas/jeigu-jiems-pavyks-ikveps-tukstancius.d?id=67083138

Brandes, P., Dharwadkar, R., & Lemesis, G. V. (2003). Effective employee stock option design: Reconciling stakeholder, strategic, and motivational factors. *The Academy of Management Perspectives*, *17*(1), 77–93. doi:10.5465/ame.2003.9474813

Bryson, A., Freeman, R. B., Lucifora, C., Pellizzari, M., & Pérotin, V. (2013). Paying for performance: incentive pay schemes and employees' financial participation. In Executive Remuneration and Employee Performance Related Pay, A Transatlantic Perspective. Oxford University Press.

Case, J., & Quarrey, M. (2019). Turning employees into owners: An analysis of policy initiatives for rebuilding the American Dream. *Journal of Participation and Employee Ownership*, *2*(3), 202–211. doi:10.1108/JPEO-09-2019-0022

Civinskas, R., & Dvorak, J. (2017). New social cooperation model in service oriented economy: The case of employee financial participation in the Baltic states. *Engineering Management in Production and Services*, *9*(3), 37–50. doi:10.1515/emj-2017-0024

Civinskas, R., & Dvorak, J. (2019). In Search of Employee Perspective: Understanding How Lithuanian Companies Use Employees Representatives in the Adoption of Company's Decisions. *Administrative Sciences*, *9*(4), 78. doi:10.3390/admsci9040078

CVbankas.lt. (2019). *Motyvacinė priemonė, kurios vertę supranta ne visi – vertė gali užaugti penkiagubai*. https://www.15min.lt/verslas/naujiena/karjera/cvbankas-lt-motyvacine-priemone-kurios-verte-supranta-ne-visi-verte-gali-uzaugti-penkiagubai-666-1245276

Damiani, M. (2009). *The Stakeholder Corporate Governance View Revisited. In Corporate Governance, Organization and the Firm*. Edward Elgar.

Eisenhardt, K. M. (1989). Agency theory: An assessment and review. *Academy of Management Review*, *14*(1), 57–74. doi:10.5465/amr.1989.4279003

Elouadi, S. (2020). The promotion of partnership value through employee share ownership and customer share ownership. In *Corporate Governance Models and Applications in Developing Economies* (pp. 192–204). IGI Global. doi:10.4018/978-1-5225-9607-3.ch010

Elouadi, S., Noamene, T. B., & Chaher, D. (2016). Employee Ownership And Employee-Shareholders Satisfaction: An Analysis Of French Companies Listed On The SBF 250. *Journal of Applied Business Research*, *32*(3), 981–994. doi:10.19030/jabr.v32i3.9647

Faleye, O., Mehrotra, V., & Morck, R. (2006). When labor has a voice in corporate governance. *Journal of Financial and Quantitative Analysis*, *41*(3), 489–510. doi:10.1017/S0022109000002519

Fama, E. F., & Jensen, M. C. (1983). Separation of ownership and control. *The Journal of Law & Economics*, *26*(2), 301–325. doi:10.1086/467037

Freeman, R. E. (1983). Strategic management: A stakeholder approach. *Advances in Strategic Management*, *1*(1), 31–60.

Freeman, R. E. (1984). Strategic management: A stakeholder theory. *Journal of Management Studies*, *39*(1), 1–21.

Freeman, R. E., Harrison, J. S., Wicks, A. C., Parmar, B. L., & De Colle, S. (2010). *Stakeholder theory: The state of the art*. Cambridge University Press.

Geczy, C., Jeffers, J. S., Musto, D. K., & Tucker, A. M. (2016). In Pursuit of Good & Gold: Data Observations of Employee Ownership & Impact Investment. *Seattle University Law Review*, *40*, 555–606.

Guedri, Z., & Hollandts, X. (2008). Beyond dichotomy: The curvilinear impact of employee ownership on firm performance. *Corporate Governance*, *16*(5), 460–474. doi:10.1111/j.1467-8683.2008.00703.x

Jaffee, J., & Freeman, J. (2000). Institutional change in real-time: The development of employee stock options for German venture capital. In *The New Institutionalism in Strategic Management* (pp. 219–246). Emerald Group Publishing Limited.

Jensen, M. C., & Meckling, W. H. (1976). Theory of the firm: Managerial behavior, agency costs and ownership structure. *Journal of Financial Economics*, *3*(4), 305–360. doi:10.1016/0304-405X(76)90026-X

Kahle, K. M. (2002). When a buyback isn'ta buyback: Open market repurchases and employee options. *Journal of Financial Economics*, *63*(2), 235–261. doi:10.1016/S0304-405X(01)00095-2

Kang, S., & Kim, A. (2019). Employee stock ownership and financial performance in European countries: The moderating effects of uncertainty avoidance and social trust. *Human Resource Management*, *58*(6), 641–655. doi:10.1002/hrm.21942

Kim, K. Y., & Patel, P. C. (2017). Employee ownership and firm performance: A variance decomposition analysis of European firms. *Journal of Business Research, 70*, 248–254. doi:10.1016/j.jbusres.2016.08.014

Kroumova, M. K., & Sesil, J. C. (2006). Intellectual capital, monitoring, and risk: What predicts the adoption of employee stock options? *Industrial Relations, 45*(4), 734–752. doi:10.1111/j.1468-232X.2006.00449.x

Kruse, D. L., Freeman, R. B., & Blasi, J. R. (Eds.). (2010). *Shared capitalism at work: Employee ownership, profit and gain sharing, and broad-based stock options*. University of Chicago Press. doi:10.7208/chicago/9780226056968.001.0001

Kurtulus, F. A., & Kruse, D. (2018). An Empirical Analysis of the Relationship between Employee Ownership and Employment Stability in the US: 1999–2011. *British Journal of Industrial Relations, 56*(2), 245–291. doi:10.1111/bjir.12254

Lamberg, J. A., Savage, G. T., & Pajunen, K. (2003). Strategic stakeholder perspective to ESOP negotiations: The case of United Airlines. *Management Decision, 41*(4), 383–393. doi:10.1108/00251740310468211

Lim, E. N., & Mccann, B. T. (2013). The influence of relative values of outside director stock options on firm strategic risk from a multiagent perspective. *Strategic Management Journal, 34*(13), 1568–1590. doi:10.1002mj.2088

Linas Agro Group. (2018). Akcijų suteikimo taisyklės, patvirtintos neeiliniame visuotiniame akcininkų susirinkime. *Protokolas, 2*.

Lowitzsch, J. (2009). *Financial Participation of Employees in the EU-27*. Springer. doi:10.1057/9780230274167

Lowitzsch, J., Dunsch, S., & Hashi, I. (2017). *Spanish Sociedades Laborales—Activating the Unemployed.* A Potential New EU Active Labour Market Policy Instrument Palgrave Macmillan.

Lowitzsch, J., & Hashi, I. (2014). *The promotion of employee ownership and participation*. Study prepared by the Inter-University Centre for European Commission's DG MARKT, 29–39.

Martin, G. P., Gomez-Mejia, L. R., & Wiseman, R. M. (2013). Executive stock options as mixed gambles: Revisiting the behavioral agency model. *Academy of Management Journal, 56*(2), 451–472. doi:10.5465/amj.2010.0967

Mathieu, M. (2017). *European Federation of Employee Share Ownership Report 2017*. European Federation of Employee Share Ownership.

Miknevičius, L. (2019). "Ad Rem" grupė vadovus "prisirišo" įmonės akcijomis. *Verslo žinios*. https://www.vz.lt/transportas-logistika/2019/02/05/ad-rem-grupe-vadovus-prisiriso-imones-akcijomis

Miller, S. D. (2012). *Buyouts: Success for Owners, Management, PEGs, ESOPs and Mergers and Acquisitions*. John Wiley & Sons. doi:10.1002/9781119205296

Poutsma, E., & Kaarsemaker, E. (2015). Added value of employee financial participation. In *Human Resource Management Practices* (pp. 181–196). Springer. doi:10.1007/978-3-319-08186-1_11

Poutsma, E., Ligthart, P. E., & Kaarsemaker, E. C. (2017). Employee Ownership and High-Performance Work Systems in Context. In Sharing in the Company: Determinants, Processes and Outcomes of Employee Participation (pp. 5–22). Emerald Publishing Limited. doi:10.1108/S0885-333920160000017004

Renneboog, L., Ter Horst, J., & Zhang, C. (2008). The price of ethics and stakeholder governance: The performance of socially responsible mutual funds. *Journal of Corporate Finance*, *14*(3), 302–322. doi:10.1016/j.jcorpfin.2008.03.009

Reynolds, J. (2014). *Sharing Profits: The ethics of remuneration, tax and shareholder returns*. Springer.

Richter, A., & Schrader, S. (2017). Levels of employee share ownership and the performance of listed companies in Europe. *British Journal of Industrial Relations*, *55*(2), 396–420. doi:10.1111/bjir.12169

Rimas, J. (2010). *Privataus kapitalo sandoriai-bendrovių teisės aspektai* (Daktaro disertacija). Vilnius universitetas.

Sahakiants, I., & Festing, M. (2019). The use of executive share-based compensation in Poland: Investigating institutional and agency-based determinants in an emerging market. *International Journal of Human Resource Management*, *30*(6), 1036–1057. doi:10.1080/09585192.2016.1172652

Sanders, W. G., & Hambrick, D. C. (2007). Swinging for the fences: The effects of CEO stock options on company risk taking and performance. *Academy of Management Journal*, *50*(5), 1055–1078. doi:10.5465/amj.2007.27156438

Shipper, F. (Ed.). (2014). *Shared entrepreneurship: A path to engaged employee ownership*. Springer.

Srivastava, A., & Bhatia, S. (2020). Influence of family ownership and governance on performance: Evidence from India. *Global Business Review*. doi:10.1177/0972150919880711

Stamkauskienė, R. (2018). Kompanija, kurioje galioja džentelmenų kodeksas. *Verslo žinios*. https://www.vz.lt/transportas-logistika/2018/09/18/kompanija-kurioje-galioja-dzentelmenu-kodeksas

Thompson, P. B., McWilliams, A., & Shanley, M. (2014). Creating competitive advantage: A stakeholder view of employee ownership. *International Journal of Strategic Change Management*, *5*(3), 262–279. doi:10.1504/IJSCM.2014.064468

Triki, T., & Ureche-Rangau, L. (2012). Stock options and firm performance: New evidence from the French market. *Journal of International Financial Management & Accounting*, *23*(2), 154–185. doi:10.1111/j.1467-646X.2012.01057.x

Ugarkovic, M. (2008). *Profit sharing and company performance*. Springer-Verlag.

Uribetxebarria, U., Garmendia, A., & Elorza, U. (2020). Does employee participation matter? An empirical study on the effects of participation on well-being and organizational performance. *Central European Journal of Operations Research*, 1–29. doi:10.100710100-020-00704-7

Wagner, S. H., Parker, C. P., & Christiansen, N. D. (2003). Employees that think and act like owners: Effects of ownership beliefs and behaviors on organizational effectiveness. *Personnel Psychology*, *56*(4), 847–871. doi:10.1111/j.1744-6570.2003.tb00242.x

Weltmann, D. (2019). The efficiency of wages, profit sharing, and stock. *Journal of Participation and Employee Ownership*, *2*(3), 222–235. doi:10.1108/JPEO-09-2019-0021

Whitfield, K., Pendleton, A., Sengupta, S., & Huxley, K. (2017). Employee share ownership and organisational performance: A tentative opening of the black box. *Personnel Review*, *46*(7), 1280–1296. doi:10.1108/PR-09-2016-0243

Wolff, F. (2012). *Employee Stock Option Compensation: A Behavioral Finance Approach* (Vol. 2). Springer Science & Business Media.

Zattoni, A. (2011). Who should control a corporation? Toward a contingency stakeholder model for allocating ownership rights. *Journal of Business Ethics*, *103*(2), 255–274. doi:10.100710551-011-0864-3

Zona, F. (2016). Agency models in different stages of CEO tenure: The effects of stock options and board independence on R&D investment. *Research Policy*, *45*(2), 560–575. doi:10.1016/j.respol.2015.10.012

ENDNOTES

1 In 2014–2017, 103 participants from the group participated in the program. The share ownership granted to them averaged 4.2 percent. This option was evaluated according to the achievement of the goals of the units. Two key performance indicators measure this: - total return on shares and EBITDA (earnings before interest, taxes, depreciation and amortization). Interestingly, one of the performance indicators was the change in the subsidiary's place in the corporation's internal ratings.

2 In 2018, AB Linas Agro Group and its subsidiaries had 2,199 employees. Including 133 managers

3 50 percent of all stock options will be valid for 3 years from the signing of the options, 25 percent - for four years, and the remaining 25 percent - for five years. As at 30 June 2019, the Group accounted for related expenses in proportion to the first period granted: a total of LTL 960 thousand. (including an amount of EUR 182 thousand that is expected to be transferred to the tax office to cover the employees' tax liability related to the payment for shares).

4 Based on data from a qualitative study. Unfortunately, it was not possible to obtain accurate data on the involvement of executives and other employees in the stock option plan.

5 In 2019, AB Linas Agro Group (LAG) incurred LTL 6.8 million. Eur. loss. In 2018, the net profit was 9.5 million. Eur.

6 This scheme is simpler than where the shares are transferred by the company. This is due to several reasons: 1) faster implementation; 2) it is more acceptable from a taxation point of view. Shares are subject to personal income tax only and there is no need to wait for a 3-year deferral period due to tax relief on social security and compulsory health insurance tax relief. Implementation goes quickly and does not require complex structures. However, a legal transaction under this scheme requires certain forms of transaction and notarial matching.

7 Analyzing the data on stock options programs in start-ups, the problem of information availability was encountered. There is no publicly available information about the applied programs, plans, and the representatives of the companies themselves (even those who agreed to participate in the qualitative study) refused to provide information on the basis of documents (such as stock option rules, draft contracts, etc.).

8 Vinted, the largest online second-hand fashion trading platform in Europe, is located in Lithuania.

Chapter 4
Understanding Employee Ownership in the Context of French Family Firms

Mohamed Ouiakoub
La Rochelle University, France

Sara Elouadi
Hassan II University, Casablanca, Morocco

ABSTRACT

Family firms, in which a family controls a majority stake in the organisation, are often considered characteristically different from non-family firms. However, our understanding of employee ownership in the specific context of family firms suffers from the concerns raised by owners of several family firms about such ownership. The decision to open the capital to its employees goes beyond the question of the ownership of family business. Nevertheless, it impacts the governance of the company and raises several concerns including the transmission of information, transparency, increased formalism, and taxation. This study aims to analyze how family firms benefit from an employee ownership plan and how governance practices impact the mechanism of employee ownership plans. This study examines the financial communication of French family firms in terms of mployee ownership activities.

DOI: 10.4018/978-1-7998-8557-3.ch004

INTRODUCTION

Employee ownership is a subject little studied on the family businesses literature. While researchers have theoretically considered the sharing of employee ownership in family businesses (Cruz et al., 2011), empirical studies have focused on employee ownership among executives, namely family managers (Gomez-Mejia, Larraza-Kintana and Makri, 2003). This is regrettable, because employee share ownership allows the majority of the company's employees, and not just managers, to become owners, thus creating a competitive advantage through the entire workforce (Rousseau & Shperling, 2004). Therefore, this study provides empirical evidence of how French family businesses approach the use of employee share plans differently.

The new PACTE law aims to reform participation and proposes to involve employees more strongly in the results and shareholding of their company. Employee shareholding is becoming more widespread in companies: with 3.7 million employee shareholders in their company (FEAS-EFES), France is the European country with the highest rate of employee (non-executive) shareholding (4%) in 2016, for a European rate of 1.6%. Leading continental European countries, ahead of Germany, which has only 700,000 employee shareholders, France is nevertheless well ahead of the United States and Great Britain (with a democratization rate of over 25%). However, while the United States is the world leader in financial participation practices (50% of employees benefit from one or more performance participation schemes), participation in governance bodies through the representation of employee shareholders on boards of directors or supervisory boards is not institutionalized like in France, where the law explicitly provides for it. France is therefore unique in terms of its employee shareholding rate, but also in terms of its legislation, which allows for the presence of employee shareholders in governance.

Employee ownership is often presented as a factor of employee motivation. It could also help to reduce conflicts between employees, managers and shareholders. However, the fact that about two thirds of all listed companies do not use employee share ownership suggests that such a formula does not only have advantages. Moreover, it seems that a link can be established between the introduction of employee ownership and the type of ownership structure. Indeed, according to a survey of large companies in the SBF250 index, only 26% of family-owned companies would be concerned, compared to 60% of their non-family-owned counterparts. The reluctance expressed by some managers of family businesses is probably not unrelated to this disparity (Hewitt Associates, 2002). They believe that employee ownership would make the management and valuation of their company more complex. In addition, employee ownership could limit the liquidity of listed shares, and could also complicate the organization of the succession of the owner-manager. Finally, some managers, fearing the risks inherent to stock market mechanisms, would refuse to allow their employees to be confronted with such risks. Given the performance of the employee share ownership, which is higher than the CAC40 and SBF250 market indices, such caution may be surprising. However, the synthesis of Arcimoles and Brillet (2000) reminds us that the relationship between employee ownership and economic performance, which is often positive, is still very uncertain.

Researchers argue that family firms are reluctant to share ownership with non-family employees due to concerns about shareholder dilution (Cruz, Firfiray, & Gomez-Mejia, 2011). This attitude is surprising insofar as family businesses consider employees to be an integral part of their long-term viability (Hoopes & Miller, 2006; Le Breton-Miller &Miller, 2006) and that employee ownership, if used, can play an instrumental role in the development of the company. Drawing upon the corporate governance and socioemotionalwealth (SEW) preservation literatures, this study seeks to address this possibility by examining whether governance practices affects the use of employee ownership in family firms. Since these governance mechanisms have been used extensivelyby family owners to maintain their control over the firm relative toother shareholders (Villalonga & Amit, 2009, 2010), we contend that these mechanisms of corporate governance may also impact the use of employee ownership. Therefore, our primary research question is: what is the relationship among governance practices impact the use of employee ownership among family firms?

This chapter is essentially devoted to an empirical examination of this issue. In this perspective, we recall that theoretical approaches to the definition of the family firm have been debated, thus establishing the impossibility of arriving at a single definition. On the basis of these theoretical elements, we set out in the research results the specificities of family firms in terms of employee ownership; we propose some avenues for future research on aspects that remain to be explored.

THEORETICAL BACKGROUND: EMPLOYEE SHAREHOLDING IN FAMILY-INFLUENCED FIRMS

Although family businesses tend to be highly committed to their employees, existing research on family businesses asserts that family owners are likely to be hesitant when it comes to broadly sharing ownership with non-family employees.

Family Businesses

There is no unanimously accepted definition of the family firm, and there are almost as many definitions as there are works on the subject. Approximately 10% of the research on the topic of family businesses is specifically concerned with definitions, concepts and research methodologies (Allouche and Amann, 2000; Arrègle and Mari, 2010), showing that the debate is far from over (readers who wish to have an overview of the variety of definitions can refer to Allouche and Amann, 2000; Chrisman et al., 2005; Sacristán-Navarro et al., 2011). The definition of a family firm chosen by the researcher is of considerable importance in interpreting the results obtained in empirical work. Indeed, how to attribute specific behavior to family firms when there may be equivocation about what precisely a family firm is? Westhead and Cowling (1998) illustrate this difficulty by showing how the chosen definition modifies the distribution of a population. Between the least restrictive definition ("top managers consider the company as family-owned") and the most restrictive ("the family owns more than 50% of the voting rights, top managers consider the company as family-owned, more than 51% of the top managers belong to the family and there is at least one second generation"), the share of family-owned companies in their sample drops from 81% to 15%!

Even if it is futile to hope to arrive at a single definition of the family business, it is nevertheless recognized that the criteria of transmission, ownership and involvement of the family in management are decisive in characterizing the family business. But what level should these criteria reach: majority control? A threshold of 10%? 20%? No minimum ownership threshold? How many family members are involved in the management of the company? Is there a family business from the first generation or does the business have to have already been passed on? Can one criterion compensate for another? (Would a fourth generation business with a low family shareholding be more "family" than a second generation business with a majority family?)

Chrisman et al (2005) identify two main categories of definitions of family firms. On the one hand, there are definitions for which family involvement (in terms of shareholding, governance, management, succession) is a sufficient condition. And on the other hand, those for which involvement is necessary but not sufficient to characterize family businesses, which must also meet less easily quantifiable conditions, which constitute the "essence" of the family business, such as the willingness to transmit (Litz, 1995), "familiness" (Habbershon and Williams, 1999), described by Arrègle et al. (2004) as the "unique resources that a firm possesses as a result of the systems of interactions between the family, family members and the business", or family social capital (Arrègle et al., 2007).

The essence of the family firm, as described by Chua et al. (1999), is its uniqueness; it is not just a matter of family members being shareholders and/or managers of a firm. What makes the family business unique is the influence that this model of ownership, governance, management and transmission has on the structure of the business, on the formulation and implementation of objectives and strategy, on the vision that a family has for a business, on the intention to develop and pursue this vision and these objectives in the future. It is illusory and certainly not necessary to arrive at a single definition. As Arrègle and Mari (2010) point out, "this heterogeneity reflects different points of view and interests. But in order to avoid misinterpretation in an empirical analysis, the definition chosen must be clearly specified. In our view, a firm is family-owned if at least two members of the same family (by marriage or blood) are shareholders and involved in the management of the firm. Insofar as empirical work has shown the sensitivity of the results to the inclusion of firms from the first generation onwards (Villalonga and Amit, 2006), we add the criterion of the willingness to pass on to the next generation for firms still run by their founders.

Finally, we can mention a proposal made by Astrachan et al (2002). The authors assume that the traditional dichotomy between family and non-family firms does not reflect the reality of family firms. In their view, it would be more accurate to use a continuous scale to measure the family character of a company, based on three dimensions: power (shareholding, governance, management), family experience (number of generations) and culture (similarity of family and company values, family involvement in the company). The use of this measure would make it possible to illustrate the diversity of family businesses and to qualify the results of empirical work aimed at explaining their specific behaviors.

Theories to Explain the Governance of Family Firms

As we have seen, family businesses are diverse by nature. It is therefore logical to find different theoretical approaches applied to their study. These cover various disciplinary fields, such as psychology, sociology, economics or strategic management. Whatever the approach, the main objectives are to define the family character and to establish the differences between family businesses and all other businesses. Within strategic management, several perspectives have been mobilized to propose a theoretical framework for the analysis of family firms. The agency theory and the stewardship theory make it possible to highlight their particularities in terms of governance. The resource-based approach and the concept of socio-emotional value highlight the specific strategic advantages of family businesses.

The application of agency theory to family firms reveals a fundamental characteristic that sets them apart from all other firms: given the involvement of the owner family in management, principal and agent are confused. However, this feature is likely to lead to both higher and lower agency costs. Family members are assumed to behave altruistically because family membership leads to decisions and behaviors based more on feelings and emotions than on simple rationality and the pursuit of self-interest. Altruism in family businesses is opposed to opportunism. Agency costs should therefore be reduced because of the existence of shared values and a relationship of trust. In addition, the proximity between family members minimizes information asymmetries and allows for consistency and unity in strategic objectives. More generally, the pursuit of interests other than purely economic in family firms reduces the problems associated with agency relationships. However, specific agency costs may arise in family firms. The family is not necessarily homogeneous and made up of individuals sharing common interests. This is all the more true when ownership is distributed between generations through succession. Dissension, information asymmetries and conflicts of interest may be even greater than in a non-family business where a majority group of shareholders share common goals. In succession situations, family members may be brought into important management positions without particular merit and without appropriate skills. Thus, a negative consequence of altruism is excessive generosity leading to not punishing the incompetence of other family members by accepting lack of expertise and decisions contrary to maximizing value creation. This is only honest incompetence. But it can even go as far as accepting opportunistic or even criminal behavior, due to a tendency to secrecy and withdrawal into the family that diminishes external control in decision-making.

However, the identification of agency costs in family firms is complex, if not impossible, because it is not necessarily relevant to apply a theoretical framework based on the idea that managers pursue only their personal interests to the detriment of shareholders' interests. Thus, another approach, the stewardship theory, appears as a theoretical perspective that can complement the agency theory and prove particularly adapted to take into account the specificities of the family character. Stewardship theory is based on a sociological and psychological approach that sees people as trustworthy, oriented towards the collective and respecting the interests of the organization in which they are located. It thus highlights the elements that lead to a convergence of interests between the principal and the agent, without limiting itself to the question of financial incentives and control by governance structures. The manager can place a high value on cooperation. This provides an intrinsic motivation to act in the interest of the organization. Commitment and motivation are the drivers of the manager's action and they result from the existence of a long-term trust between the manager and the shareholders. This type of behavior and relationship is characteristic of family businesses in which managers belong to the family or have emotional ties to it. This leads to a strong sense of commitment and motivation to act for the good of the company, not only for the family members but also for all employees. The governance characteristics of family firms highlighted by stewardship theory have been mobilized to explain the differences in performance between these firms and all other firms: resources that are not used to control agency behaviors are invested in seizing opportunities and developing performance, there is coherence and unity of purpose, there is greater strategic flexibility, and individual actions are oriented toward creating value for the firm.

Another theoretical perspective, resource theory, has also been used to highlight the specific strategic specific strategic advantages of family businesses. Family businesses have different ways of evaluating, acquiring and managing resources and management of resources that differ from those of other businesses. More specifically, five sources of advantages specific to family businesses can be identified: human capital, social capital sustainability, long-term orientation of decisions and specificity of governance structures. The system of interactions between the three levels of family, firm and individual family members creates an idiosyncratic set of resources and competencies that are deeply rooted in "familiness" and are therefore inherently difficult to imitate. The existence of long-term relationships with The existence of long-term relationships with internal and external stakeholders based on family behavior also helps explain the easy access to certain resources and the development of unique social capital. This system of relationships, tacit in nature, and this long-term orientation, conceived as sources of competitive advantages, raises the question of the transfer of these resources between generations in order to maintain the advantages. Thus, another specific capacity developed by family businesses is that of the transfer of tacit knowledge, which is favored by the personal investment of the various family members and which constitutes a fundamental asset in the creation and preservation of competitive advantages.

The performance criteria of a family business must be linked to the emotional value that a family derives from its position in the ownership and management of the company. This value goes beyond the financial aspects and is based on the exercise of personal authority, the psychological needs for belonging, identification and intimacy, the desire to preserve family values, the desire to perpetuate the dynasty and maintain the founder's legacy, the development of the family's social capital, the feeling of belonging to the clan, the trust resulting from the presence of family members in key positions within the company, and the altruistic behavior among family members. All of these elements have been grouped together under the concept of "socio-emotional wealth", which makes it possible to explain the particular character of governance and performance of family businesses. This concept can be linked to the Behavioral Agency Model. According to this model, the risk behavior dictating managers' decision-making varies according to the context. In the specific context of family businesses, the reference point for decision-making is less the maximization of added value than the protection and perpetuation of socio-emotional wealth.

The Relationship Between Family Influence and Employee Shareholding

Research, mostly Anglo-Saxon, generally concludes that the economic effects of employee ownership are positive, but uncertain. In France, the effects of employee ownership on company performance and risk remain largely unknown, and even more so in the presence of family control.

Moreover, if employee ownership could strengthen the confidence and performance of family firms, its opportunistic instrumentation cannot be excluded. Employee ownership can indeed serve to perpetuate family control of a company, with the same uncertain effects of rooting and alliance as for other companies. Thus, on the one hand, the maintenance of family control and the partial alignment of the interests of employees and shareholders can lead to a superior performance of the company. But, on the other hand, the pivotal role in the capital that employee-shareholders can play gives them a new and real power. They can use it to influence the company's strategy and to direct the policy of redistribution of wealth in their favour, by favouring, for example, an increase in wages. It is also possible that the announcement of an employee shareholding plan, by ensuring the constitution of a blocking minority, in full agreement with the owner family, may penalize the stock market value, by cancelling out any speculative anticipation of a possible takeover managerial specificities, trust and roots therefore combine to make the effects of employee shareholding on the performance of family businesses very uncertain. The same is true for risk, since it is not known to what extent employee ownership can stabilize or disrupt social relations. Under these conditions, an empirical test of the possible relationship between employee ownership and risk-performance, applied exclusively to family firms, is desirable.

Broad-based employee ownership can support the long-term viability of the firm by aligning the interests of employees with those of owners (Pfeffer, 1995). Previous human resource management studies have found that broad-based employee ownership programs are generally associated with a number of positive firm outcomes, such as increased worker productivity, improved financial performance, and higher survival rates (Carberry, 2011; Kruse, 2002). Yet, researchers argue that family firms are reluctant to share ownership with non-family employees due to concerns about ownership dilution (Cruz, Firfiray, & Gomez-Mejia, 2011). This is surprising given that family businesses view employees as integral to their long-term viability (Hoopes & Miller, 2006; Le Breton-Miller & Miller, 2006), and broad-based employee ownership programs, if used, can play a critical role.

Family firms often move from private to publicly traded status for a variety of reasons, including the need to raise equity capital when debt capital is maximized and the desire to enhance the firm's reputation (Astrachan and McConaughy, 2001). In contrast to private firms, publicly traded family firms have mixed ownership structures, consisting of both family shareholders and multiple non-family shareholders with small to large stakes and a desire to influence firm operations (Fiegener, 2010). Therefore, in order to maintain or increase their power over the firm, family owners tend to implement control-enhancing mechanisms, such as appointing a family member as CEO (Villalonga and Amit, 2006). Through this increased control, family owners exert substantial influence over the strategic actions of the firm, limiting any intervention by non-family shareholders (Villa-longa & Amit, 2006, 2010).

By guiding the strategic actions of the company, family owners are led to preserve their socio-emotional wealth rather than focusing exclusively on the accumulation of financial wealth (Gomez-Mejia, Haynes, Nunez-Nickel, Jacobson, & Moyano -Fuentes, 2007). According to Berrone, Cruz and Gomez-Mejia (2012), socio-emotional wealth represents "the stock of affect-related value that a family derives fromits controlling position in a particular firm" (p. 259). Based on behavioral agency theory (Gomez-Mejia et al., 2007), the socio-emotional wealth preservation perspective states that family owners, weighing the potential advantages and disadvantages of various actions of the family business for socio-emotional wealth, will adopt more of a loss aversion mentality, so that the family business will avoid any strategic action likely to impoverish socio-emotional wealth (Berrone et al., 2012). In their quest to preserve socio-emotional wealth, family owners pursue an agenda consisting of three underlying goals:

Keeping control and influence over the firm's opera-tions and ownership; perpetuating the family dynasty, ensuringthat the business is handed down to future generations; and sus-taining family image and reputation (Naldi et al., 2013, p. 1343).

Previous research has shown that the preservation of socio-emotional wealth has an effect on a variety of strategic actions of family businesses, including corporate social responsibility, divestments and environmental activity (Berrone, Cruz, Gomez-Mejia, & Larraza-Kintana, 2010). Nonetheless, there are two important considerations when it comes to socio-emotional wealth. First, while there are different goals of socio-emotional wealth, family control serves as a goal of supra-socio-emotional wealth that takes priority over others (Berrone et al., 2012). Gomez-Mejia et al. (2007) found that family owners were willing to take the risk of poor performance and organizational failure in order to maintain control over the family business. Second, to ensure control through socio-emotional wealth, family owners often adopt control enhancement mechanisms; however, not all mechanisms are created equal (Villalonga and Amit, 2006, 2010). Specifically, family owners who are actively involved in running the business exercise more direct control over its activities, while equity-based mechanisms, such as double-class shares, tend to provide more indirect control through shareholder voting. Therefore, these researchers suggest that the various forms of family control may affect the strategic actions of the family business differently.

By extending the perspective of socio-emotional wealth to the management of human resources, Cruz et al. (2011) argue that family businesses, in general, will be more inclined to use human resource practices that allow the preservation of socio-emotional wealth while avoiding human resource practices that could deplete socio-emotional wealth, regardless economic benefits. When it comes to employee ownership, family businesses face potential compromises in terms of socio-emotional wealth, which makes the choice to use them difficult. On the one hand, employee ownership can threaten the control and influence that family owners exercise over the business due to dilution of ownership. Family ownership can be diluted by issuing own shares for distribution to employee accounts through employee share ownership plan trusts (Rosen & Rodrick, 2013). In this case, family fears of shareholder dilution are all the more exasperated as large non-family shareholders (may become more influential if they acquire these employee shares on the stock market (Martin, Makri and Gomez-Mejia, 2011). To perpetuate the family dynasty, employee stock ownership plans can encourage employees to focus on the long-term viability of the business by providing them with long-term economic benefits rather than immediate ones tied to the performance of the business (Blinder, 2011). Regarding the reputation and image of the family related to the family business, responsible human resource practices serve to develop a positive reputation in the eyes of current and potential employees (Zellweger, Nason, Nordqvist, & Brush, 2011). For example, by offering generous salaries and benefits, family businesses let their employees know that they are highly valued (Le Breton-Miller & Miller, 2006). Likewise, employee share ownership programs can promote greater engagement and identification of the organization among employees, thereby creating a positive image of the company (Kruse, 2002). Overall, the use of employee share ownership plan represents a trade-off for the socio-emotional wealth of the family, as it can erode the socio-emotional wealth in control and preserve the socio-emotional wealth in the fields of family dynasty and reputation.

Family Businesses Around the World

The Family Business Index is a global ranking of family businesses, based on their sales revenue. Companies that have not published accounts in the last 24 months are excluded from this ranking. The family business must be managed at least by the second generation. One or more family members must be involved in the management of the business, as a member of the board of directors or management.

To meet the family business test, the family must have a substantial stake in the business. It must have at least 50% of the capital and voting rights of the company. Members of the public company family must hold at least 32% of the company's capital and voting rights.

The latest results available for the index are for the year 2019. The editors of the Family Business Index see little change in the geographic distribution of the FB500, although there is a substantial increase in German companies and a slight decrease in the representation of American companies in the index produced by EY and the University of Saint Gallen.

The number of technology companies in the index has increased significantly. New entrants to the 2019 edition are family businesses that are younger, smaller and more likely to be publicly traded.

Family businesses, whether young or old, new and existing, have boards of directors made up, for the most part, of people who are not part of the founding family.

Most of the board members are men and the gender balance of these boards is lower than that of the Fortune 500 index which contains a list of 500 global companies ranked according to the size of their revenue.

The geographic distribution of the world's largest family businesses has not changed much in 2019. Indeed, the largest number is recorded by the European continent. The number of European companies in the index goes from 224 in 2017 to 230 this year, with new entrants coming from Germany. The second place is occupied by the American continent whose number of family businesses goes from 154 in 2017 to 150 in 2019. The third place is occupied by the Asian continent with 94 family businesses, as in 2017. Finally, the African continent continues to house 4 family businesses.

The results published by the index show a strong representativeness of directors outside the founding family. Indeed, 27% of the members of the boards of directors of the family businesses in the index are part of the founding family, the rest are not.

In comparison, 22% of the board members of new companies entering the 2019 index are from the founding family, and nearly 78% are not.

Older family businesses are more likely to tap the expertise and perspectives of outside directors outside the family, but they also have fewer family members than family businesses in the third or fourth generation.

Between January 14 and March 20, 2019, Deloitte's Family Business Center conducted a survey of 791 family business leaders from 58 countries around the world. Executives were interviewed on issues relating to governance, management and prospects for family businesses.

The results are as follows: 65% of respondents would prefer ownership, management, or both to remain in the family. Indeed, 30% of respondents indicated that they would prefer to transfer ownership and management of the business to family members. 15% preferred to transfer only management and 20% would limit themselves to transferring ownership.

About a third of respondents say that non-family members make up the majority of their board of directors.

The perpetuation of family tradition and heritage is the top priority of respondents for the next 10 to 20 years. Who have mainly chosen to maintain the family inheritance and protect family capital with the desire to help the next generation understand the business and thus plan the succession.

Frensh Family Businesses

The new 2020 edition of the annual barometer - produced by the stock market operator Euronext - highlights the growing weight of families and founders in the capital of the 40 listed companies CAC 40 within the main barometer of the Parisian market. . In fact, their share increased from 10% at the end of 2016 to 14.5% at the end of 2018, which represented 207 billion euros in capitalization.

According to this latest barometer, the families and founders constituted, at the end of 2018, the second category of shareholders of the index behind the asset managers who control a quarter of the capital of the CAC 40 (precisely 24.9%), a share which has decreased since 2015 (28%).

The rise of family shareholders is mainly due to changes in the composition of the CAC 40 index, with the entries of Dassault Systèmes (40.7% controlled by the Dassault family) and Hermès (held at 54, 2% by the family holding company H51, a share to which must be added the 12.5% controlled by the family excluding the holding company and the 4.9% of Nicolas Puech, grandson of the founder Émile Hermès) to the detriment of Solvay and LafargeHolcim in 2018.

With the arrival of Hermès in the CAC40, 4 families are now among the 10 largest shareholders in the index. The surge in the valuation of LVMH (+ 130% over 3 years, + 220% over 5 years) allows the Arnault family to dominate the charts, with 4.3% of the total capitalization of the CAC.

While the Bettencourt-Meyers family (owner of L'Oréal, 2nd capitalization of the CAC 40) and the French State complete the podium, each holding 2.6% of the index. The Hermès (6th, 2.2%) and Pinault (8th, 1.5%) families also feature prominently in this ranking.

The first family business that reserves the largest share of capital for employees is the Bouygues company. For a long time, Bouygues has chosen to involve its employees in the success of their business.

It is now the first company in the CAC 40 in terms of employee shareholding, this positioning strengthens the commitment and federation of employees around the strategic objectives of the company.

Employee shareholders can play a positive role in the protection and preservation of family capital. In fact, from 1990, Martin Bouygues, founder of the group that bears his name, initiated the opening of the capital to employees, consequently, the capital held by the Bouygues family fell from 24% to 17%, this dilution of the capital for the benefit of employees has made it possible to constitute a blocking minority. In 1998, the Bouygues group neutralized a hostile takeover bid, undertaken by Vincent Bolloré, thanks to employee shareholders who worked to maintain family control.

Bouygues is a diversified industrial group organized around 4 areas of activity:

Construction (75.5% of turnover): leisure and urban development activities (46.7% of turnover; of Buildings and Public Works and public works of networks, electrical and thermal engineering and maintenance installations (45.5%; Bouygues Construction), and construction and maintenance of transport and property development infrastructure (7.8%; Bouygues Immobilier) telecommunications (18.5%; Bouygues Telecom): services mobile telephony, fixed telephony, Internet access, etc . Media (5.9%; the TF1 television channel); and others (0.1%).

The geographical revenue of sales is as follows: France (58.8%), European Union (6.7%), Europe (12.1%), North America (11.3%), Asia-Pacific (7,3%), Africa (2.6%), Central and South America (1%) and Middle East (0.2%).

The Bouygues brothers own the family holding company SCDM, the following figure details the shareholding structure of the company.

Moreover, in 2019 Bouygues received the great distinction from the French Federation of Employee Shareholder Associations (FAS)[1] for the following reasons according to the FAS: Bouygues group has developed a permanent commitment of more than 50 years from all of the company's stakeholders, an original social pact, the highest percentage of shareholding by employees in CAC40 companies, a top-up and a significant discount and the promotion of employee shareholding with the public authorities.

Figure 1. Bouygues shareholding

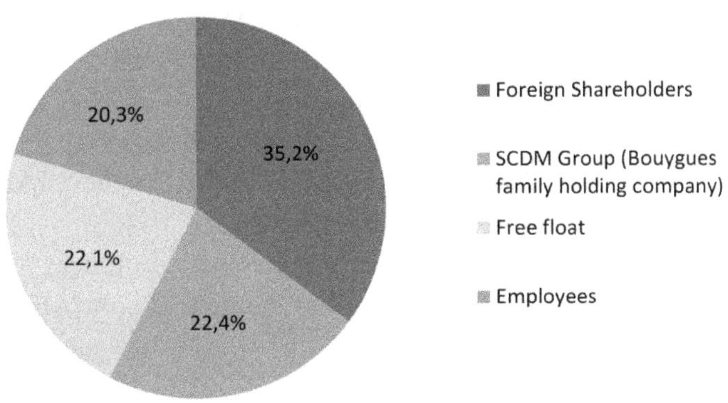

FRENCH FAMILY BUSINESSES AND EMPLOYEE SHAREHOLDING

In order to characterize French family businesses that apply employee share ownership, we used the composition of the French employee share ownership index. Indeed, in 2006 Euronext and the French Federation of Associations of Employee Shareholders and Former Employees (FAS) created an index on employee shareholding: Euronext FAS IAS®.

It measures the performance of companies with significant employee shareholding. It is the first of its kind in the world. It includes all the companies making up the CAC All-Tradable index and cumulatively meeting the following conditions:

- 3% or more of the capital is in the hands of employees;
- 15% of employees worldwide are shareholders;
- 25% of French employees are shareholders.

The performance of this index has been, since 2000, superior to that of the other indices (CAC 40, SBF 250). At the end of 2019, the index had 31 stocks and its performance had doubled over seven years. We can see in these results a reflection of the interactions between employee shareholding, trust, establishment and productivity of employees, and economic and financial performance of the company.

We have used the latest publication of the composition of the index which is currently available on the Euronext[2] web site and which dates from 04/30/2020.

The current composition brings together 31 companies. We then have to look for the shares of the capital held respectively by the employees and the founding families, if applicable by using the financial communication published by the companies and the information available on Euronext.

The maximum share of capital held by family shareholders is 69.66% and concerns the Boiron company. While the maximum share of capital held by employees is equal to 20.30% and concerns the Bouygues company. The average percentage of capital granted to employees of companies in the IAS index is equal to 6.08%. The average capital held by families within the IAS index is equal to 9.19%.

Graph 1 shows the distribution of companies in the Euronext IAS FAS index according to the capital held by family shareholders. (Figure 2)

Graph 2 shows the distribution of companies in the Euronext IAS FAS index according to the capital held by employees. (Figure 3)

And graph 3 shows the distribution of companies in the Euronext IAS FAS index according to the capital held by employees and families. (Figure 4)

Figure 2. Distribution of companies in the Euronext IAS FAS index according to the capital held by family shareholders

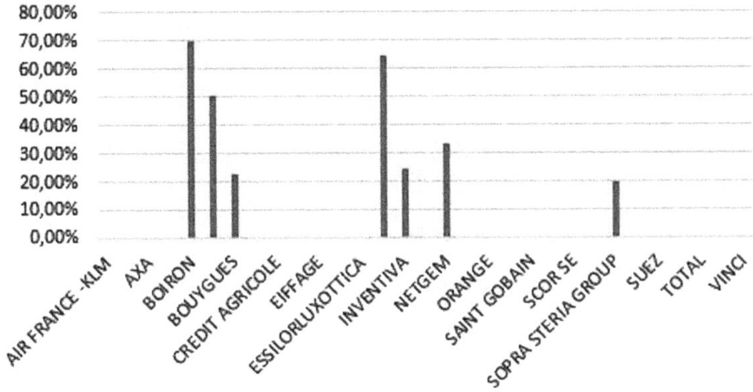

Figure 3. Distribution of companies in the Euronext IAS FAS index according to the capital held by employees

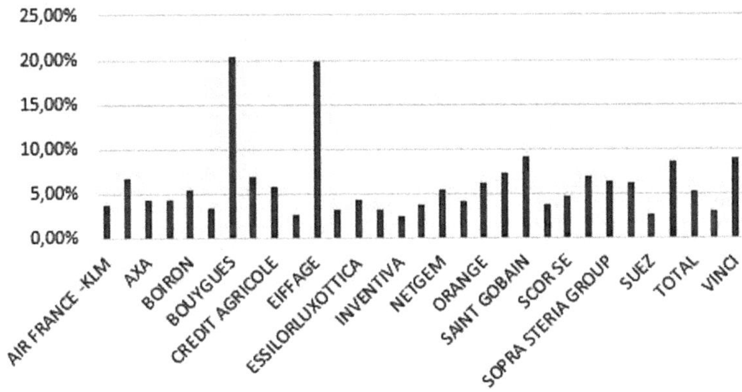

The table below summarizes the variances and standard deviations of the percentages of capital held by employees and the percentages of capital held by families within the Euronext IAS FAS index. (Table 1)

The Pearson coefficient is an index reflecting the existence of a linear relationship between two continuous variables. The correlation coefficient varies between -1 and +1, 0 reflecting a zero relationship between the two variables, a negative value (negative correlation) meaning that when one of the variables increases, the other decreases; while a positive value (positive correlation) indicates that the two variables vary together in the same direction.

Figure 4. Distribution of companies in the Euronext IAS FAS index according to the capital held by employees and families.

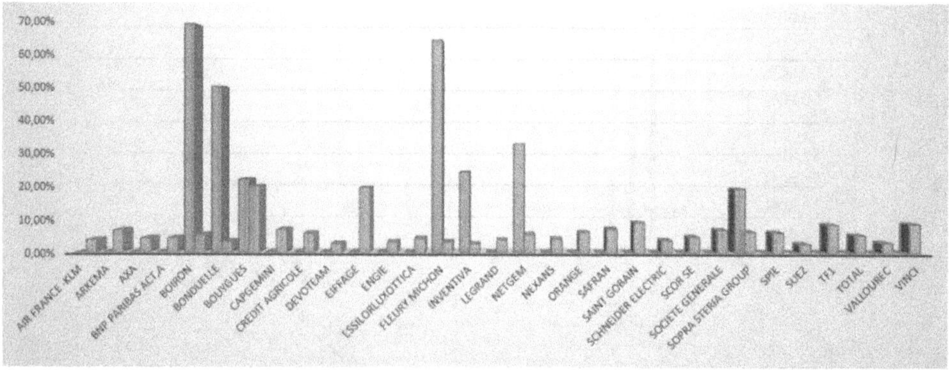

Table 1. Descriptive statistics of our sample

	Family Shareholding	Employee Shareholding
Variance	3,74%	0,17%
Standard deviation	19,66%	4,16%
Average	9,19%	6,08%
Maximum value	69,66%	20,30%
Minimum value	0,00%	2,50%

To test the Pearson correlation, we transformed our data into ordinal values. We tested in Table 2 the following two hypotheses:

H0: No correlation between the two variables: $\rho = 0$ or> 0.05
H1: there is a correlation between the two variables p <0.05

Our results reflect the presence of a negative coefficient but given that the p value is greater than the significance threshold of 0.05, we can reject H1 and conclude that there is no correlation between the percentage of family shareholding and the percentage of employee shareholding.

Family businesses occupy a prominent place in the global economy. In France, family businesses are developing a culture of protection and preservation of family capital. Our database of companies in the IAS FAS stock market index effectively reflects this finding. Indeed, among all the companies in the index, the representation of family businesses is low and does not exceed 22.5%.

Table 2. Pearson correlation statistics

		Rank Family Shareholding	Rank Employee Shareholding
Rank Family Shareholding	Pearson Correlation	1	-,190
	Sig. (bilateral)		,306
	N	31	31
Rank Employee Shareholding	Pearson Correlation	-,190	1
	Sig. (bilateral)	,306	
	N	31	31

With the exception of the Bouygues company, which is developing a culture of employee share ownership, the maximum percentage of shares given to employees is 6.3% and concerns the Sopra Steria Group company.

Our study shows that the Bouygues company cultivates a strong commitment to employees. Today, employees represent the second largest shareholder in the Group with 20.3% of the capital and 26.7% of the voting rights. The development of employee shareholding at

Bouygues is not new. The group launched its first corporate mutual fund (FCPE) in 1968. Called "Bouygues group participation", it is invested in Bouygues shares bought on the market and held 4.99% of the capital and 6.58%. voting rights at the end of 2014.

The FCPE "PEE groupe Bouygues", which collects voluntary savings from employees and the contribution paid by the company, controls 11.51% of the capital and 14.68% of the voting rights. The capital increases carried out in 2009, 2010 and 2012 also created 3 leveraged FCPEs. Finally, more modest, a last vehicle has been specially created for expatriates.

This governance structure has proven to be particularly effective in the past. In 1998, during the takeover bid launched by Vincent Bolloré, Bouygues employees joined forces with the SCDM and Ms. Francis Bouygues. Their 6.5% stake at the time (9.3% of the voting rights) had helped to make Vincent Bolloré renounce.

CONCLUSION

In conclusion, this study shows that not all family firms are reluctant to share ownership widely with their employees through employee ownership. By considering the role of different family control enhancements in framing the employee ownership decision, it is revealed that family firms led by a family CEO maintain their hesitancy toward employee ownership; however, family firms become less reluctant when dual-class share structures are in place. We hope this will encourage future research to take a more heterogeneous view of family firms when considering their human resource activities.

The topic of employee share ownership may offer a number of complementary lines of research. For example, it could be a question of confirming the existence of negative abnormal returns when employee share ownership plans are announced in order to reinforce family control. In addition, other approaches, such as longitudinal case studies, would facilitate further investigation of the interactions that may exist between family control, employee ownership, trust, embeddedness, conflicts of interest, risk and performance.

While the type of firm (family vs. non-family firms) may influence how firms benefit from an employee ownership plan, we encourage scholars to investigate how governance practices impact the mechanism of employee ownership plans in the specific context of family firms. It would be interesting, in future studies, to understand the implications of different generations of descendant CEOs (e.g. first, second, etc. generation away from the founder) versus the founding CEO on the use of employee stock own-ership plans by family businesses.

REFERENCES

Allouche, J., & Amann, B. (2000). L'entreprise familiale, un état de l'art. *Finance Contrôle Stratégie*, *3*(1), 33–79.

Anderson, R., Duru, A., & Reeb, D. (2009). Founders, heirs, and corporate opacity in the United States. *Journal of Financial Economics*, *92*(2), 205–222. doi:10.1016/j.jfineco.2008.04.006

Anderson, R., & Reeb, D. (2003). Founding-family ownership and firm per-formance. *The Journal of Finance*, *58*(3), 1301–1328. doi:10.1111/1540-6261.00567

Anderson, R., Reeb, D., & Zhao, W. (2012). Family-controlled firms and informedtrading: Evidence from short sales. *The Journal of Finance*, *67*(1), 351–385. doi:10.1111/j.1540-6261.2011.01714.x

Arrègle, J.-L., & Mari, I. (2010). Avantages ou désavantages des entreprises familiales? Principaux résultats des recherches et perspectives. *Revue Française de Gestion*, *1*(200), 87–109. doi:10.3166/rfg.200.87-109

Astrachan, J. (2010). Strategy in family business: Toward a multidimen-sional research agenda. *Journal of Family Business Strategy*, *1*(1), 6–14. doi:10.1016/j.jfbs.2010.02.001

Astrachan, J., & McConaughy, D. (2001). Venture capitalists and closelyheld IPOs: Lessons for family-controlled firms. *Family Business Review*, *14*(4), 295–311. doi:10.1111/j.1741-6248.2001.00295.x

Bazerman, M. (1984). The relevance of Kahneman and Tversky's conceptof framing to organizational behavior. *Journal of Management*, *10*(3), 333–343. doi:10.1177/014920638401000307

Berrone, P., Cruz, C., & Gomez-Mejia, L. (2012). Socioemotional wealth infamily firms: Theoretical dimensions, assessment approaches, andagenda for future research. *Family Business Review*, *25*(3), 258–279. doi:10.1177/0894486511435355

Blair, M., Kruse, D., & Blasi, J. (2000). Employee ownership: An unstableform or stabilizing force? In M. Blair & T. Kochan (Eds.), *The newrelationship: Human capital in the American corporation* (pp. 241–298). Brookings Institution. doi:10.2139srn.142146

Block, J. (2012). R&D investments in family and founder firms: An agency perspective. *Journal of Business Venturing*, *27*(2), 248–265. doi:10.1016/j.jbusvent.2010.09.003

Carberry, E. (2011). Employee ownership and shared capitalism: Assessingthe experience, research, and policy implications. In E. Carberry (Ed.), *Employee ownership and shared capitalism: New directions in research*. Labor and Employment Relations Association Series.

Chua, J., Chrisman, J., & Sharma, P. (1999). Defining the family businessby behavior. *Entrepreneurship Theory and Practice*, *23*(4), 19–40. doi:10.1177/104225879902300402

Gomez-Mejia, L., Haynes, K., Nunez-Nickel, M., Jacobson, K., & Moyano-Fuentes, J. (2007). Socioemotional wealth and business risks in family-controlled firms: Evidence from Spanish olive oil mills. *Administrative Science Quarterly*, *52*(1), 106–137. doi:10.2189/asqu.52.1.106

Hewitt Associates. (2002, Mar. 25). L'actionnariat salarié divise les entreprises patrimoniales. *La Tribune*.

Kim, E., & Ouimet, P. (2014). Broad-based employee stock ownership: Motives and outcomes. *The Journal of Finance*, *69*(3), 1273–1319. doi:10.1111/jofi.12150

Kramer, B. (2010). Employee ownership and participation effects on outcomes in firms majority employee-owned through employee stockownership plans in the US. *Economic and Industrial Democracy*, *31*(4), 449–476. doi:10.1177/0143831X10365574

Le Breton-Miller, I., & Miller, D. (2006). Why do some family businessesout-compete? Governance, long-term orientations, and sustainablecapability. *Entrepreneurship Theory and Practice*, *30*(6), 731–746.

Le Breton-Miller, I., & Miller, D. (2013). Socioemotional wealth across thefamily firm life cycle: A commentary on "Family Business Survival and theRole of Boards.". *Entrepreneurship Theory and Practice*, *37*(6), 1391–1397.

Lee, J. (2006). Family firm performance: Further evidence. *Family Business Review*, *19*(2), 103–114. doi:10.1111/j.1741-6248.2006.00060.x

Leitterstorf, M., & Rau, S. (2014). Socioemotional wealth and IPO under-pricing of family firms. *Strategic Management Journal*, *35*(5), 751–760. doi:10.1002mj.2236

Miller, D., Le Breton-Miller, I., Lester, R. H., & Cannella, A. A. Jr. (2007). Are familyfirms really superior performers? *Journal of Corporate Finance*, *13*(5), 829–858. doi:10.1016/j.jcorpfin.2007.03.004

Mullins, F. (2018). A Piece of the Pie? TheEffects of Familial Control Enhancements on the Use of Broad-Based Employee Ownership Programs in Family Firms. *Hum Resour Manage.*, *57*, 979–992. doi:10.1002/hrm.21828

Rosen, C., & Rodrick, S. (2005). *The ESOP reader: A primer on employeestock ownership plans* (4th ed.). National Center for Employee Ownership.

Rosen, C., & Rodrick, S. (2013). *Understanding ESOPs*. National Center for Employee Ownership.

Tiscini, R., & Raoli, E. (2013). Stock option plan practices in family firms:The idiosyncratic private benefits approach. *Journal of Family Business Strategy*, *4*(2), 93–105. doi:10.1016/j.jfbs.2013.03.001

Villalonga, B., & Amit, R. (2006). How do family ownership, control and management affect firm value? *Journal of Financial Economics*, *80*(2), 385–417. doi:10.1016/j.jfineco.2004.12.005

Villalonga, B., & Amit, R. (2009). How are U.S. family firms controlled? *Review of Financial Studies*, *22*(8), 3047–3091. doi:10.1093/rfs/hhn080

Villalonga, B., & Amit, R. (2010). Family control of firms and industries. *Financial Management*, *39*(3), 863–904. doi:10.1111/j.1755-053X.2010.01098.x

Weiser, J., Brody, F., & Quarrey, M. (1988). Family businesses and employee ownership. *Family Business Review*, *1*(1), 23–35. doi:10.1111/j.1741-6248.1988.00023.x

Zellweger, T., & Astrachan, J. (2008). On the emotional value of owning afirm. *Family Business Review*, *21*(4), 347–363. doi:10.1177/08944865080210040106

Zellweger, T., Nason, R., Nordqvist, M., & Brush, C. (2011). Why do family firms strive for non-financial goals? An organizational identity perspec-tive. *Entrepreneurship Theory and Practice*, *37*(2), 222–249.

ENDNOTES

1 www.fas.asso.fr

2 https://live.euronext.com

Chapter 5
International Overview of Employee Share Ownership

Paul Katuse
https://orcid.org/0000-0001-5754-4736
United States International University-Africa, Kenya

Joyce Daudi Nzulwa
Jomo Kenyatta University of Agriculture and Technology, Kenya

ABSTRACT

Business management scholars have propositioned employee share ownership as a concept bearing different perspectives. Business management practitioners have implemented the model in varying degrees suiting their organizational needs depending on the context of the organization at the particular time. Empirical research on the impact, role, and the position of employee share ownership (ESO) has produced varying results leading to far reaching conclusions as to the importance and significance of the ESO on an organization and especially at a time when a firm is undergoing through crisis. The concept of employee share ownership has led to the development of employee share ownership plans which are implemented as direct stock/share allotment, bonuses, or profit-sharing models and plans. The employer or the principal capital holder bears an exclusive discretion in making the decision of who would receive any of these options.

DOI: 10.4018/978-1-7998-8557-3.ch005

INTRODUCTION

Different scholars have substantiated the existence of some evidence linking better firm's performance with employee share ownership plans and schemes. The context of this topic is to understand how the concept of employee share Ownership is employed in different countries and whether it impacts organisational value and behavior. Several organisations in the contemporary world have implemented this concept with great success (Bradley, Estrin, & Taylor, 1990; Pendleton, 2006). However, not every organisations which has implemented ESOPs has succeeded. Most of the research relating the implementation of ESOPs and both organizational value and behaviour have also not been very clear in their conclusions. Most of these research works have attributed this connection to the existence of other factors (Pan, 2021; Derksen, 2020; Poutsma, Ligthart, & Poutsma, 2017; Whitfield, Pendleton, Sengupta, & Huxley, 2017; Kaarsemaker & Poutsma, 2006). It is with this in mind that the writers intend to clearly present ESOPs as a strategy and as an incentive plan aimed at the employees, so as to boost their morale, increase motivation, and enhance commitment, as a reward, an investment option, and for their recognition.

It is when it is premised that, committed employees will gain and benefit directly when the stock value of the firm increases in financial value for a win-win situation resulting to alignment of employee behavior to the expected value generation. Further to this, it can also be argued that employee stock ownership is a financial strategy aimed at minimizing financial outflows. The chapter will give relevant examples of how employee share ownership is carried out in different countries, how companies can use ESO to enhance productivity, faster growth, higher levels of profitability, ensure stability and a higher survival rate in turbulent market environments and lower turnover rates — benefits which spreads to all qualified and willing stakeholders which may include retirement accounts of employees and owners. For these purposes therefore, the terms employee share ownership (ESO), employee stock option plans (ESOPs) and employee share ownership schemes will be used synonymously. The literature reviewed will range from classical to contemporary literature in the area. The selection criteria of the presented documented information are on the basis of the chosen countries where the concept is being practiced and the thematic area of strategy and employee behavior towards value creation. The countries range from the US and EU where it is well documented and extensively legislated, India and south Africa whose approach to the concept slightly differs from the rest and Kenya and Ghana which have limited legislation of the concept but heavily borrow from the common law.

Employee share ownership is also known as employee stock ownership, or employee stock or share ownership. It deals with allocating the workers some amount the shares of the company. Workers would participate in share acquisition through a stock option plan, however such stock options plan at times would be selective, not allowing all the employees to participate. Hieu (2020) is of the opinion that when as organization adopts an employee share ownership plan, or scheme, the employees instantly become shareholders and this changes the power relationship between the management and the workforce. This tends to give workers more bargaining power and the realization that they work for themselves and hence they don't just have to comply by performing their tasks to the basic required minimum but enhancing their contribution to have a better financial reward. It can also help in resolving some human relations conflicts since the component of the 'ownership' makes the worker have a different approach and attitude to their work. Gamble (2000), Faccio and Lang (2002) however, postulated that employee ownership can also be regarded as a strategy by managers in order to safeguard their positions. In the context of the managers owning shares through an employee share ownership plan or scheme, the shareholders would have a challenge in organizing a contrary vote to the managements proposals or even at times they may find it hard to get the requisite momentum to change corporate-level managers. It is in this line of argument that some studies found out that industry reacts adversely when the scheme or plan for employee share ownership is viewed as an entrenchment by the management (Dhillon & Ramírez, 1994; Hallock, Salazar, & Venneman, 2004; Lamberg, Savage, & Pajunen, 2003).

REASONS FOR ADOPTION OF ESOPS

Scholars who advocate for employee ownership plans and schemes have claimed that, the adoption would lead to an improvement in the overall way a company performs; the augmentation of firm's productivity, enhanced participation of the workers, and boosting of morale of the employee. Most of the organisations which implement employee ownership plan are privately owned (Kaplan & Ludwig, 1985), this has since changed (Appiah-Kubi, 2001). Weyher and Knott (1985) argued that, organisations adopt employee share ownership because of many reasons, some of the most important reasons are; (a) to facilitate an employee with benefits, (b) to offer an incentive for an employee's efforts, (c) to satisfy the management's philosophical obligation to the shared ownership, (d) to benefit from tax waivers and advantages, (e) to underwrite capital acquisitions, (f) to acquire the stock of a retiring employee, (g) to fund worker acquisition of the firm in case of a corporate divestiture, or (h) when transferring ownership from public owned to private owned.

Literature on employee ownership suggests that there are three options of employee ownership models which are targeted to the psyche of the employee, these alternatives are however not mutually exclusive. These models are; the intrinsic satisfaction model of employee ownership (Ren, Xiao, Yang, & Liu, 2019); the instrumental satisfaction model of employee ownership (Pendleton, Wilson, & Wright, 1998; Kuvaas, 2003) and the model of employee ownership effects (Basterretxea & Storey, 2018). The premise under each alternative model is that, when workforce is satisfied with the employee ownership plan, there will be more commitment to the organisation and workers will be more motivated to keep on working in the organisation. Each of the models projects that distinct employee ownership contexts are related with high levels of employee commitment and satisfaction with share ownership, enhanced organizational fidelity, and minimal employee turnover and inclinations to work contrary to the organisations expectations.

Further to this, the three models are also consistent with economic literature on the relationship between a principal and an agent (Pierce, Rubenfeld, & Morgan, 1991; Aubert, Kern, & Hollandts, 2017; Mullins, 2018; Kim & Patel, 2020), which submits that, incentives of the financial type for instance gainsharing, merit pay and—by addendum—employee ownership, may cause agents' (in this case the employees) functional interests to be well matched with those of the principal (in this case the owner of the organisation). Sometimes, the direct acquisition of employee buyouts, or employee stock option plans are types of employee ownership which require the employees to acquire stock directly through a conversion of part of their incomes from their salaries. These in most cases are often times meant to be a part of turnaround strategy for a firm which is financially performing below expectation.

Within the specifics of the basic principles of the agency theory, the employee share ownership concept, whereby a part of the employee income mostly salary is connected directly to the firms profitability, has clearly shown its capacity to repress employees self-seeking conduct in the workforce (Paterson & Welbourne, 2019; Palmer & Wiseman, 1999) by alleviating the workers proclivity to underinvest in organisation-specific human capital (Wang, He, & Mahoney, 2009) and also at the same time making the employees' risk choices indistinguishable to those of the other shareholders (Kim & Han, 2019). Further to this economic perspective of the agency theory, employee share ownership brings forth positive psychological effects for instance employees' sense of control for their destiny (Basterretxea, Heras-Saizarbitoria, & Lertxundi, 2019) and focused and a more closer identification with the organizational goals (Yoon & Sengupta, 2019; Fitzroy & Nolan, 2020; Bogićević-Milikić & Došenović, 2020),which result into productive conduct from the employee and eventually lead to a comparatively enhanced performance by the firm.

ESOP AS A STRATEGY

Gonza and Ellerman (2020) argue that, among many strategies which and organisation can undertake, employee share ownership in one such strategy. In the contemporary industry, most employee share ownership schemes and plans are held by big companies. The mechanism also presents management succession problem with a ready solution and especially where there is lack of interest and capacity to take over the running of the company, this happens when an employee has acquired enough shares to qualify for a claim on the board. The mechanism also helps in anchoring the organization to the local community by encouraging community buy in and also rewarding performing and loyal employees who have helped sustain the organization. In this manner the employee share ownership specifically through employee stock option plans (ESOPs) is proving to be an attractive alternative for the founder owners of small-and-medium-sized firms (SMEs) as they divest in a manner which secures a fair worth for their investment while still rewarding their workforce and retaining their jobs, tax base, and general wages within the local community.

Earlier in the United States, the employee stock option plans were implemented specifically as an exceptional type or simply a “carve-out” for private pension retirement plans, this meant therefore that employee-owners could not receive any cash out of their ownership until when nearing or at retirement (Jan & Fabo, 2016). This has also been used as an exit strategy by the management, since by nature in the US it is a tax-exempted, clearly defined retirement plan contribution, where the shares of a company’s stock are bought from the owner-manager and held on behalf of the organisation’s employees. This would make employees gain twice, through their salaries and pay outs of dividends or matured shares. With such an expectation, the loyalty and commitment levels of the workers increases.

Gordon and Pound (1990) posited that, employee shared option plan and schemes have been used as a business takeover defense mechanism involving the dual shift of the long-term corporate strategy and a change within the ownership or the voting structure of the organisation. This important duality of cause – guarantees an organisation some sustainability, the challenges of the same notwithstanding. ESOPs would therefore be implemented fundamentally to anchor long-term organisational performance and also to protect the organization from takeovers. An employee share ownership plan can improve an organizational performance, by putting in place an impetus based system which is pay-for-performance connects employees’ wealth to the organisation’s share-price performance.

However, Johnson, Pratt and Stewart (1982) felt that, even though the claims that ESOPs lead to a positive performance and a win-win situation for both owner and employee, the claims may be difficult to appraise due to several reasons. One of the reasons is that the implementation of an ESOP is a composite transaction. Such undertakings (including bond refunding, leasing, and stock repurchase) join two decisions to form a solitary transaction. In the same way leasing puts together acquisition of assets and financing, an ESOP combines a stock sale and a plan for retirement. Due to the fact that analytical techniques of finance are focused on analyzing single decision separately, challenges will always be encountered in a context where decisions cannot be isolated like in compound transactions. Such business transactions will always appear to be encompassed by controversy as to how desirable they are (McDaniel, Madura, & Wiant, 1995; Riaz, Razzaq, & Waqar, 2017; Schneider, 2020; Kruse, Freeman, & Blasi, 2010)

ESOP AND BUSINESS SUSTAINABILITY

As a strategic welfare and growth policy, employee stock ownership plan or scheme has enabled employees of an organization practicing it to participate in the sharing of the firm's profits and company growth benefits by way of owning a portion of the ordinary shares of the enterprise. Wen, Li, Zhang and Shen (2021) while citing Kim and Ouimet (2014) posited that, employee stock ownership plan (ESOP) comes from the concept of diversification of capital ownership as propounded by Louis Kelso in 1958. Most of the existing literature and research on the subject of employee stock ownership plan and schemes mainly focus on the processes of the implementation of employee stock ownership plan and the attendant economic outcomes. Research has shown that, when firms ran short of cash for operations or are undergoing unmitigated competition, the inclination to spread risk and save by minimizing funds outflow by launching ESOP is very high. This is focused at saving cash wages and avoiding the loss of corporate control occasioned by liquidity risks (Bradley, Estrin, & Taylor, 1990; Faccio & Lang, 2002; Aubert, Kern, & Hollandts, 2017; Kim & Patel (2020). In their research, Blasi, Freeman, & Kruse (2016) found out that the main purpose of use of ESOP by many organisations is to increase the motivation levels of employees towards their participation in decision making for the company and also sharing of internal information, which if done appropriately can greatly enhance overall corporate performance.

Sustainable growth for an organization may refer to the continual increment of an enterprise and the maintenance of an appropriate growth rate which can not only keep acceptable development in the contemporary time, but also not dim the interests and expectations of the forecasted development. Higgins (1977) proposed a model of sustainable growth rate (SGR), which focused on the maximum growth rate a firm can realise only through selling its products and services without running out of its financial resources. This proposed Model was based on accounting identities and putting in place financial indicators. Its main purpose was to appraise the optimal growth rate realised by organisations which only rely on retained earnings and the extent of retention of internal earnings. Sustainable growth of an organisation is highly affected by its internal financial factors, besides by its corporate governance, which goes to mean that, if the internal financials of an organisations are well management and corporate governance principles which to some extent are hinged on the principle agent theory are adhered to, then sustainability will be achieved.

In the initial years of the concept, employee stock option plans were mostly given to the core workers of the organisation or those knowledgeable and technically skilled core workers who in the past had made critical contribution to the organization, however in the contemporary times this has since changed to include willingness and time factor. These technically skilled core workers used to form the fundamental component of the human assets of the firm (Zhou, Huang, & Zhao, 2019). As an incentive to these employees, it used to help enhance their level of affinity and identity within the firm, and therefore reducing those kinds of behaviors which infringed on the concerns of the firm and brought down agency cost. The low levels of agency cost are conducive to the improvement of the efficiency of capital operation and the provision of more funds for organisational innovation. Organisational innovation is a critical component of the sustainable growth capacity of the firm. This therefore means that, with an improved innovation ability, an enterprise will be in a position of improving its sustainable growth. Besides that, the reduced agency cost may also minimise resources wastage, rent-seeking expenses and hidden costs as a result of in-service expenditure by senior executives, which in turn can effectively minimise the internal communications cost and general organizations running cost, increase the overall capability of the organisation, making it the right recipe for the organization's sustainable growth.

ESOPS IN EUROPE

Hieu (2018) says that, since the early 1990s, the European Union through its commission has been on a spree of research and the promotion of employee stock option plans in Europe. Its approach on this has been through the laying of emphasis on how employee stock option plans would benefit the participants and the citizens of the European Union who are employed. The Commission has been encouraging the member countries of the EU to put in place a sustainable business environment in order to enhance the growth of ESOPs by the provision of supportive mechanisms and measures, for instance, legislative measures (creating legal framework for fit for adoption of ESOPs by companies), fiscal mechanisms (employment of tax and financial inducements for the benefit of ESOPs participating parties) and socio-political measures (encouraging positive social attitudes when it comes to ESOPs) (The European Commission., 2014).

Most of European union member states tax gains accrued from employee stock options whenever the option is exercised. The base of the tax is the difference between the worth of the acquired stock and the value in price which the purchasing employee is supposed to pay to acquire the share. The gain is mostly taxed as part of the employee's income, i.e. employee's social security contributions and his or her income taxes. Further, a lot of countries also tax any other subsequent gain arising out of the sale of the stock as income coming from capital. However, in other cases, taxes would only be levied when the options are granted or when they vest (i.e. at the first time of exercising the options). In some EU member states, taxes are only levied when the final sale of the stocks happen (The European Union, 2020). It should be noted that, the tax rates may not be uniform, different countries differ in terms of the rates, the tax rate reflect the taxation policies of the different countries in the EU. In the EU, there are high tax countries and low tax countries. For instance, Denmark, Sweden and Finland are at the category of high tax rates, whereas Luxembourg, Austria and, Greece are at the category of low tax rates (The European Union, 2021).

Through the use of survey data obtained from firms in the European union, the European commission has clearly shown that there is a lot of evidence connecting citizenry benefits like employment, savings and economic growth to enhanced ESOPs adoption for productivity (The Catholic University of Brussels, 2000; The European Commission, 2003; Palmer, Mawad, & Treyz, 2020; Burke, 2021). This evidence corroborates previously existing empirical literature (Blasi et al., 2016; Aubert et al., 2017; Bradley, Estrin, & Taylor, 1990; Hallock, Salazar, & Venneman, 2004). Mathieu (2020) notes that, employee ownership stake and held capital in European companies has been steadily increasing, in 2006 it was 2.33% and in 2020 it moved to 3.05% representing about Euro 310 billion as of May 2020 and over Euro 420 billion in the first quarter of 2021. European firms with employee share plans have grown steadily. In 2020, 88 percent of large European firms had employee share plans compared to 33% in 2006. Some of these firms are as Amag Austria Metall in Austria, Royal Mail in the UK, Allianz in German, Crédit Suisse in Switzerland (Economic Survey of Employee Share Ownership, 2020).

The general Introduction of employee stock option plans as a part of a privatisation model, links the strategic interest of the organisation to the workers and also the citizenry. It increases the organizational safeguards consequently when an organisation is owned by the state and also when an organisations is owned privately by a foreign investor. In Europe, employee stock option plans have clearly proven as one of the highly efficient business models for many enterprises. The model also positively scores high when it comes to environmental and social responsibility. Empirical evidence has shown that employee stock option plans increase the worth in wealth (Blasi & Kruse, 2019) and the wages of participating employees (Basterretxea et al., 2019). Furthermore, employee stock option plans improve employees' life quality and performance (Bryson, Clark, Freeman, & Green, 2016; Erdal, 2014). Empirically it has been established that those firms having employee ownership tend to be more successful comparatively (Blasi & Kruse, 2019; National Center for Employee Ownership, 2019), they enjoy high levels of productivity and register faster phases of growth (Blasi et al.,2016). In their research, Kruse, Freeman, and Blasi, (2010) established that, employees who have bought employee stock option plans in their oerganisations are unlikely to seek for employment elsewhere.

ESOPS IN THE US AND CANADA

The development and implementation of the concept of ESOP in the United States has been strongly encouraged by a various Federal and state legislative laws. Among the most significant of these enactments is a sequence of big Federal tax subsidies created since the mid-1970's (Yale Law Journal Company, Inc, 1990). The North American concept of ESOP slightly differs from that in operation in India and south Africa, but somehow similar to that which is operation in some parts of Europe and China. ESOPs in the US and Canada go hand in hand with Employee stock purchase plans (ESPP). Though these two concepts seem related, they differ in terms of their operation. The main concept under ESOPs is to specifically reward workforce by offering them with access to get portion of the company ownership where as an ESPP deals only with availing the employee and opportunity to buy stock of the organization through a set purchase program. Some of the firms which have adopted ESOPs are as google, Microsoft and Amazon in the technology sector (Martechseries, 2021) others are Publix Super Markets and Penmac which is 100 percent owned by employees (NCEO, 2020).

From the American tax law point of view, the Internal Revenue Service defines ESOP as a qualified defined contribution plan that is a stock bonus plan or a stock bonus/money purchase plan (IRS, 2021). In this context an employee stock option plan has to be designed in such a way that it is meant to only invest primarily in the qualifying employer securities as defined by the IRC section 4975(e)(8) and must adhere to certain conditions of the code and directives. There are no different types of ESOPs under the US law, however given the different practice options and utility of the alternatives, they can be categorized into three. All those transactions or qualified plans entailing the ESOPS are just variations of these three types.

These variations are; (1) Non leveraged ESOP, (2) Leveraged buyout ESOP, (3) Issuance ESOP.

1. Non Leveraged ESOP

The non-leveraged type of ESOP entails a funded contribution of finances or stock directly from the sponsoring employer, it does not include any funds borrowed to buy the sponsoring employer's stock (Derksen, 2020). The ordinary shares contributed by the organisation are "newly issued shares." The newly shares are issued to the ESOP and a deduction is taken by the corporation for their appraised fair market value as of the date of contribution. Alternatively, cash can be contributed to the plan in annual discretionary amounts as cash flow permits, to purchase shares at a later date, or simultaneously, from either the corporation or from another shareholder.

In a more general outlook, a non-leveraged employee stock option plan is put up in place in order to encourage benefit to the firm's sponsor by way of tax deductions creation with the newly issued stock, therefore enhancing the flow of cash and minimizing taxes (Bogićević-Milikić & Došenović, 2020). This is also one among many of the better strategies for measured accretion of benefits for retirement connected to the worth of worker share or stock and also for the promotion of participation in the management formation. The reason for having an employee stock option plan may be to acquire shares or stock from an existing shareholder or stockholder in terms of the basis of the cash flow by the tax inducements attributed to the leveraged ESOPs. In this context, employee stock option plans may not require borrowing funds (Kim & Han, 2019). The use of non-leveraged employee stock option plan helps the firm evade the negative impact debt and borrowing may have on the firm's worth and in the balance sheet. Further to this, financing an employee stock option plan on the basis of cash flow gives an indication of the firm's commitment to buy shares from those participating employees who are departing from the organization, either through human resource separation or otherwise. This approach in itself is more easy to manage in comparison to the leverages version. This form of firm's commitment goes by the name repurchase liability.

2. Leveraged Buyout ESOP

Leveraged buyout employee stock option plan is similar to general issuance employee stock option plan, however, this kind of funding is used to acquire stock from an employee who is already selling due to the fact that he or she may be retiring from active service of the organization. This kind of transaction has become one of the most favored strategy of succession for closely held businesses. The inducement of tax that the organization allowing the performance of this encompass tax favored investments and financing and tax deferred capital gains (Aubert et al., 2017). These are very riveting to the point of view of planning for succession and estate planning.

An employee who plans for his or her transactions appropriately, may offer his or her stock to employee stock option plan and avoid the capital tax gains immediately after the sale. The seller may again re-invest the process from the transaction inside the period of 12 months after the sale to the ESOP and adjourn the liability of capital gains tax in an indefinite manner. This is similar to the option of reinvesting the sale proceeds of a house for instance. Consequently, the one who has sold will bear all the deferred taxes at his or her work in his or her investment portfolio (Yale Law Journal Company, Inc, 1990). The firm, sequentially will have made good the price of the purchase fully in pre-tax settlements.

In this context, just as in a normal issuance employee stock option plan, the debt principal is made good by the pre-tax money. An outcome of this may be that the firm's liability to repurchase in the future, may be equal to the fair market worth of the share or stock bought through the plan (Yale Law Journal Company, Inc, 1990). However, contrary to the Issuance of employee stock option plan, the existing stockholders will not have their ownership diluted in any way.

There is however a disadvantage to those stockholders who do not offload their shares to the employee stock option plan. They would always find it more challenging to transact on their shares in the future as they will be in direct competition with the organization. This challenge takes prominence when there is substantial growth in the value of the stock, or the repurchase liability, or when both of these factors are combined resulting into an unmitigated cash outflow from the companies' coffers. From the managements perspective, it may not be a very prudent move to overload the firm with an ESOP liability (Mullins, 2018).

3. Issuance ESOP

In an Issuance employee stock option plan happens when a participating employee has shares allocated to his or her account as a loan. The Issuance uses financing to purchase shares from the sponsoring employer. In the process of repaying, the ESOP account which is called 'suspense account' releases share to the accounts of the employee participating in the ESOP in accordance with the IRS formula (IRS, 2021).

The benefits of accruing to an organization through an Issuance employee stock option plan entail the creation of tax favored funding for acquiring capital goods, for growth through mergers and acquisitions, or generally formation of capital. The amount borrowed for the process of buying stock automatically becomes tax deductible because of the way it is paid by way of plan cost or contribution (Gonza & Ellerman, 2020). The organisation is therefore able to benefit by borrowing to finance ESOPs on a completely deductible manner.

The Issuance ESOP is however not a panacea; it also has some demerits. The negative aspects of ESOPs are not mutually exclusive with the benefits thereof. To begin with, they possess a diluting impact on the current shareholders when the worth of the firm does not increase at a faster rate in comparison to the percentage value of the shares sold to the employee stock option plan. There is also the presence of repurchase liability which may be a challenge for the planned future retirement benefits. Once ESOPs are in place, the organisation may be required in the future to repurchase those shares distributed from the plan to the participating employees. So, generally the employee stock option plan may allow the organisation to ''take a debt from the retirement plan'', by allowing the deductions at the given time to be used as contributions for the organisation's capital. This may possibly be allowed until all the benefits are paid. This may improve the organisation's cash inflows, subject to the requisite retirement or any other future planned distribution and repurchasing.

ESOPS IN AFRICA (A FEW CHOSEN COUNTRIES)

Of all the 54 countries of the African continent, just a few can compare the vibrancy of their economies and business to most in the developed economies. This however doesn't mean that ESOPs are not practiced. The practice however may be slightly different from the rest of the world. Roux (2005) says that, employee share-ownership plans (ESOPs) have become the biggest strategy and tool in South Africa to implement the government sponsored broad based black economic empowerment (BBBEE) program. The black based empowerment framework entails several components, which are; employment equity, equity ownership, preferential procurement, skill development, enterprise development, Management and other residual components, however the score card against which organizations are measures are five. These are equity and ownership at 20 percent, skills development at 15 percent, employment equity at 15 percent, preferential procurement at 20 percent, enterprise development at 15 percent and socio-economic development at 5 percent (BEE Empowered, 2021). It is within the ambit of this broad based worker empowerment that the fluidity and simplicity of employee shared ownership plan in the Republic of South Africa, has become very attractive.

The leading protagonists of employee stock option plans in South Africa argue that, the main reason for the need of ESOPs is because since independence there still is a high concentration of capital on a few citizens and therefore the need for de-concentration. Secondly, and close to the first reason, is the need for democratization, to a greater extent, of the organisations assets, which includes unrolling and sharing the ownership of the organization amidst individual stockholders within the private sector and finally the requirement to encourage employee ownership and economic empowerment (Industrial Development Corporation, 2021). Nomafu (2018) says that, organisations which have adopted employee stock option plans tend to have a better performance in comparison to those which haven't. Employee stock option plans in South Africa can be acquired through credit, without transacting in cash or even deducting the employee's salary at source. In order to encourage this, the government of the republic of South Africa put in place the Broad-based Black Economic Empowerment Act 53 of 2003 (BEE Empowered, 2021; South African

Government, 2021) which the objectives to; formulate a legislative framework in order to promote black economic empowerment; and empowering the minister in charge with capacity to issue codes of good practice among organisations and publishing transformation charters; and establishing of the Black Economic Empowerment Advisory Council (BEEAC) and finally for the provision of matters related thereof. Since then there have been several amendments to the law.

When this Law was put in place, it changed the country's way of taxing amounts got from the broad based employee stock options plans in favour of both employers and employees. Before the enactment of the legislation, the way tax was treated never encouraged the transference of free or discounted stock insides of the confinement of the broad based plans. This was a very big problem to affordability of the shares and posed a huge threat to employees receiving low incomes since they were cut off from ever participating in such and could not afford the payment of tax on the free or the discounted stock without selling their stake. This made it necessary to have special tax rules in order to encourage and promote the long term and strategic broad based employee empowerment by making the employees participate in the growth and success of their employing organization with minimal tax cost (Kim & Patel, 2020).

Further amendments of this legislation makes an employee's qualifying shares to have a tax free treatment in spite of the fact that shares might been acquired free of charge or where acquired when discounted. The Law lays down that, for equity to qualify for tax free treatment, they need to have the following qualifications; the worker needs to receive the shares on the basis of broad based employee share plan and the total number of shares acquired within the plan should not exceed three thousand South African Rands (SAR3 000) in total worth within a 12-month period (South African Government, 2021).

Existing empirical studies have shown that there are higher levels of productivity associated with organisations which have ESOPs. However, the productivity benefits are dependent on several other factors for instance the size company size. These benefits thereof are mostly higher for the smaller companies (Aubert et al., 2017; Philip, 2003). Employee stock option plans acts a synergist to enhanced worker commitment and worker engagement. Worker engagement means a work environment where employees are highly committed to the goals and values of the organisation, are well motivated and have a high level of morale which leads to effective contribution to the organisation's success as well as having a sense of pride and wellbeing. Some studies (Sinenhlanhla, 2019; Lampel, Bhalla, & Jha, 2012) tend to suggest that ESOPs does drive innovation, this is because employees who own the organisation focus more, and have a higher attachment to the growth of the organisation through suggestions of innovative ideas. A few examples of South

African firms which have adopted ESOPs are as Anglo American, De Beers and Afrisam (Transcend, 2021).

In Kenya, employee stock options plan nowadays are becoming a most sought after form of the structure of an organisation's privatization program and especially with infrastructure based organisations. In Kenya there are several laws which govern ESOPs, these include; the Companies Act 2015 section 446 (b)(c); the Income Tax Act (Cap 470); the Finance Act; the Trustees Act; the common law and Capital Markets Authority Collective Investment Schemes Regulations, 2001; however, due to the fact that the Kenyan ESOP regulations are still in their nascent stage, the United Kingdom's statutory schemes regulations also gives requisite guidelines to the form and structure of almost all the schemes in use in the contemporary Kenyan business sphere (Ayugi & Wanaju, 2018; Public-Private Infrastructure Advisory Facility (PPIAF), 2021). In Kenya a common practice is the use of a trust which has well defined rules in terms of how shares are distributed transferred and bought back. Set up in a form of a legal entity (mostly a trust), a separate organization, buys the shares of the firm, on the place of the workers, with a clear manner which describes the way the shares will be distributed. These trusts are structured in such way that they get maximum benefits from tax laws such that the plans are made tax efficient for both the company employing and the employees participating. For example, the Kenya Airways privatization ESOP, was done in such way that a unit trust for the purposes of tax was set up (Abdallah & Cheluget, 2020), however the Safaricom IPO which was also part of the compaies privatization didn't have a similar arrangement especially for the employees even though they were allowed to bug equity (Wanjiku, 2008). Other firms which have adopted ESOPs are ARM cement and Equity bank ((Kenyan Wall Street, 2016).

TYPES OF ESOPS

In Kenya thus far, only 3 types of ESOP schemes are in use;

1. **Profit sharing scheme** – this is made possible through a trust, which has to be put in place because of that purpose. The trustees get payments from the organisation and use the money to acquire the shares offered on the ESOPs. The shares will then be 'appropriated' by the trustees to those employees who are eligible in line with the trust deed and regulations of the scheme.
2. **Share option schemes related to Savings** – this type is connected to a contract on employee savings. The employees who are eligible have options offered to then to take up the ESOP stocks at the market price or payable at the time when the option is granted.

3. **Share option scheme** – participating employees are given options to buy ESOPs shares at particular times of the organisations operations. The buying price is set up at the time of the employee stock option grant. Regulatory provisions requiring the exercise of the given option to be taken within certain time limit may be in pace.

These types of ESOPs are designed to take advantage of national tax laws so that the plans are tax efficient both for employees and for the companies. For example, the ESOP for Kenya Airways privatization was structured as a unit trust for tax reasons (Megginson, Nash, & Randenborgh, 1994). These trusts are established by the employee organisations, which bestow the trust with either cash to acquire existing equity or through allocation of new stock. In Kenya, the establishment of an ESOP may be challenging and especially for small organisations. It requires professions assistance. Other than in the case where the worker or executives acquires an infrastructure oriented unit, the ownership through ESOPs is allowed up to between 5 to 15 percent of the worth of the organization. For levels higher than 15 percent ownership, there would be a claim on the board which may discourage private foreign investors who may believe that more labour law adjustments may be made hence opening up the management.

The Public-Private Infrastructure Advisory Facility (PPIAF), 2021) says that, in Kenya, for the success of an ESOP program to be made certain, some key undertakings that the agency implementing it should follow. These undertakings are as follows;

ISSUES ON PARTICIPATION TO THE ESOPS

1. It should be made possible for all employees to participate in the ESOPs after they are found to be qualified after having served the organization for at least 12 months continuously.
2. The stake for management and that of the rest of the labour force should have minimal or no discrepancy.
3. Voting rights should be similar.
4. Dividend rights should be similar.
5. Employee trust aids should be used to guarantee sustainability of the plan for a longer period.
6. There should be transparency especially in the first allocation, such that at least every one knows what everyone got.
7. The importance of free shares, should not be discounted so as to make every willing employee shareholder.
8. Other form of benefits and incomes should not be forfeited for share allocation.

9. After separation, workers should be let free to transfer or sell their stock to the trust.
10. The trustee should be run by a balanced make up of both management and employees to avoid over dominance by one side

ISSUES ON THE MANAGEMENT

1. It is essential to engage an expert who is knowledgeable on matters ESOPs, taxation and trust law.
2. For success of the ESOP, the management style of participation should be adopted
3. Clear communication with the employees is necessary, in order to get their buy in hence cultivating enthusiasm for the long term.
4. Total consultation with everyone in the employ should be done.
5. There should organization culture change to facilitate the co-existence in the co-ownership. This should be spearheaded by the management.
6. Employees should have a clear understanding of the distinction between rights and duties as workers, because this at times may cloud the relationships.
7. Management should have adequate inducement or incentives which must be transparent. In most cases, a good share option plan should allow employees to get extra shares should they meet set targets, both for organizational and individual.
8. Management should ensure that the running of the organization happens within the laid out policy frameworks and legislation.

TECHNICAL AND STRUCTURAL ISSUES

For a smooth and seamless operation of ESOPs in Kenya, the following important aspects need clear understanding; the shares source (whether they are from the government or they are new shares); the rules which denote the eligibility status for instance, the amount and worth of the shares per person, when to offer, and the offer price of the shares; compliance with the various legal requirements; keeping of employee's income and conditions thereof separate from share ownership.

Further to the above, it should be noted that;

1. The representatives of workers have a right of advice by a knowledgeable expert in the field.
2. ESOP Sustainability features should be built in so as to ensure that those who leave the organization at the time of separation find it easy to transfer or sell.

3. Clarification should be given in terms of how an employee decides to acquire the shares, some employees would pull resources together (*the Harambee system* – a form resource consolidation) and buy under the name of one of them, with their own arrangement as to their sharing ratios.
4. Advice on tax efficient share plans should be clearly given, to ensure that employees make better decisions.

Within the organization, what is called the internal market, some individuals among the company's employ, would want to acquire or sell. This is allowed within private organisations on a basis which is matched with the buyer's capacity, if the plan has been going on for some time. Depending on the amount of shares employees have acquired, they may have the entitlement of having a representative at the organisations board as a rule of thumb. Mostly if they hold anything in excess of 25 percent of the total equity.

Though there are few instances in Kenya, if an employee stock option is decided upon before public-private initiative of privatization, then clarity should be made as to whether the ESOP serves as an incentive related to performance, or otherwise stipulated.

ESOPS IN GHANA

Since 1985, when the government of Ghana begun its public enterprise reforms program, several public sector enterprises have been privatized. Part of this privatization has entailed the use of employee stock option plans. In Ghana most of the ESOPs have been through Initial Public Offers (IPOs) which have been found to be efficient towards developing the local domestic capital markets by broadening share ownership whereby both small investors and institutional investors are invited to participate in the process of privatization (Appiah-Kubi, 2001; ESMAP, 2003). With Ghana's basic trust law, the requirements to have an ESOP in place is have a definition and full recognition of the law dealing with the type of ESOP trust. The law is supposed to stipulate the contexts such a trust is supposed to serve if incase it has to be under the law's protection (Abduali & Shafiwu, 2014). Further, other supplementary qualifications and legal requirements are included which give the participating employees the rights of determining the way in which the stock in their ESOP are voted on particular organizational issues, their rights on particular information dealing with the trust operation, and the legal entitlement to demand for the benefits to be distributed as employer securities. The ESOP should also give independent annual valuations of securities belonging to the employer and give an allowance to the employee to repurchase any employer held securities in case those securities are not freely traded in the open market (ESMAP, 2003).Even though ESOPs in Ghana have not grown tremendously, some of the firms which have opted for it are as AngloAshanti and MTN Ghana (Ghana Stock Exchange, 2020) (Industriall global union, 2009)

ESOPS IN INDIA

The field of employee stock option plans in India is well researched and practiced. There is a plethora of empirical research on different perspectives, ranging from product launch (Agnihotri & Bahttacharya, 2020), employee motivation (Bhattacheryay, 2020), entrepreneurship development (Biswas & Dey, 2021), corporate social responsibility (Samantara & Dhawan, 2020) to compensation strategies (Ayyagar, 2021), employee skill and competence management (Chandra, 2021), financial performance (Ramchandani & Pandya, 2019), Corporate governance and risk bundling (Gupta & Mittal, 2020) etc. The legal provisions in India covering ESOPs are under the Securities and Exchange Board of India and the Indian Companies Act 20013.

Katoch (2017) while citing Dhar and De (2009) argued that ESOPs in India are highly charged up as an issue because of the aggressive increment of the use of the plans by big business entities within the south east Asian region to defuse risks and diversify ownership. His study showed that there is a very big diversity when it comes to the reporting of the practices of ESOPs related information in different organizations in India. Majority of ESOPs in India are by IT start ups, some of these are as Razorpay and Paytm in financial services (Majumdar, 2021).

CONCLUSION

The chapter concludes that, ESOPs have been adopted as a business strategy for different reasons depending on the context. Several countries have extensively localized the legislation on the concept of ESOPs. The adoption of the concept is gradually increasing but at different paces world over. The adoption of the concept has an effect on employee behavior which may lead to less employee turnover, more commitment, increased efficiency and eventually sustainable performance of the firm.

REFERENCES

Abdallah, K., & Cheluget, J. (2020). Determinants of Participation in Employee Share Ownership Plans in the Banking Sector: A Case of Listed Commercial Banks in Kenya. *Journal of Human Resource & Leadership*, 60-75.

Abduali, I. A., & Shafiwu, A. B. (2014). Participatory Decision Making and Employee Productivity. A Case Study of Community Banks in the Upper East region of Ghana. *Business and Economics Journal*, 35-50.

Agnihotri, A., & Bahttacharya, S. (2020). ESOPs and New Product Launch: Conditional Effects of Financial Slack and Ownership Concentration. *International Journal of Innovation Management*, 1022–1040.

Appiah-Kubi, K. (2001). State-Owned Enterprises and Privatisation in Ghana. *The Journal of Modern African Studies*, 197–229.

Aubert, N., Kern, A., & Hollandts, X. (2017). Employee stock ownership and the cost of capital. *Research in International Business and Finance*, 67–78.

Ayugi, C., & Wanaju, E. U. (2018). *MMAN Advocates Website*. Retrieved from Creating a Bigger Pie or Golden Handcuffs? Employee Share Ownership Plans in Kenya: https://mman.co.ke/content/creating-bigger-pie-or-golden-handcuffs-employee-share-ownership-plans-kenya

Ayyagar, K. C. (2021). In the Human Resource Management and Compansation Strategies adopted adopted across IT and ITES Industries due to COVID-19 in India. *KC Ayyagar - International Journal of Modern Agriculture*, 1472 - 1482.

Basterretxea, I., Heras-Saizarbitoria, I., & Lertxundi, A. (2019). Can employee ownership and human resource management policies clash in worker cooperatives? Lessons from a defunct cooperative. *Human Resource Management*, 585-601.

Basterretxea, I., & Storey, J. (2018). Do Employee-Owned Firms Produce More Positive Employee Behavioural Outcomes? If Not Why Not? A British-Spanish Comparative Analysis. *British Journal of Industrial Relations*, 292–319.

BEE Empowered. (2021). *The elements of the BEE Scorecard*. Retrieved from Bee Empowered Website: https://bempowered.net/information/the-elements-of-the-bee-scorecard/

Bhattacheryay, S. (2020). Multinational enterprises motivational factors in capitalizing emerging market opportunities and preparedness of India. *Journal of Financial Economic Policy*, 609-640.

Biswas, D., & Dey, C. (2021). *Entrepreneurship Development in India*. Routledge.

Blasi, J., Freeman, R., & Kruse, D. (2016). Do Broadbased Employee Ownership, Profit Sharing and Stock Options Help the Best Firms Do Even Better? *British Journal of Industrial Relations*, 55–82.

Blasi, J., & Kruse, D. (2019). *Building the Assets of Low and Moderate Income Workers and Their Families: The Role of Employee Ownership*. Institute for the Study of Employee Ownership and Profit Sharing, Rutgers University.

Bogićević-Milikić, B., & Došenović, D. (2020). Moderators of the relationship between intrinsic rewards and job satisfaction: The evidence from the Republic of Srpska. *Sociologija*, 416–437.

Bradley, K., Estrin, S., & Taylor, S. (1990). Employee Ownership and Company Performance. *Industrial Relations*, 385–402.

Bryson, A., Clark, A., Freeman, R., & Green, C. (2016). Share Capitalism and Worker Wellbeing. *Labour Economics*, 151–158.

Burke, E. (2021). *5 European countries with better stock options than the US*. Retrieved from https://www.siliconrepublic.com/start-ups/stock-options-europe-latvia-lithuania-estonia-france-uk

Chandra, V. (2021). *Work-Life Balance in India: Policy, Practices and the Road Ahead -Work-Life Interface: Non-Western Perspectives*. Springer Nature.

Derksen, R. (2020). *Employee share ownership and firm performance: The mediation effect of employee turnover*. Radboud University.

Dhar, S., & De, S. (2009). ESOP Accounting in India: Measurement and Disclosure issues. *Journal of Business and Economic Issues*, 45-61.

Dhillon, U. S., & Ramírez, G. G. (1994). Employee stock ownership and corporate control: An empirical study. *Journal of Banking & Finance*, 9–25.

Economic Survey of Employee Share Ownership. (2020). *New progression in Europe*. European Federation of Employee Share Ownership.

Erdal, D. (2014). Employee Ownership and Health: An Initial Study. In S. Novkovic & T. Webb (Eds.), *Co-Operatives in a Post-Growth Era: Creating Co-Operative Economics* (pp. 210–220). Zed Books.

ESMAP. (2003). *Ghana: Corporatization of Distribution Concessions through Capitalization*. ESMAP-Energy Sector Management Assistance Program.

Faccio, M., & Lang, L. H. (2002). The ultimate ownership of Western European corporations. *Journal of Financial Economics*, 365–395.

Fitzroy, F. R., & Nolan, M. A. (2020). *Towards Economic Democracy and Social Justice: Profit Sharing, Co-Determination, and Employee Ownership*. IZA Discussion Paper No. 13238, 15-30.

Gamble, J. E. (2000). Management commitment to innovation and esop stock concentration. *Journal of Business Venturing*, 433–447.

Ghana Stock Exchange. (2020). *MTN Ghana Limited (MTNGH) - Notice of Virtual Extraordinary General Meeting of Shareholders*. MTN Ghana.

Gonza, T., & Ellerman, D. P. (2020). *Turning Platform Workers into Owners: ESOP-Type Buyouts for the Labor-Based Platforms*. University of Ljubljana.

Gordon, L. A., & Pound, J. (1990). ESOPs and corporate control. *Journal of Financial Economics*, 525–555.

Gupta, P., & Mittal, P. (2020). Corporate Governance and Risk Bundling: Evidence from Indian Compannies. *European Journal of Science & Technology*, 37-52.

Hallock, D. E., Salazar, R. J., & Venneman, S. (2004). Demographic and Attitudinal Correlates of Employee Satisfaction with an ESOP. *British Journal of Management*, 78–99.

Hieu, P. H. (2018). *The determinants of employee stock ownership plans (ESOPs)*. Université de Limoges.

Hieu, T. P. (2020). Effectiveness of policy measures to promote employee share ownership programs in banks. *Université de Limoges*, 100-125.

Higgins, R. C. (1977). How Much Growth Can a Firm Afford? *Financial Management*, 7–16.

Industrial Development Corporation. (2021). *Broad-based Black Economic Empowerment (BBBEE)*. Industrial Development Corporation.

IndustriALL Global Union. (2009). *ESOP Accord reached Between Ghana Mineworkers and AngloGold, Averting Industrial Actions*. Retrieved from IndustriALL Global Union Web Site: http://www.industriall-union.org/

IRS. (2021a). *Employee Stock Ownership Plans (ESOPs)*. Retrieved from Internal Revenue Service-Government: https://www.irs.gov/retirement-plans/employee-stock-ownership-plans-esops

IRS. (2021b). *Stocks (Options, Splits, Traders)*. Retrieved from IRS Web site: https://www.irs.gov/faqs/capital-gains-losses-and-sale-of-home/stocks-options-splits-traders

Jan, D., & Fabo, B. (2016). The Platform Economy and the Disruption of the Employment Relationship. *Social Science Research Network*, 35-53.

Johnson, R. E., Pratt, R. T., & Stewart, S. S. (1982). The Economic Consequences of ESOPs. *Journal of Financial Research*, 75–83.

Kaarsemaker, E. C., & Poutsma, E. (2006). The fit of employee ownership with other human resource management practices: Theoretical and empirical suggestions regarding the existence of an ownership high-performance work system. *Economic and Industrial Democracy*, 669–685.

Kaplan, J., & Ludwig, R. (1985). *ESOP*. Tax Management.

Katoch, R. (2017). Accounting Mechanism of Employee Stock Options in India: A Case Study of Wipro Limited, an IT Service Provider Company in India. *International Journal of Management, IT & Engineering*, 433-553.

Kenyan Wall Street. (2016). *CMA Approves ARM Cement to give employees 21Million shares via ESOP*. Hisa Technologies Ltd.

Kim, A., & Han, K. (2019). All for one and one for all: A mechanism through which broad-based employee stock ownership and employee-perceived involvement practice create a productive workforce. *Human Resource Management*, 571–584.

Kim, E. H., & Ouimet, P. (2014). Broad-Based Employee Stock Ownership: Motives and Outcomes. *The Journal of Finance*, 1273–1319.

Kim, K. Y., & Patel, P. C. (2020). A multilevel contingency model of employee ownership and firm productivity: The moderating roles of industry growth and instability. *Organization Science*, 1–25.

Kruse, D., Freeman, R., & Blasi, J. (2010). Shared Capitalism at Work: Employee Ownership, Profit and Gain Sharing, and Broad-based Stock Options. National Bureau of Economic Research, 257-289.

Kuvaas, B. (2003). Employee ownership and affective organizational commitment: Employees' perceptions of fairness and their preference for company shares over cash. *Scandinavian Journal of Management*, 193–212.

Lamberg, J.-A., Savage, G. T., & Pajunen, K. (2003). Strategic stakeholder perspective to ESOP negotiations: The case of United Airlines. *Management Decision*, 383–393.

Lampel, J., Bhalla, A., & Jha, P. P. (2012). The Employee Owned Business Model During Growth and Adversity: How Well Does it Hold Up? *European Business Review*, 20–25.

Majumdar, R. (2021). *Paytm Expands ESOP Scheme To $604 Mn, Largest Among Indian Startups*. New Delhi: inc42.

Martechseries. (2021). *Insights*. Retrieved from Martechseries Web Site: https://martechseries.com/mts-insights/staff-writers/top-tech-companies-successful-esop-processes-plans/

Mathieu, M. (2020). *Annual Economic Survey of Employee Share Ownership in European Countries*. European Federation of Share Ownership.

McDaniel, W. R., Madura, J., & Wiant, J. K. (1995). Performance following ESOP formations by publicly-held corporations. *Journal of Economics and Finance*, 147–169.

Megginson, W., Nash, R., & Randenborgh, M. V. (1994). The financial and operatingperformance of newly privatized firms: An international empirical analysis. *The Journal of Finance*, 122–145.

Mullins, F. (2018). A piece of the pie? The effects of familial control enhancements on the use of broad-based employee ownership programs in family firms. *Human Resource Management*, 979–992.

National Center for Employee Ownership. (2019). *A Statistical Profile of Employee Ownership*. National Center for Employee Ownership.

NCEO. (2020, July 5). *Publications*. Retrieved from NCEO Web Site: https://www.nceo.org/articles/employee-ownership-100

Nomafu, Z. (2018). *Why Companies Need to Support ESOP Initiatives*. Dadelane Wastewater Solutions.

Palmer, M., Mawad, M., & Treyz, C. (2020). Europe loosens rules on stock options, but employees are still sceptical. *Financial Times*. Retrieved from https://sifted.eu/articles/stock-option-changes-europe/

Palmer, T. B., & Wiseman, R. M. (1999). Decoupling risk taking from income stream uncertainty: A holistic model of risk. *Strategic Management Journal*, 1037–1062.

Pan, H. (2021). Core-Staff-Based ESOPs: a new concept of employee share ownership in China. Lorraine: University of Lorraine: European Centre for Research in Financial Economics and Business Management.

Paterson, T. A., & Welbourne, T. M. (2019). I am therefore I own: Implications of organization-based identity for employee stock ownership. *Human Resource Management*, 175–183.

Pendleton, A. (2006). Incentives, Monitoring and Employee Stock Ownership Plans: New *Industrial Relations*. Academic Press.

Pendleton, A., Wilson, N., & Wright, M. (1998). The Perception and Effects of Share Ownership: Empirical Evidence from Employee Buy-Outs. *British Journal of Industrial Relations*, 99–123.

Philip, K. (2003). *Co-operatives in South Africa: Their Role in Job Creation and Poverty Reduction*. South African Foundation.

Pierce, J. L., Rubenfeld, S. A., & Morgan, S. (1991). *Employee ownership: A conceptual model of process and effects*. Academic Press.

Poutsma, F., Ligthart, P. E., & Poutsma, E. (2017). *Sharing in the Company: Determinants, Processes and Outcomes of Employee Participation*. Emerald Group Publishing Limited.

Public-Private Infrastructure Advisory Facility (PPIAF). (2021). *Key Elements of a Labor Program*. Retrieved from Public-Private Infrastructure Advisory Facility (PPIAF) Website: https://ppiaf.org/sites/ppiaf.org/files/documents/toolkits/LaborToolkit/Toolkit/module5/employee.html

Ramchandani, S. B., & Pandya, H. B. (2019). *Evaluating the Effect of Employee Stock Option Plans on the Financial Performance of Indian Construction & Infrastructure Companies*. Academic Press.

Ren, T., Xiao, Y., Yang, H., & Liu, S. (2019). Employee ownership heterogeneity and firm performance in China. *Human Resource Management*, 621–639.

Riaz, F., Razzaq, A., & Waqar, A. (2017). Effect of Employee Stock Ownership Plans (ESOPs) on the performance of Small business in Karachi. *International Journal of Applied Business and Management Studies*, 1-16.

Roux, H. L. (2005). Esops emerging as key to broad-based empowerment. *Engineering News*. Retrieved from https://www.engineeringnews.co.za/article/esops-emerging-as-key-to-broadbased-empowerment-2005-06-06/rep_id:4136

Samantara, R., & Dhawan, S. (2020). Corporate social responsibility in India: Issues and challenges. *IIMS Journal of Management Science*, 91-103.

Schneider, N. (2020). Broad-Based Stakeholder Ownership in Journalism: Co-ops, ESOPs, Blockchains. *Media Industries Journal*, 123-140.

Sinenhlanhla, S. (2019). *Unpacking Employee Share Ownership Plans ESOPs*. Sam Tambni Research Institute.

South African Government. (2021). *Broad-based Black Economic Empowerment Act 53 of 2003*. Retrieved from South African Government Website: https://www.gov.za/documents/broad-based-black-economic-empowerment-act

The Catholic University of Brussels. (2000). *A company perspective on financial participation in the European Union: objectives and obstacles*. The Catholic University of Brussels.

The European Commission. (2003). *The legal and administrative environment for Employee*. The European Commission.

The European Commission. (2014). *The Promotion of Employee Ownership and Participation*. The European Commission.

The European Union. (2020). *Employee Involvement - Employment, Social Affairs & Inclusion - European Commission*. Brussels: The European Union.

The European Union. (2021). *Start Up Europe*. Brussels: The European Union.

Transcend. (2021, July 5). *Our Clients*. Retrieved from Transcend Web Site: https://www.transcend.co.za

Wang, H. C., He, J., & Mahoney, J. T. (2009). Firm-specific knowledge resources and competitive advantage: The roles of economic-and relationship-based employee governance mechanisms. *Strategic Management*, 1265–1285.

Wanjiku, R. (2008, June 4). Kenya's Safaricom IPO disappoints small investors. *Ntework World*, p. 1. Retrieved May 25, 2021, from https://www.networkworld.com/article/2280772/kenya-s-safaricom-ipo-disappoints-small-investors.html

Wen, X., Li, Z., Zhang, Y., & Shen, S. (2021). ESOP and Corporate Sustainable Growth. *Web of Conferences*, 1-6.

Weyher, H., & Knott, H. (1985). *The employee stock ownership plan*. Commerce Clearinghouse.

Whitfield, K., Pendleton, A., Sengupta, S., & Huxley, K. (2017). Employee share ownership and organizational performance: A tentative opening of the black box. *Personnel Review*, 123–140.

Yale Law Journal Company, Inc. (1990). When Does Worker Ownership Work? ESOPs, Law Firms, Codetermination, and Economic Democracy. *The Yale Law Journal*, 1749–1816.

Yoon, Y., & Sengupta, S. (2019). Employee share ownership, training, and early promotion policy as a bundle in enhancing labor productivity: A test of the three-way interaction effect. *Human Resource Management*, 603–620.

Zhou, D., Huang, J., & Zhao, Y. (2019). Employee Stock Ownership Plans and Corporate Innovation. *Journal of Accounting Research*, 63–70.

Section 3

Special Issues of Employee Stock Ownership Plans in Morocco

Chapter 6
Analysis of the Effects of Employee Share Ownership on the Creation of Financial Value of Moroccan Companies Listed on the Stock Exchange

Houssam Errommani
Hassan II University, Casablanca, Morocco

Hicham Elbouanani
Hassan II University, Casablanca, Morocco

ABSTRACT

Employee share ownership (ESOP) is a highly acclaimed international incentive and motivation mechanism for employees thanks to its virtuous impact on company performance and organizational behavior. The work proposes to study the effects of this practice on the financial performance of Moroccan companies in order to assess the impact of employee participation on the creation of financial value. To this end, the authors conducted an empirical study based on two analytical methods using SPSS software. The sample is made up of 33 companies that have published and carried out at least one employee shareholding operation in Morocco since their IPO. The financial data was extracted from the accounting statements of each company for the period from 2015 to 2019. The results show that ESOP is weakly practiced by companies, and the tests do not allow to confirm of the existence of its impact on the performance of the companies studied.

DOI: 10.4018/978-1-7998-8557-3.ch006

INTRODUCTION

Employee share ownership is a widely known and internationally acclaimed practice. The United States is the global pioneer of employee Savings Plans and currently has 14 million salaried shareholders. France is considered the European champion in terms of the democratization of employee shareholding and has nearly 3.2 million salaried shareholders, followed by United kingdom, which has almost 2 million employee shareholders. While in Germany, 700,000 employees own the shares of their companies. This enthusiasm for employee shareholding schemes is shared by European companies, which total 10 million salaried shareholders in 2019.

This growing economic interest is accompanied by a real political awareness through devoting more tax incentives to promote the introduction of employee shareholding by companies. In France, the PACTE -Action Plan for Business Growth and Transformation Act enacted in the spring of 2019 has put in place numerous incentives and reductions to expand the adoption of employee shareholding by French companies. And the French Minister of Economy and Finance, Bruno Le Maire, has set a government target of granting 10% of the capital of French companies to employees by 2030.

Moroccan companies are no exception to the rule and have set up some employee shareholding operations. However, these participation plans remain the preserve of large market capitalizations and suffer from the lack of knowledge of its mechanisms and its effects on the value of companies and the attitudes of employees. To this end, the academic world must encourage the development of this virtuous phenomenon for the Moroccan economy by devoting more empirical research to the benefits of employee shareholding, which remain, in particular, very laconic in Morocco.

As such, our work questions the development of employee shareholding in the Kingdom of morocco and proposes to provide elements of answer to the following problem: What companies practice employee shareholding in Morocco and does employee shareholding influence their financial performance?

To answer our problem, we present, first, a theoretical analysis of employee shareholding, then we present an empirical synthesis of previous studies that have focused on the link between the performance of the company and employee shareholding. Second, we present the chosen research methodology for this study, as well as the results and discussion of these. At the end, the conclusion will recall the objectives and results of the study. And will explain, on one hand, the theoretical, methodological and managerial inputs and, on the other hand, the limits and prospects for future research.

THEORETICAL AND CONCEPTUAL FRAMEWORK OF EMPLOYEE OWNERSHIP

Within the framework of the traditional and financial approach to corporate governance, employee share ownership finds a better frame of reference for analysis in agency theory. This theory considers the firm as a real node of contracts through which the relationship between the agent "manager" and the principal "shareholder" is established. This relationship is called an agency relationship, defined by (Jensen & Meckling, 1976) as a contract by which the shareholders appoint a manager to carry out a task on their behalf, namely the management of the firm. This implies, of course, a certain delegation of decision-making power. However, this agency relationship presents many problems related to the divergence of interests between the principal and the agent, which can have a negative impact on the performance of the company and on the financial interests of the shareholders. Generally, this divergence of interests between the principal and the agent can generate costs called "agency costs", due mainly to opportunism caused by the incompleteness of contracts, uncertainty, imperfect observability of the efforts made by the agent, as well as informational asymmetry (Caby & Hirigoyen, 2001; Desbrières, 2002).

(Jensen & Meckling, 1976) classify these costs according to three types, namely: "control costs" or monitoring costs incurred by the principal to limit any opportunistic behavior by the agent during his management of the firm, "obligation costs" incurred by the agent to reassure the principal and persuade him to act in his interests. And "opportunity costs" which represent the residual loss, due to the loss of utility suffered by the principal because of the divergence of interests with the agent.

In response to these circumstances, which can lead to a decline in quality, productivity and performance, and in order to ensure that the interests of the employee-managers are consistent with those of the shareholders, control instruments and incentive mechanisms can be established, including employee share ownership.

In this perspective, (Hansman, 1996) considers that when companies disseminate employee share ownership plans in a very broad manner, they encourage employees to control themselves and the efforts of other employees. In other words, employee stock ownership plans create a culture of collective responsibility (Whyte, 1978). Employee ownership can help build positive working relationships, including awareness of common interests and shared goals (Lawler, 1977), and the promotion of cooperation (Long, 1978) between employees (Weitzman & Kruse, 1990).

In this sense, (Long, 1980) affirms that employee ownership can provide a sense of common purpose, a sense of belonging to an organization, and a sense of loyalty. Informally, this can only encourage the establishment of a system of trust (Poulain-Rehm, 2006) within the company. Thus, employee ownership is not only a source of incentive and motivation for employees, but also helps to involve them in the company by generating a high level of commitment and reducing absenteeism, conflicts and turnover.

As a result, it will certainly increase productivity and increase the company's competitiveness and profitability. In these perspectives, there has been a great deal of research into the impact of employee ownership on financial and organizational performance. Most of these studies have demonstrated the positive relationship between employee ownership and company performance, notably the studies of "(Conte & Tannenbaum, 1978); (Wagner & Rosen, 1985); (Rosen and al., 1986) and (Marsh & Mc Allister, 1981)". In fact, according to (Rotondi, 1975) this performance is linked to the emanation of three interdependent factors but induced by the ESOPs, namely the convergence of interest of the employees, loyalty and the feeling of belonging to the company.

On the other hand, employee participation in governance bodies is likely to lead to better decision-making. Employees usually have information that senior managers do not. In addition, employee ownership allows different opinions to be expressed, which can concretely reduce the risk of group mentality (Garfatta, 2010).

Finally, for any company, the interest of employee ownership is to enhance employee motivation and to ensure the reconciliation of individual interests (Desbrières, 1997), in the search for better performance (Garfatta, 2010). This was corroborated by the Altedia-COB study of June (1999), which concluded that the most important reason for companies to adopt employee share ownership is to motivate employees, reconcile interests and reduce turnover.

The considerable interest in employee share ownership has prompted us to analyze the place of this mechanism in Morocco, in order to remedy the lack of Moroccan academic research on the subject. For this reason, we choose in the framework of this study to provide answers to the financial aspect of value creation, mainly through the analysis of the impact of the employee shareholding on the financial and accounting performance of companies.

SUMMARY OF EMPIRICAL WORK ON FINANCIAL PERFORMANCE AND EMPLOYEE OWNERSHIP

Employee ownership is a phenomenon that has generated a lot of debate in the academic and political world. As such, many studies have been conducted on the relationship between employee share ownership and firm performance. Four categories of literature seem to emerge, the first one arguing that there is a negative relationship between employee share ownership and company performance. The second category affirms that employee shareholding has no effect on performance. The third, and most dominant, category argues that there is a positive relationship between employee ownership and performance. And finally, there is a fourth category that explains that employee ownership has a curvilinear impact on financial value. We present in what follows a synthesis of these empirical works.

Few empirical studies assert the existence of a negative relationship between employee share ownership and performance. This is the case, for example, of (Livingston & Henry, 1980) who find a negative effect on profitability. Similarly, (Park & Song, 1995) report a negative effect on economic and stock market performance. As for (Faleye, and al., 2006), they show that companies with a high level of employee ownership (more than 5% of capital) have a lower performance than those with a low level of employee ownership (less than 5% of capital). The authors call this phenomenon the "Dark Side" of employee ownership and attribute it to the entrenchment of managers and the instrumentalization of employees.

The second category of studies shows that employee share ownership has no effect on performance. According to these studies, employee share ownership has no significant impact on the economic performance of the company (Bloom, 1986) and (Borstadt & Zwirlein, 1995). The General Accounting Office (1986) found that Employee Stock Ownership Plans (ESOPs) will only have an effect on performance if they are combined with participative management, because in the United States the granting of shares is not always accompanied by voting rights. In France, (Vaughan-Whitehead, 1992) did not prove the existence of a significant impact on financial performance and income. Also, (Trébucq, 2002) shows that employee share ownership has no influence on shareholder value. Moreover, (Poulain-Rehm, 2006) pointed out in a study carried out in the French context on a sample of 131 listed companies, that employee ownership does not affect shareholder and partnership value.

The third category of studies reveals positive links between employee share ownership and performance. More precisely, these studies show that employee ownership has a positive impact on financial performance (Fitzroy & Kraft, 1987), on turnover, economic and financial performance (Wagner & Rosen, 1985) and on profitability (Conte & Tannenbaum, 1978). In France, a longitudinal study carried out by (Kumbhakar & Dunbar, 1993) over a period of six years (1982-1987), covering a sample of 120 companies, showed that employee shareholding has a positive and significant effect on performance (measured by sales).

Also, (Jones & Kato, 1993) affirm the existence of a positive and significant correlation between employee ownership and economic performance, according to a study of a sample of 320 Japanese companies that had ESOPs. More recently, the study carried out by (Aubert, et al., 2016) in a French context on the 900 subsidiaries of a group listed on the CAC 40, shows that employee shareholding has a positive influence on economic performance. Likewise, the study conducted by (Basterretxea & Storey, 2018) explains that Employee Share Ownership generates an increase in productivity and a decrease in turnover of the two joint-owned companies in Great

Britain and Spain. In another context, the research realized by (Alimi, 2019) affirms that employee shareholding contributes to increasing the shareholder value of the Cameroonian companies studied.

In the Moroccan context, we did not find any studies that explicitly investigated the link between employee ownership and performance. Nevertheless, the research of Azzouzi and Haoudi (2020) found, in a different framework, that the presence of family shareholding positively influences the performance of Moroccan listed firms.

The fourth category shows that the relationship between employee ownership and performance is curvilinear. In France, (Dondi, 1992) studied the financial profitability of a sample of 105 French companies listed over a period of four years (1985-1988), and found that financial profitability gradually increases, as long as the shareholding rate employee does not exceed 10% of the company's capital. However, financial profitability decreases when employee ownership exceeds the 10% threshold. Therefore, the relationship between employee ownership and financial profitability tends to take an inverted U shape. In this sense, (Guedri & Hollandts, 2008), demonstrate from their study which was based on a sample of 189 French companies over a period of four years (2001-2004), that there is a curvilinear relationship between employee ownership and the economic performance of the company.

If the literature does not seem to be unanimous on the nature of the impact of employee share ownership on financial value, we can nevertheless note that the vast majority of studies show the existence of a positive link, and we can add to these studies the plurality of studies that highlight the role of employee shareholding in the emergence of positive behaviors at work such as increased organizational involvement, job satisfaction, the decrease of departure intentions (Elouadi, 2015) and the favorable role of employee shareholding in the development of employees' human capital and their potential at work (Elouadi, 2016).

Referring to the empirical results of the previous studies mentioned above, we intend to examine the following hypotheses:

H0: Employee share ownership would have no effect on the creation of financial value in companies.

H1: Employee share ownership would have a positive effect on the creation of financial value in companies.

H2: Employee share ownership would have a negative effect on the creation of financial value in companies.

EMPIRICAL METHODOLOGY

The first constraint we face in wanting to analyze the impact of employee share ownership on the financial value of companies is the lack of information on Moroccan companies that associate employees to their capital. We then decided to establish a list of these companies (Annexes N ° 1). For this, we used several data sources available on the website of the Casablanca Stock Exchange and the website of the Moroccan capital market authority, AMMC.

These documents include press releases, financial statements, information documents and technical results. Our study population consists of companies listed on the Casablanca stock exchange and included in the Masi index, which includes 75 companies as of 31/12/2019. The analysis allowed us to have a sample of 33 companies among the seventy-five, which have mediated and carried out at least one employee share ownership operation in Morocco (Annex N°1). This database contains the following information: the name of the company, its sector of activity, the date of listing on the stock exchange, the date of the employee share ownership operations, the number of shares offered to employees and the percentage of capital, the discount granted by this company, the period of unavailability of the shares, the number of employee share ownership operations carried out by this company and the modalities of dissemination of the employee share ownership scheme.

After having identified all the companies practicing employee share ownership in Morocco, we extracted their financial data from the websites of the Casablanca Stock Exchange and the AMMC[1]. They concern the following information: the net results of five years (2015-2019), the annual sales of five years (2015-2019), the share capital of the companies practicing employee share ownership as of 31/12/2019. Finally, for the variable: type of governance (family or non-family): we exploited the work of (Korichi & Alaoui Mdaghri, 2018) which aimed to identify family and non-family companies listed on the Casablanca Stock Exchange.

Measurement of Variables

Referring to the literature and previous studies that have examined the relationship between ESOPs and corporate financial performance, we find that several measures have been advocated to examine this relationship. Indeed, for the variable “financial value creation” which constitutes our dependent variable, (Trébucq, 2002) retained “economic value added”, while (Poulain-Rehm, 2006) used “value added”. And (Ngongang, 2013) used “the average positive value added of two years”. Other measures have also been exploited by researchers such as “return on investment (ROI)”, “Tobin’s Q ratio” and “Marris’ ratio” (Garfatta, 2010). In the context of our study, we retain two measurement indicators, namely: “the average net profitability ratio over five years", which measures the average profitability of the company over five years (2015-2019), and "the average net result over five years" (Table N°1).

Table 1. Selected measure of financial creation value

Dependent Variable	Indicator	Name
Financial value creation	average net profitability ratio over five years (2015-2019)	ANPR
	Average net result over five years (2015-2019)	ANR

Source: Authors

Furthermore, "employee ownership", which is our explanatory variable, has been measured by the literature in different ways. Table 2 summarizes the measures recommended by previous empirical work.

Table 2. ESOPs measurement indicators in previous studies

Authors	ESOPs Measurement Indicators
(Hammer & Stern, 1980)	- Percentage of capital held by employee shareholders
(Klein, 1987) ; (Faley, and al., 2006)	- Percentage of voting rights held by employee shareholders.
(Chaplinsky & Niehaus, 1994)	- Increase of percentage held by ESOPs. - Percentage of capital held by employee shareholders
(Welbourne &Cyr, 1999)	- Percentage of shares held by employees and other managers (binary variable). - Coding of the nature of shareholding.

Source: (Garfatta, 2010, p.179)

Looking at previous studies, we can see that employee ownership has been measured by many indicators. In this paper, we focus on the frequency of adoption as an indicator of employee ownership, which corresponds to the number of employee share ownership operations carried out by the companies in our sample since their IPO.

This choice is justified by the absence of data corresponding to the share of capital held by employees for all companies. Similarly, we extracted from previous work, notably the study by (Garfatta, 2010), control indicators or moderating variables likely to have an influence on the relationship between employee ownership and financial value creation, namely seniority, capital and type of governance. We summarize all the measures used in this study in the following table (Table 3).

Table 3. Summary table of the variables selected in this study

Variables	Indicators	Denomination
Average net profitability ratio over five years (2015-2019)	Average 5-year net result / average 5-year sales. This ratio is used as an indicator to measure financial value creation in our first analysis method.	ANPR
average net result of five-year (2015-2019)	average net result of five-year is an indicator of financial value creation in our second analysis method.	ANR
Employee share ownership	Measured by the number of employee share ownership operations carried out by the company since its IPO	FREQUENCY
Seniority	This is the company's existence duration since its initial public offering (number of years)	SENIO
Capital	This is the company's share capital on 31/12/2019 (MMAD)	CAPITAL
Type of governance	It is a categorical data that distinguishes if the company is family or non-family	TYPGOV

Source: Authors

METHODOLOGY OF THE EMPIRICAL TESTS

In order to conduct our empirical study, and test the relationship between employee ownership and financial value creation. We borrow the methodology of (Ngongang, 2013) who used the average of financial indicators to test the relationship between employee ownership and value creation in the Cameroonian context for the years 2008 and 2009. In this regard, we adopt a quantitative approach based on a set of inference tests to answer our hypothesis H1 using SPSS software. For this reason, we structure our study around two methods of analysis: The first method, corresponds to an empirical analysis of a t-test for an independent sample in order to compare the financial performance of companies that practice employee ownership in Morocco (33 companies). For this aim, we decompose companies with employee ownership into two subgroups, namely those with a frequency strictly below 2 and those with a frequency greater than or equal to 2. The purpose of this test is to examine the hypothesis that companies with a sustained frequency of adoption of employee ownership have a higher financial performance than those with a lower frequency of adoption.

In the second method, we plan to carry out an independent samples t-test comparing, this time, the financial performance of companies that practice employee ownership in Morocco to companies that do not. We select a sample of 66 companies (of which 33 companies do not practice employee ownership).

The objective of this test is to examine the hypothesis that companies with employee ownership plans in Morocco have a better financial performance than those that do not practice it. Indeed, we perform these inference tests, while respecting the premises of the t-test for independent samples, namely: the normality test of the distribution and the homogeneity test of variances.

Descriptive Analysis and Characteristics of Our Sample

Our study covers a sample of 66 listed companies between 2015-2019, of which 33 companies practice employee ownership. According to our data, the majority of companies that practice employee ownership in Morocco chose to interest their employees during the IPO, through the reservation of a tranche for their employees (26 operations). Capital increases come in second place with 9 operations. And only 5 public offers of sales (OFS) enabled the establishment of employee shareholding. Moreover, the large foreign groups holding subsidiaries in Morocco choose to interest their Moroccan employees through the FCPEs (Company mutual funds), of which we have listed 3 operations. Finally, only one employee shareholding plan was planned in the framework of privatization operations. Moreover, 78.79% of the companies practicing employee share ownership in Morocco have carried out only one employee share ownership operation since their IPO. While 12.12% have carried out two operations, and only 9.09% have implemented more than three operations. The majority of companies that practice employee share ownership in Morocco are family-owned companies, mentioning a percentage of 54.55% against 45.45% for non-family-owned companies. And 28 companies that have issued employee share ownership plans have a seniority of (1 year to 21 years), 4 companies have a seniority of (38 years to 50 years) and only one company has more than 70 years. Also, 27 companies practicing employee ownership in Morocco have a capital of (1 to 1500 MMAD), 4 companies have a capital of (1500 to 2500 MMAD) and 2 companies have a capital of (3000 to 5500 MMAD).

EMPIRICAL RESULTS AND DISCUSSION

In order to analyze the relationship between employee ownership (measured by the frequency of adoption of employee ownership) and financial value creation (measured by the average net profitability ratio over five years and the average net result over 5 years) we proceed by checking the normality of the distribution of our sample (Table N°4).

Table 4. Sample normality test

Sample Normality Test							
	Frequency	Kolmogorov-Smirnov[a]			Shapiro-Wilk		
		Statistics	DF	Signification	Statistics	DF	Signification
Capital	1	,233	26	,001	,760	26	,000
	2	,428	4	.	,657	4	,003
	3	,296	3	.	,919	3	,448
Seniority	1	,299	26	,000	,687	26	,000
	2	,350	4	.	,830	4	,168
	3	,180	3	.	,999	3	,946
ANPR	1	,428	26	,000	,331	26	,056
	2	,170	4	.	,984	4	,928
	3	,312	3	.	,895	3	,371

a. Correction of the signification of Lilliefors
Source: Authors, SPSS

According to the table above (Table N°4), there are two tests to examine the normality of the distribution, namely: the Kolmogorov-Smirnov test and the Shapiro-Wilk test. In view of the size of our sample, we choose the Shapiro-Wilk test, which applies to relatively small samples. The results show a P-value above the 5% threshold for our variables of interest (FREQENCE-ANPR). Therefore, H0 is credible and our distribution follows a normal distribution. We then examine the homogeneity of the variances: Homoscedasticity or heteroscedasticity (Tables 5 and 6).

According to Table N°5 and N°6: Levene's test for our variables of interest (FREQUENCY-ANPR), we notice that the P-value>0.05. Therefore, we do not reject the null hypothesis (hypothesis of homoscedasticity). And we affirm the homogeneity of the variances.

After having validated the two criterias of parametric tests, namely the normality of the distribution and the homogeneity of variances. We carry out a t-test for independent samples, in order to answer our hypotheses. First, we decompose our sample into two independent subgroups: the first subgroup, which we call group 1, corresponds to companies with an adoption frequency strictly lower than two. The second subgroup, called group 2, corresponds to companies with an adoption frequency greater than or equal to two. The following tables show the main results of this study (Tables 7 and 8).

Table 5. Homogeneity of variances

The One-way ANOVA						
		Sum of Squares	**df**	**The Mean Square**	**F**	**Signification**
Capital	Inter-groups	701584156973292 9500,000	2	3507920784866 464800,000	2,985	,066
	Intra-groups	352502320557444 26000,000	30	1175007735191 480830,000		
	Total	422660736254773 60000,000	32			
Seniority	Inter-groups	2623,604	2	1311,802	8,042	,002
	Intra-groups	4893,365	30	163,112		
	Total	7516,970	32			
ANPR	Inter-groups	,289	2	,144	,225	,800
	Intra-groups	19,219	30	,641		
	Total	19,508	32			

Source: Authors, SPSS

Table 6. Homogeneite of variances

Test of Homogeneity of Variances				
	Levene's Statistics	**df1**	**df2**	**Signification**
Capital	10,133	2	30	,000
Seniority	3,819	2	30	,033
ANPR	,523	2	30	,598

Source: Authors, SPSS

Table 7. Test-t statistics

Group Statistics					
	Frequency	**N**	**Mean**	**Standard Deviation**	**Standard Error**
ANPR	1	26	-,09753009842	,876439232903	,171883875041
	2	7	,12170390400	,080446456043	,030405902364

Source: Authors, SPSS

The results show that the mean of the net profitability ratio is (-0.09) for group 1 and (0.1) for group 2. Similarly, the standard deviation of the ANPR is (0.87) for group 1 and (0.08) for group 2. Thus, we see a large variability in the distribution of the ANPR of group 1 companies. (Table N°7).

Table 8. Levene's test of equality of variance

Independent Samples Test			
		Levene's Test for Equality of Variances	
		F	Sig.
ANPR	Hypothesis of equal variances	,932	,342
	Hypothesis of unequal variances		

Source: Authors, SPSS

The table above (Table N°8), presents the test of equality of variances. The Levene test compares the variance of the two groups. We notice that the Levene's test is superior to the P-value: 0.342>0.05 (significance level= 5%). Therefore, we do not reject the null hypothesis of equality of variances. We must conclude that the variance of the companies belonging to group 1 is equal to the variance of the companies belonging to group 2.

Table 9. Test-t for equality of means

t-Test for Equality of Means						
t	df	Sig. (bilateral)	Average Difference	Difference Standard Deviation	95% Confidence Interval of the Difference	
					Inferior	Superior
-,653	31	,518	-,219234002423	,335483273606	-,903456649983	,464988645136
-1,256	26,481	,220	-,219234002423	,174552529049	-,577714890447	,139246885601

Source: Authors, SPSS

The t-test table for equality of means (Table N°9) shows us that the p-value 0.220 is greater than 0.05 (significance level = 5%). Therefore, we cannot reject the null hypothesis of equality of means of the NRN of the two groups. It is likely that at the 5% level, firms belonging to group 1 and group 2 have the same net profitability ratio.

Results of the Independent Samples T-Test: (*comparison of the financial performance of companies that practice employee share ownership and companies that do not*)

In the following, we present the results of the independent sample t-test comparing the financial value creation of companies that practice employee share ownership and companies that do not in Morocco. In this regard, we retain 66 companies to respect the parity of the sample (Poulain-Rehm, 2006).

Table 10. Test-t statistics

Group Statistics					
	Frequency	**N**	**Mean**	**Standard Deviation**	**Standard Error**
ANI MMAD	1	33	582,7998	1328,34079	231,23445
	0	33	198,1073	365,22448	63,57742

Source: Authors, SPSS

The table above (Table N°10) gives us the sample size for each group. Sample 1 corresponds to companies that have carried out and publicized at least one employee share ownership operation and sample 0 corresponds to companies that have never practiced employee share ownership. The average net result is (582.79 MMAD) for group 1 and (198.10 MMAD) for group 0. Similarly, the standard deviation of the ANR is (1328.30 MMAD) for group 1 and (365.22 MMAD) for group 0. Thus, we see a large variability in the distribution of ANR in favour of companies that introduce employee ownership.

Table 11. Levene's test of equality of variance

		Levene's Test for Equality of Variances	
		F	**Sig.**
ANI MMAD	Hypothesis of equal variances	8,583	,005
	Hypothesis of unequal variances		

Source: Authors, SPSS

According to Table N°11, we notice that the P-value of Levene's test is lower than 5% (significance level). The null hypothesis of equality of variances is rejected. We have to conclude that the variance of the companies which introduce employee ownership is not equal to the variance of the companies which do not introduce it.

According to Table N°12, we can see that the P value of the t-test is higher than the significance level of 5%. (0.117>0.05). The null hypothesis of equality of the means of the net result of the two groups cannot be rejected. Therefore, it can be stated that at the 5% level, it is likely that companies that practice employee ownership and companies that do not practice employee ownership have the same ANR. It can be concluded that the results of the independent samples t-test do not support hypothesis H1, nor hypothesis H2.

Table 12. Test for equality of means

Independent Samples Test						
t-Test for Equality of Means						
t	df	Sig. (bilateral)	Average Difference	Difference Standard Deviation	95% Confidence Interval of the Difference	
					Inferior	Superior
1,604	64	,114	384,69253	239,81547	-94,39395	863,77901
1,604	36,811	,117	384,69253	239,81547	-101,30414	870,68920

Source: Authors, SPSS

Our results show that employee ownership does not induce any effect on the financial value creation of companies. This confirms the work of the part of the literature that supports the absence of impact of employee ownership on performance.

CONCLUSION

The objective of this study was to empirically verify the nature of the relationship between employee ownership and financial value creation in Moroccan companies. In a first part, we tested the hypothesis that companies with a sustained frequency of adoption of employee ownership have a higher financial performance than other companies in our sample. And in a second part, we examined the hypothesis that firms that practice employee ownership in Morocco have a higher financial performance than those that do not. The results of the independent samples t-test do not support hypothesis H1. Indeed, the inference tests conducted reveal that a sustained frequency of adoption of employee ownership does not translate into higher value creation. Similarly, companies that practice employee ownership and those that do not, have the same net result average. These results confirm the studies of (Borstadt & Zwirlein, 1995), who find that employee ownership has no effect on company performance. Similarly, our results confirm the work of Trébucq, (2002) who shows that employee ownership has no influence on shareholder value. Also, (Poulain-Rehm, 2006) underlined in a study carried out in the French context on a sample of 131 listed companies, that employee ownership does not affect shareholder and partnership value. Nevertheless, we believe that the insignificance of the empirical results is due to the measurement variable of employee ownership adopted in our study, namely "Frequency", which does not really reflect the employees' share of the capital. The main theoretical contribution of our study lies in enriching the scientific framework of employee savings in Morocco. Indeed, the subject of our research is a crucial lever for the development of the Moroccan economy and remains unfortunately very poorly invested by Moroccan researchers. This study allowed us to establish a framework for employee ownership in Morocco through the design of a database that includes all companies that have carried out employee ownership operations in Morocco. Similarly, our study has a great managerial interest. Indeed, Moroccan companies are called to join the global momentum by adopting more and more employee ownership because the practice remains unknown and a minority in Morocco. Indeed, only 7 companies out of 33 that practice employee ownership in Morocco have renewed the operation more than twice. While 78.8% of the companies practicing employee, ownership have done it only once. The figures for employee share ownership adoption in Morocco are not sufficient to analyze the empirical impact of participation on the financial value of companies. A considerable effort must be made, jointly, by academics, politicians and professional prescribers in order to encourage employers to share capital with employees and enjoy the beneficial effects of this mechanism, which is widely recognized internationally.

Despite the above-mentioned contributions, our research is not without its limitations. The main limitation is the scarcity and unavailability of data on employee ownership in Morocco. The unavailability of the variable "share of capital held by employees" led us to use the variable "Frequency of adoption" as an indicator to measure our variable of interest "Employee shareholding". We invite future researches to study the topic of employee ownership from different empirical facets. Indeed, our work can be complemented by interviews with managers and professional prescribers, to analyse in depth the particularity of employee ownership in Morocco. Likewise, it would have been wise to use the variable "percentage of capital held by employees" as a dependent variable in order to analyze the impact more precisely. Also, the literature shows that the adoption of the variable "percentage of voting rights held by employees" is more satisfactory because it is a measure that best reflects the effective participation of employee shareholders in voting rights. And according to several empirical studies, the expected effects of ESOPs are not automatic and depend on the presence of mediating variables including political presence in decision-making bodies (Elouadi, 2020), we strongly invite researchers to devote importance to these incentive variables.

REFERENCES

Alimi, O., & Victor, T. (2019). L'actionnariat Salarié Et La Création De Valeur Partenariale. Dans Les Entreprises Au Cameroun. European Scientific Journal, 15(34), 250.

Azzouzi, B., & Haoudi, A. (2020). Actionnariat familial et performance financière: le cas Marocain. *Revue Du contrôle, De La Comptabilité Et De l'audit, 4*(2).

Basterretxea, I., & Storey, J. (2018). Do employee-owned firms produce more positive employee behavioural outcomes? If not why not? A British-Spanish comparative analysis. *British Journal of Industrial Relations, 56*(2), 292–319. doi:10.1111/bjir.12247

Bloom, S. (1986). *Employee Ownership and Firm Performance*. Harvard University Press.

Borstadt, L., & Zwirlein, T. (1995). ESOPs in Publicly Held Companies: Evidence on Productivity and Firm Performance. *Journal of Financial and Strategic Decision Making, 8*(1), 1–13.

Caby, J., & Hirigoyen, G. (2001). *La création de valeur actionnariale*. Academic Press.

Chaplinsky, S., & Niehaus, G. (1994, September). The Role of ESOPs in Takeover Contests. *The Journal of Finance, XLIX*(4), 1451–1470. doi:10.1111/j.1540-6261.1994.tb02461.x

Conte, M., & Tannenbaum, A. S. (1978). Employee-owned companies: Is the difference measurable. *Monthly Labor Review, 101*, 23.

Desbrières, Ph. (1997a), Le rôle de l'actionnariat des salariés non-dirigeants dans le système de gouvernement de l'entreprise. In Recherche en Gestion. Economica.

Desbrières, Ph. (2002). Les Actionnaires – Salariés. *Revue Française De Gestion, 141*.

Dondi, J. (1992). *Contribution à la connaissance de l'actionnariat des salariés dans les entreprises françaises* (Doctoral dissertation). Bordeaux 1.

Elouadi, S. (2015). Les effets attitudinaux de l'actionnariat salarié: une étude empirique dans le contexte des entreprises françaises du SBF 250. *Question (s) de Management*, (3), 11-24.

Elouadi, S. (2020). L'influence des variables incitatives sur la satisfaction des actionnaires salariés: une modélisation par équations structurelles. *Question(s) de Management, 2*(2), 35-49. doi:10.3917/qdm.202.0035

Elouadi, S., Noamene, T. B., & Chaher, D. (2016). Employee Ownership And Employee- Shareholders Satisfaction: An Analysis Of French Companies Listed On The SBF 250. *Journal of Applied Business Research, 32*(3), 981–994. doi:10.19030/jabr.v32i3.9647

Faleye, O., Mehrotra, V., & Morck, R. (2006). When Labor Has a Voice in Corporate Governance. *Journal of Financial and Quantitative Analysis*, *41*(3), 489–510. doi:10.1017/S0022109000002519

FitzRoy, F. R., & Kraft, K. (1987). Cooperation, productivity, and profit sharing. *The Quarterly Journal of Economics*, *102*(1), 23–35. doi:10.2307/1884678

Garfatta, R. (2010). *Actionnariat salarié et création de valeur dans le cadre d'une gouvernance actionnariale et partenariale: application au contexte française*. Academic Press.

Hammer, T. H., & Stern, R. N. (1980, March). Employee Ownership: Implications for the organisational distribution of power. *Academy of Management Journal*, *23*(1), 78–100.

Hansmann, H. (1996). *The ownership of enterprise*. Harvard University Press.

Hollandts, X. & Guedri, Z. (2008). Les salariés capitalistes et la performance de l'entreprise. *Revue Française de Gestion, 183*(3), 35-50.

Jensen, M. C., & Et Meckling, W. H. (1976). Theory of The Firm: Managerial Behavior, Agency Costs and Ownership Structure. *Journal of Financial Economics*, *3*(10), 305–360. doi:10.1016/0304-405X(76)90026-X

Jones, D. C., & Kato, T. (1993). The scope, nature, and effects of employee stock ownership plans in Japan. *Industrial & Labor Relations Review*, *46*(2), 352–367. doi:10.1177/001979399304600209

Klein, K. (1987). Employee Stock Ownership and Employee Attitudes: A Test of Three Models. *The Journal of Applied Psychology*, *72*(2), 319–332. doi:10.1037/0021-9010.72.2.319 PMID:3583982

Kumbhakar, S. C., & Dunbar, A. E. (1993). The elusive ESOP—Productivity link: Evidence from US firm-level data. *Journal of Public Economics*, *52*(2), 273–283. doi:10.1016/0047-2727(93)90024-N

Lawler, E. E. (1977). Job and work satisfaction. In W. C. Hamner & F. L. Schmidt (Eds.), *Comtemporary problems in personnel*. St. Clair Press.

Livingston, D., & Henry, J. (1980). The effects of employee stock ownership on corporate profits. *The Journal of Risk and Insurance*, *47*(3), 491–505. doi:10.2307/252634

Long, R. J. (1978). The Relative Effects of Share Ownership Versus Control on Job Attitudes in An Employee-Owned Company. *Human Relations*, *31*(9), 753–763. doi:10.1177/001872677803100901

Long, R. J. (1980). Job Attitudes and Organizational Performance under Employee Ownership. *Academy of Management Journal*, *23*(4).

Ngongang, D. (2013). Actionnariat salarié comme levier de création de valeur ajoutée et de productivité dans les entreprises camerounaises. *La Revue Gestion et Organisation*, *5*(1), 1–8. doi:10.1016/j.rgo.2013.10.001

Park, S., & Song, M. H. (1995). Employee Stock Ownership Plans, Firm Performance and Monitoring by Outside Blockholders. *Financial Management*, *24*(4), 52–65. doi:10.2307/3665950

Poulain-Rehm, T. (2006), *L'actionnariat des salariés en France, un facteur de création de valeur?* Note de recherche, www.iae.Univpoitiers.Fr/affi2006/coms/130.pdf

Rotondi, T. Jr. (1975). Organizational identification: Issues and implications. *Organizational Performance and Human Behavior*, *13*(1), 95–109. doi:10.1016/0030-5073(75)90007-0

Trébucq, S. (2002). L'actionnariat salarié dans les entreprises familiales du SBF 250: Un outil de création de valeur Revue Finance, Contrôle. *Stratégie*, *5*(4), 107–135.

Vaughan-Whitehead, D., & Barre, R., & Barre, R. (1992). Intéressement, participation, actionnariat: Impacts économiques dans l'entreprise. *Economica.*

Wagner, I., & Rosen, C. (1985). Employee ownership: Its effects on corporate performance. *Employment Relations Today*, *12*(1), 77–82.

Weitzman, M., & Kruse, D. (1990). *Profit sharing and productivity*. Academic Press.

Welbourne, T., & Cyr, L. (1999). Using ownership as an incentive. *Group & Organization Management*, *24*(4), 438–460. doi:10.1177/1059601199244003

Whyte, W. F. (1978). In support of voluntary employee ownership. *Society*, *15*(6), 73–82. doi:10.1007/BF02697780

APPENDIX

Table 13. List of companies implementing ESOPS in Morocco

Libelle
AFMA
ATLANTA
UNIMER
ATTIJARIWAFA BANK
BANK OF AFRIKA
BCP
BMCI
CDM
COLORADO
JET CONTRACTORS
LABEL VIE
STOKVIS NORD AFRIQUE
NEXANS MAROC
SOTHEMA
DELATTRE LEVIVIER MAROC
STROC
RISMA
DISWAY
HPS
IB MAROC, COM
INVOLYS
M2M
S2M MONETIQUE
MANAGEM
ALLIANCES
DOUJA PROMOTION ADDOHA
RES DAR SAADA
TOTAL MAROC
LYDEC
MARSA MAROC
SALAFIN
MAROC TELECOM
TIMAR

[1]Moroccan Capital Market Authority

Chapter 7
Exploratory Study of the Attitudinal Effects of Employee Shareholding in Morocco

Sara Elouadi
https://orcid.org/0000-0001-5412-2714
Hassan II University, Casablanca, Morocco

Meriem El Kerbani
Hassan II University, Casablanca, Morocco

ABSTRACT

The authors conducted an empirical study in the form of a questionnaire distributed to Moroccan employees. It was completed by 217 employees and relates to the year 2020. The data collected was analyzed by the method of structural equations. The authors continued the methodology of Anderson and Gerbing. The two authors proposed a two-step analysis method. This first involves performing a confirmatory analysis of the measurement model to improve its convergent validity and discriminant validity. The results of the questionnaire survey show that there is a positive and strong link between employee share ownership on the one hand and work motivation and organizational involvement on the other. Also, the tests carried out show that employee share ownership contributes significantly to reducing the departure intention.

DOI: 10.4018/978-1-7998-8557-3.ch007

INTRODUCTION

The Covid-19 pandemic has confronted the world's economies with an abysmal financial crisis. Indeed, the fear of the spread of the virus has paralyzed the productive system, forcing many companies to file for bankruptcy, unable to absorb the shortfall in demand. This unprecedented situation is characterized by the simultaneous contraction of supply and demand, and has plunged governments into a climate of uncertainty and opacity regarding the long-term effects of the disease.

The need is felt, more than ever, for a real recovery plan to bail out the Moroccan economy and save businesses from certain death. This rescue plan must pass, inescapably, by the reconstitution of the economic capacities of our country to instill a climate of confidence between the employees and the companies. A change of governance and management codes within companies is necessary by giving voice and the right to action to employees.

All over the world, managers and politicians are in favor of employee share ownership because it has many virtues for employees, the company and the state. Indeed, ownership of shares brings a lot of satisfaction to employees and induces positive changes in work behaviors, including improved productivity, motivation and organizational commitment. Also, the funds brought by employee shareholders for the purchase of shares are likely to feed the treasuries of the companies and, thus, instill a new financial dynamic.

The State will also benefit from the virtues of employee shareholding because of the increase in tax revenue linked to the safeguarding of employment and the stimulation of economic activity.

Employee share ownership is booming in Europe, according to the French Federation of Employee Shareholder Associations, the number of employee shareholders in Europe amounts to 10 millions. And the share of employees in large European companies has continued to increase throughout the European crisis, from 2.37% in 2006 to 2.85% in 2019, or 350 billion euros in May 2019, and increased to 400 billion in early 2020. Also, the number and percentage of large European companies with employee stock ownership plans continues to grow. In 2019, 89% of companies had employee stock ownership plans, 62% had stock option plans and 52% organized plans for all employees. The Coronavirus pandemic seems to make employee share ownership more concrete among French companies, which see it as a real asset for economic recovery. The Minister of Public Accounts, Gérald Darmanin, has expressed his willingness to generalize the practice and proposes to "resurrect the great idea of profit-sharing: employees become shareholders of their company, they receive their share of the profits it makes, and they increase their purchasing power, in addition to their salaries, through profit-sharing".

Moreover, in most large European companies, the increase of employee share ownership is evident. The percentage of large companies with significant employee ownership has risen from 46.5% in 2006 to 56.5% in 2019.

In the United States, there are currently 14 million employee shareholders in the famous ESOP (Employee Stock Ownership Plan) model launched in 1974. More recently and in order to stem the deleterious effects of the crisis on the American economy, Ron Johnson, one of the most conservative members of Congress, and Representative Alexandria Ocasio-Cortez, one of the most liberal, have both presented radical proposals to expand employee ownership in the United States.

In Morocco, employee shareholding operations are not common and almost exclusively concern large national groups and subsidiaries of foreign multinationals. At national level, employee shareholding operations generally accompany the first Initial public offerings and suffer from their low occurrence.

Indeed, over the last five years, nearly 79% of Moroccan companies having introduced employee share ownership have set up a single employee ownership plan and this at the time of their first Initial public offerings. Capital increases are the second most common way of granting shares to employees. The third position is occupied by Public Sales Offers.

We believe that the unpopularity of employee ownership in Morocco is due to three main reasons. The first one is the legislative delay and the lack of an incentive framework for employee savings. For it is only in 2013 that a law was voted for the implementation of the Company Savings Plan.

The second reason is related to the nature of the Moroccan economic fabric, which is composed of nearly 90% of family businesses. This type of company is characterized by a long and unshakeable culture of confidentiality, which manifests itself, in particular, in the refusal to share decision-making power and to grant shares to employees. The third reason is the lack of knowledge about the effects of employee ownership. Indeed, managers are unaware of the beneficial effects of employee ownership on the individual, organizational and financial performance of companies. In this respect, we ask for the mutual commitment of employers, legislators, researchers and professional prescribers such as consulting firms in order to promote the development of employee ownership in Morocco and to make the Kingdom's economy benefit from the fruits of capital sharing with employees.

Our research has invested this objective by conducting an empirical study on the behavioral effects of employee ownership in Moroccan companies. First, we propose a theoretical analysis of employee ownership through the prism of agency theory. Second, we present a synthesis of empirical work on the behavioral effects of employee ownership. Finally, we present our empirical methodology and the results of our investigation.

Agency Theory and Employee Ownership

To analyze the attitudinal effects of employee ownership, we used agency theory. This theory focuses mainly on behavior and incentives within firms. Agency theory presents employee ownership as an incentive to limit the sources of divergence of interest between managers and employees. By providing privileged access to the sharing of the wealth created, employee ownership allows, according to this theory, the reconciliation of interests by reducing sources of conflict. Consequently, the agency theory offers an interesting framework to analyze the practice of employee ownership. The employee ownership is, then, considered as an incentive tool which can lead to a better convergence of interests within the company and thus solve the problems in an agency relationship.

The first work on agency theory was done by Ross (1973, p. 136), who explains the agency relationship as the relationship that arises when one of the two parties, designated as agent, acts either on behalf of or in the name of the other, designated as principal, in a particular area of decision-making.

According to Eisenhardt (1989), the agency theory aims to solve two major problems, the first concerns the conflicts inherent in the divergence of interests between the principal and the agent and the second is related to the difficulty of the principal to control the agent's work. Indeed, it is costly and difficult for the principal to verify whether the agent's behavior is adapted to the organization's objectives. This is related to the problem of risk sharing that arises when the agent and the principal have different perceptions of risk.

Indeed, the company must reconcile the following divergent expectations and objectives:

- Those of the shareholders who seek to maximize profitability and the value of the equity invested;
- Those of the managers aiming at maximizing the value of the company through, for example, the increase of the turnover;

Agency Theory at the Heart of Employee Ownership

According to the principles of agency theory, employee ownership leads to an alignment of interests within the company. Indeed, the dual privileged status of shareholder-employee allows to accumulate the advantages linked to the status of shareholder to those linked to the status of employee.

Moreover, this status constitutes an incentive mechanism aiming at aligning the interests of employees and shareholders and consequently limiting the sources of conflicts and thus reducing agency costs. Employee ownership in the context of the agency relationship is multifaceted. According to Hollandts (2007), the employee shareholder is, first of all, an employee who undertakes to perform work on behalf of the manager, in exchange for a previously agreed remuneration represented by the salary. However, the employee shareholder is at the same time a shareholder of the firm, and therefore has a financial and political right vis-à-vis the manager, which gives him the possibility to control the manager.

The interest of employee ownership is then to give them a certain number of rights that allow them to safeguard their interests. But also, to exercise a right of control over the strategic decisions of the company and the behavior of the managers, by attending the board of directors or supervisory board Desbrières (1997).

On the other hand, employee ownership is also a solution to agency problems. Desbrières (2002), Dondi (1993) and Gamble et al. (2002) explain that employee ownership allows:

- The reduction of agency costs, the alignment of employees' interests with those of shareholders.
- Higher cooperation between employees and managers.
- -And the decline of conflicts within the organization.

As Desbrières (1997) points out, being a shareholder allows companies to go further than simple participative management. According to him, employee shareholding allows the confrontation of different sources of information to limit the propensity of managers to adopt opportunistic behavior, in addition to the possibility of political participation that it confers.

The examination of employee ownership in an agency framework leads to the conclusion that employee ownership has a positive influence on organizational behavior.

Summary of Empirical Work

The majority of empirical studies dealing with the effects of employee ownership on organizational attitudes show that participation contributes to the emergence of productive behavior. Long (1978a, 1978b, 1980 and 1982) found in his work that employee shareholders were more motivated, mainly because of their perceived participation in decisions.

According to the work of Klein (1987), employee ownership contributes positively to the appearance of three distinct levels of satisfaction. First, there is the intrinsic satisfaction linked to shareholder status. According to this understanding, ownership provides a psychological feeling of satisfaction.

Then, there is instrumental satisfaction, which is concerned with the indirect effects of employee ownership; the authors cite, in particular, the participation in decision-making that shareholder status offers.

Finally, extrinsic satisfaction highlights the importance of the prospect of monetary gain. According to the literature, employee share ownership offers a feeling of satisfaction if it is financially rewarding.

The direct link between motivation and performance has been studied by Russell et al (1979), their results show the existence of a better quality of work for employee shareholders, explained by a clear decrease in customer complaints.

Also, the survey conducted by Dondi (1994) indicates that for French companies, motivation is the first objective assigned to employee ownership.

And as a direct result of motivation, productivity is one of the most relayed effects of a policy based on employee ownership. In this respect, Jones and Kato (1995) find an increase in productivity of 4% to 5% only 3 to 4 years after the introduction of employee share ownership plans.

And in the context of French companies, the study by Vaughan-Whitehead (1992) affirms that the introduction of employee share ownership plans induces positive organizational effects, including improved motivation, involvement, quality of work and production, and generates a decrease in absenteeism and turnover.

Similarly, Caramelli's (2006) international attitudinal study shows that employee ownership has positive effects on emotional involvement, job satisfaction, motivation and employee retention.

Studies by Elouadi (2015) and Elouadi et al. (2016, 2017) in the context of French SBF 250 companies show that employee ownership leads to higher employee shareholder satisfaction, better organizational commitment, and lower intent to leave.

In addition, a recent study of two large condominium retailers in Spain and Great Britain reveals that employee ownership is linked to higher productivity and lower attrition. However, the study highlights other attitudinal effects such as increased absenteeism (Basterretxea and Storey, 2018).

In another context, a recent study of Cameroonian firms explains that the average level of shareholder wealth creation tends to increase for firms with the highest shareholding. The study concludes, then, that employee ownership is a lever for shareholder wealth creation in Cameroonian firms (Alim, 2019).

More recently, a study conducted in the French context of SBF 250 companies (Elouadi, 2020) shows that the emanation of positive effects of employee ownership is not automatic and is conditioned by the presence of incentive variables. These are the granting of matching contributions, the presence of employee shareholder directors and the existence of an employee shareholder association.

The majority of studies on the effects of employee share ownership establish the existence of positive effects on organizational behavior. On the other hand, other studies assert the contingency of the effects induced by ownership, which differ according to the level of capital held by employees, the perceived participation and the purposes of the employee ownership operations (Poulain-Rehm, 2007).

Greenberg's (1980) study provides evidence of high satisfaction among cooperative employees. However, the results of Hammer et al (1982) are more mixed and reveal that satisfaction is not related to the adoption of employee ownership.

Similarly, studies by Buchko (1993) and French and Rosenstein (1984) reveal that the perceived influence of employee ownership positively affects satisfaction. The authors conclude that the volume of shares granted to employees has no significant effect on employee satisfaction.

According to Kruse (1984), employee ownership is not always linked to improved motivation among employee shareholders. Nevertheless, Conte and Svejnar (1988) explain that the positive impacts of employee ownership are related only to lower levels of employee ownership. Also, Bloom's (1986) study of 609 publicly traded companies with employee ownership programs concluded that ownership had no significant effect on firm economic performance.

The results of Poulain-Rehm (2006), whose work focuses on a sample of 131 French listed companies for a three-year period from 1999 to 2001, do not corroborate the positive impact of employee ownership on value creation, in particular, by reducing conflicts and agency costs.

A little later, the study by Poulain-Rehm and Lepers (2013) indicates that employee share ownership plans in the context of 163 French companies do not influence partnership and shareholder value creation.

Furthermore, some studies that have tested the link between employee ownership and performance conclude that there is a curvilinear and non-monotonic effect of employee participation. This research states that performance increases for low and medium levels of employee ownership, and decreases for high to very high levels, and points to the existence of an inflection point that varies across companies.

This is the study by Dondi (1992), Guedri and Hollandts (2008) and Garfatta (2010). We can add to this category the study of Aubert et al (2009) who show, in their model, the presence of an optimal level of employee share ownership transfer that satisfies employee preferences and is accompanied by an incentive effect for the firm.

Another part of the literature highlights the existence of negative effects of ownership on organizational performance. This is the study by Livingston and Henry (1980) and the study by Chang (1990). The latter reveal that the adoption of employee stock ownership plans as an anti-takeover shield generates negative performance. In parallel, the studies of Gordon and pound (1990), Chang and Mayers (1992) and Blasi et al. (1996) confirm the negative impact on value of the introduction of employee share ownership in a defensive setting.

And by studying 226 companies with more than 5% employee ownership and 188 companies with less than 5%, Faleye et al. (2006) find that there is a dark side to employee ownership, namely that beyond 5% employee ownership, the company becomes less successful.

These results, despite their apparent divergence, mostly link employee ownership to the emergence of positive organizational effects. This leads us to formulate the following research hypotheses:

H0: Share ownership has no effect on organizational behavior;
H1: Employee ownership improves organizational commitment;
H2: Employee ownership improves work motivation;
H3: Employee ownership leads to a decrease in the departure intention.

RESEARCH METHODOLOGY AND RESULTS

Through this empirical study, we aim to collect up-to-date data to fill the information gap on the current situation of employee ownership in the Moroccan company. We seek, thus, to study the effects of employee ownership on organizational attitudes.

The survey is carried out online by e-mail by sending the web link of the questionnaire to Moroccan employees. The data refer to the year 2020. Our questionnaire includes questions that will allow us to describe the status and characteristics of the Moroccan employee shareholder.

Construction and Validation of the Measurement Instruments

The purpose of this section is to provide the measurement instruments for the variables used in our research hypotheses. It is generally recommended to use existing measurement scales as much as possible (Churchill, 1979), as the construction of measurement instruments is a complex task (Hinkin, 1995). Moreover, the use of different instruments in the literature to measure the same variable makes it difficult to integrate the different results obtained.

We retain three existing measurement instruments. These are the Affective Involvement (AI) scale by Meyer (1991), the Work Motivation (WM) scale by Roussel (1996), and the Intent to Quit (IQ) scale by Pendleton et al. These three scales were chosen first because they consist of a small number of items (6, 5, and 3 respectively). We tried to limit the size of the questionnaire as much as possible to increase the chances of collecting responses.

The Descriptive Variable of the Employee Ownership Construct

In the employee ownership literature, ownership of company stock can be measured either through binary or continuous variables. Binary variables distinguish employee shareholders from non-shareholders in the same company (Tucker, 1989). With respect to the use of continuous variables, share ownership is measured, at the individual level, as the number of shares held by the employee (Pendleton, 2001). Because of the difficulty of accessing information on the exact number of shares held, we have chosen the binary form based on the employees' declaration. We thus ask the following question: Are you a shareholder in your company?

1. Yes
2. No

Descriptive Variables of Employees' Attitudes

Variable 1: Employees' Preference for Company Stock

This variable indicates the extent to which employees tend to invest money in their companies' stock rather than for other purposes. This variable was only used by Kuvaas (2003), the scale used was composed of two items. However, it is generally recommended to use a scale with at least three items in order to have valid and reliable measurement instruments (Hinkin, 1995). Therefore, we decided not to use this scale, which contains only two items, and we adopted the scale developed by Caramelli (2006). According to Elouadi (2020, p.40), "This variable makes it possible to appreciate the preference of the employees for the shares of their companies and translates their confidence in the future and the attractiveness of the securities of their companies".

Investment Preference Scale: Please indicate your level of agreement or disagreement with the following statements (1- Strongly agree to 5- Strongly disagree)

Pf1: In general, I prefer to invest my profit-sharing bonuses in shares of my company
Pf2: When I receive a dividend, I prefer to invest it in my company's shares rather than receive the money
Pf3: When there is an offer of shares in the company, I usually participate;
Pf4: When possible, I invest money in shares of my company;
Pf5: I usually sell my company's stock as soon as I can;
Pf6: When the next offer comes along, I will definitely buy stock in my company.

Variable 2: Work Motivation

Motivation is the least studied attitude in the empirical literature on employee ownership, this variable is used to assess the extent to which employees put in more effort when they become shareholders. We therefore decided to build on the work of Roussel (1996) to define and implement the concept of motivation.

Motivation Scale: Please indicate your level of agreement or diesgreement with the following statements (1 - strongly agree to 5 - strongly disagree)

Mot 1: For reasons of my own, I no longer give my best to my work.
Mot 2: In the coming months, given my motivation, I intend to work very hard.
Mot 3: If I had the opportunity to change jobs, I would put more effort into them than I currently do in my job.
Mot 4: The number of tasks that I want to spend a lot of time on has decreased over time.
Mot5: Since you have been in this position, (when you reflect on all the changes you have experienced), do you feel that the level of intensity of your efforts has:(1- decreased a lot, 5- increased a lot)

Variable 3: Affective Organizational Involvement

This refers to the emotional attachment and commitment employees have to their organization. This construct includes sensitivity to issues facing the company and whether employees want to stay with the company.

In the employee ownership literature, commitment is typically measured using the Organizational Commitment Questionnaire by Mowday, Sters, and Porter (1979), and is generally considered a measure of emotional commitment (Meyer, 1997). In our research, we chose to use Meyer and Allen's affective involvement facet. This scale was developed in a 6-item version (Meyer, 1993) and in another 8-item version (Meyer and Allen, 1997). In order to limit the size of the questionnaire, we will keep the shorter version while retaining the French version of Caramelli (2006).

Organizational Involvement Scale: Please indicate the extent to which you agree with the following statements (1 - strongly agree to 5 - strongly disagree)

Implic1: I would be very happy to stay at this company for the rest of my career;
Implic2: I really consider the problems of this company as if they were my own;
Implic3: I don't feel like a ≪ family member ≫ in this company;
Implic4: I don't feel emotionally attached to this company;
Implic5: This company means a lot to me;
Implic6: I don't feel a strong sense of belonging to my company.

Variable 4: Intention to Quit the Company

Intention to quit the company is typically measured in the employee ownership literature using items from the (Cammann, 1983) questionnaire. We will use three items from the questionnaire to measure this variable.

Intention to Leave Scale: Please indicate the extent to which you agree with the following statements (1 - strongly agree to 5 - strongly disagree)

Qu1: I often think about leaving this job;
Qu2: If I were offered a similar job at another company, I would accept it;
Qu3: I will definitely look for a new job within the next year.

Data Collection and Sample Construction

The base population of our sample is composed of all Moroccan employees who are shareholders or not in the different Moroccan companies. The data were collected during the third quarter of 2020. We collected a total of 217 responses, 54.4% of which were filled in by employees of companies that apply employee ownership. The results show that 27.6% of the employees surveyed own shares in their companies.

Data Analysis and Results

After the data collection, we proceeded to the validity and reliability analysis using the principal component analysis (PCA) method. The KMO index of our data obtains 0.790 and Bartlett's test is significant ($P < 0.0005$). This shows that the correlations between the variables are of good quality. The principal component analysis generated 5 factors, which were confirmed by the eigenvalue graph. In addition, the items Pf5 and Mot5 were removed by the software from the eigenvalue matrix.

- Factor 1 entitled "Preference to invest in the company" has 5 items:
  - **Pf1:** In general, I prefer to invest my profit-sharing bonuses in shares of my company
  - **Pf2:** When I receive a dividend, I prefer to invest it in shares of my company rather than receive the money
  - **Pf3:** When there is an offer of shares in the company, I usually participate;
  - **Pf4:** When possible, I invest money in shares of my company;
  - **Pf5:** I will definitely buy shares in my company in the next offering.
- Factor 2 consists of 3 items that we call affective importance
  - **Reverse-Impli3:** I do not feel like a family member in this company;
  - **Reverse-Impli4:** I do not feel emotionally attached to this company;

    - **Reverse-Impli6:** I do not feel a strong sense of belonging to my company.
- Factor 3 contains four items and we call it affective involvement
    - **Implic1:** I would be very happy to stay in this company for the rest of my career;
    - **Implic2:** I really consider the problems of this company as if they were my own;
    - **Implic5:** This company means a lot to me;
    - **Mot2**: for the next few months, given my motivations, I intend to work very hard.
- Factor 4 consists of three items, it is the departure intention:
    - **Reverse- Qu1:** I often think about leaving this job;
    - **Reverse- Qu2:** If I were offered a similar job in another company I would accept it;
    - **Reverse- Qu3:** I will definitely look for a new job within the next year.
- Factor 5 which we call work motivation, includes three items:
    - **Reverse-Mot1.** For reasons that are personal to me, I no longer give my best in my work;
    - **Reverse-Mot3.** If I had the opportunity to change jobs, I would put more effort into them than I currently do in my job;
    - **Reverse-Mot4.** The number of tasks that I want to spend a lot of effort on has decreased over time;

After assessing the validity of our measurement tools, we need to evaluate their reliability before we can permanently retain them. Below we present the results of the analysis of the five extracted factors. The table reflects good alpha coefficients, except for factor 5 which has a Cronbach's Alpha of 0.523. Due to the small number of items that make up this factor, we decide to remove it from our analysis.

Table 1. Factor Reliability Analysis

Factor	Cronbach Alpha	Number of Elements
1	,893	5
2	,800	3
3	,755	4
4	,763	3
5	,523	3

Confirmatory Analysis of Each Factor

We then carried out a confirmatory analysis of the 4 factors with the Amos software. We present the correlation coefficients and the adjustment indices of the 4 selected factors.

For the analysis of the data in structural equations, we keep the items of the intention to leave construct without recoding in order to show its negative links with employee ownership. In fact, all the items that make up the intention to leave construct are in the negative form. Nevertheless, we kept the coding of the items of factor 2 named affective importance in order to homogenize the answers with the essence of the construct. Also, for the same reasons, we kept the coding of the Pf6-inverted item.

Table 2. The correlation coefficients of the factors

Structural Relations	Correlation Coefficient
Factor 1 Preference to invest in the company <-Employee Ownership	,790
Pf1<--- Preference to invest in the company	,834
Pf2<--- Preference to invest in the company	,853
Pf3<--- Preference to invest in the company	,964
Pf4<--- Preference to invest in the company	,986
Reverse -Pf6 <--- Preference to invest in the company	,766
Factor 2 Affective Importance <--- Employee Ownership	,957
Reverse-Implic3 <---Affective Importance	,842
Reverse-Implic4<--- Affective Importance	,949
Reverse-Implic6-<--- Affective Importance	,798
Factor 3 Affective Implication <--- Employee Ownership	,797
Implic1<--- Affective Implication	,616
Implic2<--- Affective Implication	,792
Implic5<--- Affective Implication	,729
Mot2<--- Affective Implication	,648
Factor 4 Departure intention <--- Employee Ownership	-,678
Qu1 <--- Departure intention	,758
Qu2 <--- Departure intention	,746
Qu3 <--- Departure intention	,841

In addition to the quality of the adjustment indices obtained, the verification of the acceptability of the estimates is also based on the absence of negative variances and standardized coefficients greater than 1 (Roussel et al. 2002, p. 220). The table shows that all relationships are significant.

The table of regression coefficients shows that the items contribute strongly to explaining the latent constructs they measure. And the regression coefficients linking employee ownership to the 4 factors reflect the existence of strong significant relationships.

Table 3. Factor fit indices

Factors	NFI	TLI	CFI	RSMEA
Factor 1	,968	,928	,976	,070
Factor 2	0,986	,972	0,994	,043
Factor 3	,913	,793	,931	, 096
Factor 4	,998	1,048	1,000	0,

The fit indices show that the partial structural models represented by the 4 factors are acceptable and that the parameter estimates are reliable.

The global structural model allows to combine the different constructs that have been subject to a step by step structural analysis, the following global model includes all the constructs.

Figure 1. The linear model of the relationship between employee share ownership and organizational commitment, work motivation, and intention to leave.

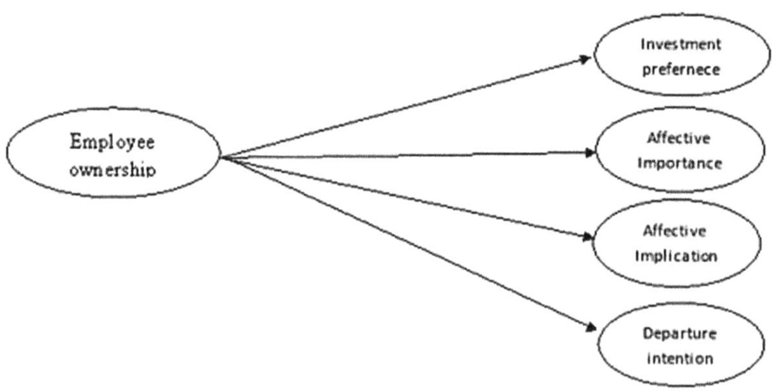

The overall structural model allows for the merging of the different constructs that are subject to structural analysis. It will allow to distinguish, first, the structural relationships that link the potential components to the employee ownership variables, and then to connect the observable variables to their potential components to measure them.

Figure 2. The overall structural model for departure intention, organizational commitment and job satisfaction

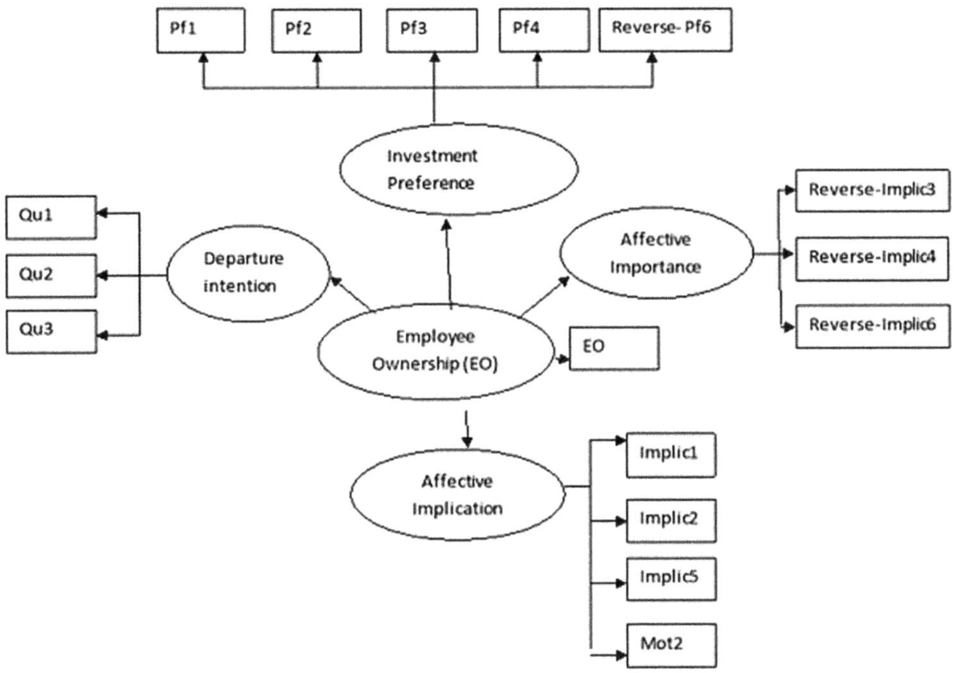

In Table 4, we present the results of the fit indices for the global model.

Table 4. Correlation coefficients of the global model

Structural Relations	Correlation Coefficients
Preference to invest<--- Employee Ownership	,792
Affective Importance <--- Employee Ownership	,754
Affective Implication <--- Employee Ownership	,906
Departure Intention <--- Employee Ownership	-,767

According to the regression coefficient table, employee ownership has a positive impact on the latent variables: Affective Involvement, Affective Importance and Investment Preference. Also, employee ownership significantly reduces the departure intention. These results support our hypotheses H1 and H3 and negate the null hypothesis H0.

Table 5. Fit indices of the overall structural model

NFI	TLI	CFI	RSMEA
, 827	,836	, 885	,068

The fit indices related to the overall model show that the model is fairly consistent with the empirical data, we believe that our model is acceptable.

Discussion of the Results

One of the main interests of this research work was to see if the principles that emerged from studies conducted in the European and American context were transposable to the case of employee ownership in Morocco. However, through our present research work, we have tried to unveil the practice of employee ownership in Morocco through the experience of a number of employees from different sectors and different groups of companies, to this effect. The adoption of employee ownership by the company is based on a vision of social development and motivation of its staff.

The results confirm that one of the reasons why employee ownership is implemented is the belief that it positively impacts employee behavior and leads to additional performance for the company. A large number of empirical studies have been conducted to test this relationship. They have been conducted by economists and financiers who have studied the relationship between various indicators of employee ownership and various measures of performance, and by researchers in social psychology or human resource management who have studied the impact of employee ownership on employees' attitudes and behaviors at work.

Our results are consistent with these recent studies. Indeed, the recent study by Degbey et al (2020) states that in the context of mergers and acquisitions, employee ownership through the psychological sense of belonging plays a positive role in employee retention with direct and mediating effects such as employee commitment and involvement. Similarly, the study conducted by Saylor (2017) in the specific context of accounting firms (CPA companies) finds the existence of positive effects of employee ownership on the retention of the best employees and the improvement of performance, acting in particular, on productivity, sales and growth.

Other previous works confirm the positive attitudinal effects of ownership, for example the study of Tucker et al (1989) carried out in a longitudinal framework, the results highlight the positive role that employee ownership plays in improving satisfaction and organizational commitment. Also, the works of Buchko (1992, 1993), Frohlich et al (1998) and Hallock et al (2003) highlight the existence of a positive relationship between ownership and organizational commitment of employees.

Also, employee ownership significantly reduces the intention of employee shareholders to leave, as such the works of Fakhfakh (2004), Vaughan-Whitehead (1992), Caramelli (2006) and Elouadi (2015) find that employee ownership exerts positive effects on organizational behavior.

In review of the results we obtained on our study, it seemed to us that the effects of employee ownership in the context do not escape from the previously outlined theory. Some dimensions indicate that employee ownership has an effect in one way or another on employees and the company, with the figures changing according to occupational category and culture on employee ownership and the financial markets.

CONCLUSION

One of the main objectives of this research work was to see if the implications that emerged from studies conducted in the European and American contexts were transposable to Moroccan companies.

The analysis of the results of the questionnaire administered to Moroccan employees reveals that employee ownership reinforces the investment preference and the organizational involvement of employee shareholders while decreasing their intention to leave. These results are clearly in line with international studies and show that employee ownership is a relevant mechanism for companies. And to stem the negative effects of the Covid-19 crisis, our economy needs a mutual commitment from employees and managers towards the integration of a pluralist governance based on the equitable sharing of power and value created.

Our results must be understood and interpreted with various theoretical and methodological limitations in mind. At the methodological level. It is generally advisable to test several different structural models and to select the one that best fits the data (Hair et al. 2006). In our study, we tested only one model and retained it because its fit seemed acceptable. Also, it would have been important to test a number of mediating effects in order to establish, with more rigor, the determinants of the attitudinal effects of employee ownership Elouadi (2020).

At the theoretical level, one of the most important issues that we have not been able to address here is to understand the extent to which employees are themselves willing to invest in the company's decision-making process through equity participation and the extent to which managers are willing to open up the capital to employees. It seems to us that the employee ownership will only be a real tool of power for employees if these two wills meet.

We are also considering broadening the scope of the questionnaire to include a larger number of respondents. For all these reasons, we invite Moroccan researchers to invest more in studies on employee ownership in order to enrich the empirical work and to propose to managers elements of answers concerning its induced effects on work behavior and organizational performance.

REFERENCES

Alim, O. (2019). Employee ownership in companies in Cameroon. *Journal of Participation and Employee Ownership.*, *2*(2), 93–114. doi:10.1108/JPEO-05-2019-0012

Anderson, J. C., & Gerbing, D. W. (1988). Structural equation modeling in practice: A review and recommended two-step approach. *Psychological Bulletin*, *103*(3), 411–423. doi:10.1037/0033-2909.103.3.411

Aubert, N., Grand, B., Lapied, A., & Rousseau, P. (2009). Is employee ownership so senseless. *Finance*, *30*(2), 5–29. doi:10.3917/fina.302.0005

Autenne, A. (2005). Quelle gouvernance des plans d'actionnariat employee ownership larié? *Revue internationale de droit économique, 1.*

Basterretxea, I., & Storey, J. (2018). Do employee-owned firms produce more positive employee behavioural outcomes? If not why not? A British-Spanish comparative analysis. *British Journal of Industrial Relations*, *56*(2), 292–319. doi:10.1111/bjir.12247

Blasi, J. R., Conte, M., & Kruse, D. L. (1996). Employee stock ownership and corporate performance among public companies. *Industrial & Labor Relations Review*, *50*(1), 60–79. doi:10.1177/001979399605000104

Buchko, A. (1992). Employee Ownership, Attitudes and Turnover: An Empirical Assessment. *Human Relations*, *45*(7), 711–733. doi:10.1177/001872679204500704

Buchko, A. (1993). The effects of employee ownership on employee attitudes: An integrated cauemployee ownership1model and path analysis. *Journal of Management Studies*, *30*, 633–657. doi:10.1111/j.1467-6486.1993.tb00319.x

Cammann, C., Fichman, M., Jenkins, G. D., & Klesh, J. R. (1983). Assessing the attitudes and per-ceptions of organizational members. In S. E. Seashore, E. E. Lawler, P. H. Mirvis, & C. Cammann (Eds.), *Assessing organizational change: A guide to methods, measures, and practices* (pp. 71–138). John Wiley & Sons.

Caramelli, M. (2006). *Une étude des effets de l'actionnariat employee ownership larie dans le contexte de l'entreprise multinationale: une approche attitudinale interculturelle* (Doctorat en sciences de gestion). Montpellier: Université Montpellier II sciences et Techniques.

Chang, S. (1990). Employee stock ownership plans and shareholder wealth: An empirical Investigation. *Financial Management*, *19*(1), 48–58. doi:10.2307/3666036

Chang, S., & Mayers, D. (1992). Managerial Vote Ownership and Shareholder Wealth: Evidence from Employee Stock Ownership Plans. *Journal of Financial Economics*, *32*(1), 103–131. doi:10.1016/0304-405X(92)90027-U

Charreaux, G. (1998). *La théorie positive de l'agence: lecture et relectures*. IAE DIJON -CREGO / LATEC.

Charreaux, G. (2000). La théorie positive de l'agence: Positionnement et apports. *Revue d'Economie Industrielle*, *92*(1), 193–214. doi:10.3406/rei.2000.1046

Charreaux, G. (2002). L'actionnaire comme apporteur de ressources cognitives. *Revue française de gestion*, (5), 77-107.

Churchill, G. A. Jr. (1979). A paradigm for developing better measures of marketing constructs. *JMR, Journal of Marketing Research*, *16*(1), 64–73. doi:10.1177/002224377901600110

Conte, M. A., & Svejnar, J. (1988). Productivity Effects of Worker Participation in Management, Profit-Sharing. Worker Ownership of Assets and Unionization in U.S Firms. *International Journal of Industrial Organization*, *6*(1), 139–151. doi:10.1016/0167-7187(88)90011-2

Degbey, W. Y., Rodgers, P., Kromah, M. D., & Weber, Y. (2020). The impact of psychological ownership on employee retention in mergers and acquisitions. *Human Resource Management Review*, *31*(3), 100745. doi:10.1016/j.hrmr.2020.100745

Desbrières, P. (1997). Le rôle de lactionnariat des employee ownership lariés non-dirigeants dans le système de gouvernement de l'entreprise. In G. Charreaux (Ed.), *Le gouvernement des entreprises: Corporate Governance, theories et faits*. Economica.

Desbrières, P. (2002). Les actionnaires employee ownership lariés. *Revue Française de Gestion, 141*, 255–281.

Dondi, J. (1993). *L'Actionnariat des Employee ownership lariés dans les Entreprises Françaises: Résultats Empiriques. Travaux de Recherche n° I.9302*. IAE de Bordeaux.

Dondi, J. (1994). L'actionnariat des employee ownership laries dans les entreprises françaises: L'identification de son rôle à laide de résultats empiriques. *Personnel, 347*, 56–64.

Eisenhardt, K. (1989). Agency Theory. An Assessment and Review. *Academy of Management Review, 14*(1), 57–74. doi:10.5465/amr.1989.4279003

Elouadi, S. (2015). Les effets attitudinaux de l'actionnariat employee ownership larié: une étude empirique dans le contexte des entreprises françaises du SBF 250. *Question (s) de Management*, (3), 11-24.

Elouadi, S. (2020). L'influence des variables incitatives sur la employee ownership tisfaction des actionnaires employee ownership lariés: une modéliemployee ownership tion par équations structurelles. *Question (s) de Management*, (2), 35-49.

Elouadi, S., Ben Noamene, T., & Chaher, D. (2016). Employee Ownership And Employee -Shareholders Employee ownership tisfaction: An Analysis Of French Companies Listed On The SBF 250. *Journal of Applied Business Research, 32*(3), 981–994. doi:10.19030/jabr.v32i3.9647

Elouadi & Ben Noamene. (2017). Does Employee Ownership Reduce the Intention to Leave? In *Handbook of Research on Human Resources Strategies for the New Millennial Workforce*. IGI Global.

Faleye, O., Mehrotra, V., & Morck, R. (2006). When labor has a voice in corporate governance. *Journal of Financial and Quantitative Analysis, 41*(3), 489–510. doi:10.1017/S0022109000002519

French, J. L., & Rosenstein, J. (1984). Employee ownership, work attitudes, and power relationships. *Academy of Management Journal, 27*(4), 861–869.

Frohlich, F., Godard, J., Oppenheimer, J. A., & Starke, F. A. (1998). Employee versus conventionally-owned and controlled firms: An experimental analysis. *Managerial and Decision Economics, 19*(4-5), 311–326. doi:10.1002/(SICI)1099-1468(199806/08)19:4/5<311::AID-MDE893>3.0.CO;2-I

Gamble, J., Culpepper, R., & Blubaugh, M. (2002). ESOPs and Employee Attitudes: The Importance of Empowerment and Financial Value. *Personnel Review*, *31*(1), 9–26. doi:10.1108/00483480210412391

Garfatta, R. (2010). *Actionnariat employee ownership larié et création de valeur dans le cadre d'une gouvernance actionnariale et partenariale: application au contexte français* (Doctorat en sciences de gestion). Bourgogne: Université de Bourgogne.

Gordon, L., & Pound, J. (1990). ESOPs and Corporate Control. *Journal of Financial Economics*, *27*(2), 525–555. doi:10.1016/0304-405X(90)90066-9

Guedri, Z., & Hollandts, X. (2008). Beyond dichotomy: The curvilinear impact of employee ownership on firm performance. *Corporate Governance*, *16*(5), 460–474. doi:10.1111/j.1467-8683.2008.00703.x

Hair, J. F. (2006). *Multivariate Data Analysis*. Auflage.

Hallock, D. (2003). A Research Model to Investigate the Organiemployee ownership tional Impact of an ESOP. *The International Journal of Sociology and Social Policy*, *12*(23), 47–63. doi:10.1108/01443330310790390

Hinkin, T. R. (1995). A review of scale development practices in the study of organizations. *Journal of Management*, *21*(5), 967–988. doi:10.1177/014920639502100509

Hollandts, X. (2007). *Les effets de participation des employee ownership lariés sur la performance de l'entreprise*. Doctorat en sciences de gestion.

Jones, D. C., & Kato, T. (1995). The productivity effects of employee stock ownership plans and bonuses: Evidence from Japanese panel data. *The American Economic Review*, *3*, 391–414.

Kruse, D. (1984). *Employee ownership and employee attitudes: Two case studies*. Norwood Editions.

Kuvaas, B. (2003). Employee ownership and affective organizational commitment: Employees' perceptions of fairness and their preference for company shares over cash. *Scandinavian Journal of Management*, *19*(2), 193–212. doi:10.1016/S0956-5221(01)00044-6

Livingston, D., & Henry, J. (1980). The Effect of Employee Stock Ownership on Corporate Profits. *The Journal of Risk and Insurance*, *47*(3), 491–505. doi:10.2307/252634

Long, R. J. (1978a). The effects of employee ownership on organizational identification, employee attitudes, and organizational performance: A tentative framework and empirical findings. *Human Relations*, *31*(1), 29–38. doi:10.1177/001872677803100102

Long, R. J. (1978b). The relative effects of share ownership vs. control on job attitudes in an employee owned company. *Human Relations*, *31*(9), 753–763. doi:10.1177/001872677803100901

Long, R. J. (1980). Job attitudes and organizational performance under employee ownership. *Academy of Management Journal*, *23*, 726–737.

Long, R. J. (1982). Worker ownership and job attitudes: A field study. *Industrial Relations*, *21*(2), 196–215. doi:10.1111/j.1468-232X.1982.tb00228.x

Meyer, J., & Allen, N. (1997). *Commitment in the Workplace: Theory, Research, and Application.* Employee Ownership ge Publications.

Meyer, J., Allen, N., & Smith, C. (1993). Commitment to organizations and occupations: Extension and test of a three-component conceptualization. *The Journal of Applied Psychology*, *78*(4), 538–551. doi:10.1037/0021-9010.78.4.538

Mowday, R., Steers, R., & Porter, L. (1979). The measurement of organizational commitment. *Journal of Vocational Behavior*, *14*(2), 224–247. doi:10.1016/0001-8791(79)90072-1

Pendleton, A. (2001). Employee ownership, participation and governance: a study of ESOPs in the UK. Routledge.

Pendleton, A., Wilson, N., & Wright, M. (1998). The Perception and Effects of Share Ownership: Empirical Evidence from Employee Buy-Outs. *British Journal of Industrial Relations*, *36*(1), 99–123. doi:10.1111/1467-8543.00082

Poulain-Rehm, T. (2006). Qu'est-ce qu'une entreprise familiale? *La Revue des Sciences de Gestion*, *219*(3), 77–88. doi:10.3917/rsg.219.0077

Poulain-Rehm, T. (2007). L'actionnariat des employee ownership lariés en France, un facteur de création de valeur. *Bankers Markets and Investors*, *88*, 25–36.

Poulain-Rehm, T., & Lepers, X. (2013). Does employee ownership benefit value creation? The case of France (2001–2005). *Journal of Business Ethics*, *112*(2), 325–340. doi:10.100710551-012-1255-0

Rottenberg, S. (1962). Property in work. *Industrial & Labor Relations Review*, *15*(3), 402–405. doi:10.1177/001979396201500306

Roussel, P. (1996). *Rémunération, motivation et employee ownership tisfaction au travail*. Editions Economica.

Roussel, P., Durieu, F., Campoy, E., & El Akremi, A. (2002). *Méthodes d'équations structurelles: recherche et applications en gestion*. Économica.

Russell, R., Hochner, A., & Perry, S. (1979). Participation, influence, and worker ownership. *Industrial Relations*, *3*(3), 330–341. doi:10.1111/j.1468-232X.1997.tb00932.x

Taylor, T. (2017). ESOPs Help Some CPA Firms with Retention, Succession: Employee Stock Ownership Plans Can Boost a Firm's Productivity and Growth. *Journal of Accountancy, 223*(5), 51.

Tucker, J., Nock, S., & Toscano, D. (1989). Employee ownership and perceptions of work. *Work and Occupations*, *16*(1), 26–42. doi:10.1177/0730888489016001002

Vandenberg, R. J., & Lance, C. E. (2000). *A Review and Synthesis of the Measurement Invariance Literature: Suggestions, Practices, and Recommendations for Organizational Research*. Organizational Research Methods.

Vaughan-Whitehead, D. (1992). *Interessement, participation, actionnariat: impacts économiques dans l'entreprise*. Economica.

Chapter 8
Employee Stock Ownership in Morocco:
Between Legal Reality and Need for Evolution

Asmaa Boukhima
Hassan II University, Casablanca, Morocco

Tahar Khallouki
FSJES, Morocco

ABSTRACT

Today, the notion of social interest occupies an essential place in legal science. For a long time limited to the shareholders' own interests, today a large part of the legal doctrine insists on the necessity to take into consideration all the interests that contribute to the prosperity of the company, such as its employees, its suppliers, its customers. This is the sense in which the current debate on corporate governance and CSR (corporate social responsibility) is heading. In the context of this study, attention will be focused on the case of the employee. How does one take into consideration the interest of the latter in the company? Both forms of involvement are important, but the authors limit themselves to the second one, namely employee stock ownership.

DOI: 10.4018/978-1-7998-8557-3.ch008

INTRODUCTION

Today, the notion of social interest occupies an essential place in legal science.

For a long time limited to the shareholders' own interests, today a large part of the legal doctrine insists on the necessity to take into consideration all the interests that contribute to the prosperity of the company, such as its employees, its suppliers, its customers...

This is the sense in which the current debate on corporate governance and CSR (Corporate Social Responsibility) is heading.

In the context of this study, attention will be focused on the case of the employee. How to take into consideration the interest of the latter in the company?

Both forms of involvement are important, but we will limit ourselves to the second one, namely employee stock ownership.

The latter concerns any employee holding one or more securities that give him/her access to the capital of the company in which he/she works. This participation can take several forms: it can take the form of stock options, capital increases reserved for employees or even the allocation of free shares to employees. It differs from profit-sharing scheme, which includes profit-sharing, employee savings plans and dividends.

Employee stock ownership has several advantages for the employee and for the company.

For the employee, his or her participation in the capital allows him or her to benefit from more information about the company, to participate in the determination of the company's orientations and to take part in decision-making, which gives him or her more motivation and a greater feeling of belonging to the company.

For the company, employee stock ownership allows it to develop its team cohesion while benefiting from a stable, involved and better consolidated shareholder base.

In spite of this importance, employee ownership suffers from an almost legal vacuum. Contrary to what happens in other countries, the Moroccan legislator has given little interest to employee stock ownership, making the institution a poorly developed practice.

What are the causes of this lack of interest or delay of the Moroccan legislator in terms of employee stock ownership? What explains this very modest legal and practical reality? How to make employee stock ownership a tool to improve company performance, especially in this period of crisis? Can we transpose the French model in the Moroccan context?

We will try to answer all these questions.

After a general overview of the legal and practical reality of employee stock ownership in Morocco (first part), we will try to analyze the French legal model and its possible exportation in our country (second part).

THE CURRENT STATE OF EMPLOYEE OWNERSHIP IN MOROCCO

Employee stock ownership is a very underdeveloped culture in Morocco. This can be explained by two reasons: the lack of awareness of the benefits of employee stock ownership (A) and the passivity of the legislator (B).

Lack of Awareness of the Benefits of Employee Stock Ownership

Employee share stock ownership has advantages both for the company and for the employees.

For the Company

Employee share stock contributes to the recruitment and retention policy of employees. It allows the company to motivate and give confidence to its employees by making them participate in the company's benefits.

In other words, thanks to share stock ownership, the company can retain the best qualified employees. The latter, attracted by the shares, do not think of changing the company to go to another. Their primary concern becomes the continuity of the company, which will allow them financial satisfaction.

In the same way, the share stock ownership contributes to the performance of the company. In fact, several studies have been carried out and have led to the conclusion that there is a link between share stock ownership and performance (Wagner and Rosen 1983).

For his part, Vaughan Whited (1992) emphasized that share stock ownership has a positive influence on the value added by each employee.

This is explained by the fact that employees are more involved, more committed, more attached to future monetary gain, which makes it possible to increase the company's productivity.

A study has shown that productivity increases by 4 to 5% in companies that have implemented share stock ownership mechanisms, and this only 3 to 4 years after their introduction (Jones and Kato 1995). This is a logical finding, since employees become owners of the firm and are more involved in achieving the social interest.

For the Employee

The share stock ownership allows the employee to become a shareholder of the company at a lower cost. Indeed, whatever the formula used, the employee has an advantage over third parties.

The share stock ownership allows the employee to exercise two types of rights: a right to information and a right to action (Moroccan law 17-95 of the public limited company).

The right to information allows to know the social situation and to be able to vote within the general assembly with full knowledge of the facts.

Thus, the employee stock ownership, like all other shareholders, has the right to take cognizance of several documents at the company's registered office from the time of convening the ordinary general meeting: the agenda of the meeting; the text and presentation of the draft resolutions presented by the board of directors or the management board; the list of directors on the board of directors, the members of the management board and the supervisory board; the inventory, the summary statements of the past financial year drawn up by the board of directors or the management board; the management report of the board of directors or the management board; the report of the statutory auditor(s); the draft appropriation of results...

Similarly, by becoming a shareholder, the employee has a right to intervene in the life of the company. Thus, under certain conditions, they can convene the general meeting, challenge or dismiss the auditor, and put a draft resolution on the agenda of the meeting. He can even initiate a warning procedure if he notices facts likely to compromise the continuity of the operation. This right is open to him without any requirement to represent any share of the share capital.

Its right of action also allows it to request the annulment of acts and deliberations for abuse of majority. To do so, the decision taken must be contrary to the general interest of the company and must be guided by the sole purpose of favoring members of the majority to the detriment of members of the minority.

Finally, the employee stock ownership can take action against the directors and engage their civil or criminal liability.

Thus, through this right to information and action, the employee stock ownership can act, influence the course of events, participate in the decision-making process regarding the company's orientations, which can change his view of the company and involve him more in its performance.

Very Brief Legal Framework

In Morocco, the legal framework is very basic. There is no complete text dedicated to the institution. The few scattered provisions in different laws do not allow for the promotion of employee stock ownership and its inclusion in a global development strategy.

The first premises of employee stock ownership in Morocco began with the law on privatization (law n°39-89 authorizing the transfer of public enterprises to the private sector).

Indeed, this law authorized in its article 7 the participation of the employees of the company concerned by the privatization according to the conditions determined by the decree of October 16, 1990 taken for the application of the article 7, as it was modified and supplemented by decree of May 14, 1999.

Thus, it is provided that a part of the transfers will be reserved for the employees of the company or the establishment subject to the transfer who can prove a seniority of at least one year. In this context, the employees benefit from a maximum discount of 15% on the transfer price.

However, in return, the shares acquired by the employees may not be sold before three years from the date of their acquisition.

In case of non-compliance with this provision, the employee is obliged to repay the amount of the discount granted.

After these few provisions provided for by the 39-89 law, we had to wait for the 2013 finance law which introduced the company savings plan allowing employees to build up, with the help of their company, a complementary medium-term savings plan, within an advantageous tax and social framework.

Indeed, the contribution paid by the company to the employee in order to help him/her to build up his/her savings does not replace a salary element insofar as it is not considered as a salary supplement. Similarly, it is not taxable on income except when it exceeds 10% of the annual taxable salary.

Another advantage of the PEE is related to the exemption of the gains and incomes realized. However, this tax advantage is conditioned by a ceiling on payments of 600,000 dhs and by the unavailability of the sums saved in the PEE for a minimum period of 5 years. The products generated by the portfolio must be kept during the 5 year period.

With the exception of these few provisions favoring SA, the latter remains very little developed in comparison with European countries. The proof is that the practice of SA is limited to large groups that carry out capital increases reserved for their employees (as in the case of BCP via a capital increase of 2.2 billion dh ; Maroc Telecom, which offered 0.3% of its capital at a price of 117.7 dh against 125.3 dh for the general public), as well as subsidiaries of foreign multinationals for which the use of employee savings schemes is firmly anchored in the parent companies (e.g. Veolia, Tui, Vinci, Total, Airbus SE).

Based on this legal and practical aspect, the AS in Morocco remains in an embryonic state. Its success would depend on the combination of a certain number of conditions to be satisfied at the level of those who conceive it, those who will ensure its good application and those who will benefit from it. Does the French model allow for this outcome? Can it be transposed to the Moroccan context? This is what we will try to analyze in the second part.

THE FRENCH MODEL AND ITS POSSIBLE TRANSPOSITION IN THE MOROCCAN CONTEXT

If in France, which has always been a source of inspiration for the Moroccan legislator, employee stock ownership has been successful (A), nothing guarantees its success elsewhere. In Morocco, employee stock ownership has recently started to attract the attention of both researchers and professionals; both are wondering about the possibility of developing such a mechanism, especially at a time when the national company needs financial and social stability in order to be able to act in a more and more disruptive environment. In this regard, should we transpose the French model while adapting it to the Moroccan context or on the contrary conceive a typically Moroccan model? (B).

Employee Share Ownership in France, a Successful Model

In France, employee stock ownership has been a notable success. This success can be explained by a variety of factors related to both the legislation in force and the context of its application. The results achieved seem to have met the expectations of the various actors involved.

A Well Adapted French Legislation

The development of employee share ownership in France is essentially due to the political will of General de Gaulle to promote employee participation in the company's results in order to strengthen its equity and to limit social conflicts within the company. The traditionally conflictual relationship between capital and labor must give way to a relationship of coalition and understanding. With this ambition in mind, the French legislator set about establishing favorable legislation that has continued to develop over time. It is constantly subject to revision in order to remain in conformity with the requirements of the context of its application. For more than fifty years, we have witnessed a succession of laws and ordinances; each of them tries to remedy the inadequacies of the one that preceded it. In this regard, it seems important to give a brief overview of the legislative effort accomplished. Thus, we can retain:

The ordinances of August 17, 1967 which founded collective employee shareholding in France. These are, in fact, two ordinances n° 67-693 and 67-694. The first one related to the participation of employees in the results of the company; applicable in companies with a workforce of more than 100 employees reduced to 50 by a law dated November 7, 1990. The second one dealt with the creation of company savings plans (PEE) which could receive both SICAV shares and securities issued by any company with more than 100 employees. Its objective is therefore to promote the creation and circulation of these securities through the adoption of a financing mechanism that would be adapted and adaptable to future developments.

The law of August 6, 1986, which governed privatization operations. This law opened a new stage in terms of employee shareholding. It prescribed in its article 11 that in case of transfer of a State participation, 10% of the amount transferred must be offered to the employees of the company concerned and to those of its subsidiaries as well as to its former employees having worked at least five years in the company or its subsidiaries. Various facilities were then granted to the employees in order to facilitate the success of the expected objectives (discounts of up to 20%, payment deadlines,...). This law has in fact, considerably developed the employee stock ownership in the companies of the public sector especially since the public authorities have amply adhered to its good translation at the field level. They have accompanied it by two important measures, namely the conditional allocation of free shares and the possibility of subscribing in formulas allowing the coexistence of a collective shareholding and an individual employee stock ownership.

The ordinance of October 21, 1986, which restructured the 1967 ordinances on employee savings and shareholding, allowing companies to issue new shares for subscription by their employees within the framework of reserved offers, thus enabling these companies to strengthen their equity capital.

The law of July 25, 1994, which marked a first step in the participation of employee stock ownership in the governance of their companies. When they hold a given percentage of the share capital (5% reduced to 3% by the law of January 17, 2002), they can periodically submit a resolution to the company's Extraordinary General Meeting to introduce an employee shareholder director on the Board of Directors or the Management Board.

The law of February 19, 2001, known as the "Fabius law", which aims to encourage capital increases reserved for employees both at the level of the parent company and its subsidiaries, and even at the level of the Small and medium-sized enterprises (SMEs), which seems to have had a certain revival of interest.

The law of August 6, 2015, known as the "Macron" law, which had, in a way, put an end to the situation generated by the unfavorable provisions of the finance law of 2005. This law marked the return to a much more favorable regime. Under this law, the social security contribution payable by companies, paid at the time of the final acquisition of shares, is fixed at 20% for allocations authorized by an Extraordinary General Meeting as from January 1, 2018 and even abolished for SMEs that have not distributed dividends since the date of their incorporation.

The so-called "Breton" law, which introduced many provisions concerning the takeover of a company by its employees, the use of shares bought back by the company and no longer only new shares for an offer reserved for its personnel, the possibility, under certain conditions, of placing free shares at the time of their definitive acquisition in a PEE (company savings plan)... So many advantages that are supposed to give a new lease of life to employee stock ownership.

The law of May 22, 2019 relating to the growth and transformation of companies, known as the "PACTE law", which has set itself the objective of giving a strong boost to employee stock ownership; the goal being to reach the fraction of 10% of the capital of French companies held by their employees. This law is further complemented by the 2019 law on the financing of social security, which includes measures to strengthen employee participation in the governance of their companies. Particular attention has been paid to SMEs.

In short, it is clear that the legislator has not skimped on the means to be implemented to give employee stock ownership all the means to flourish; as shown by the number of laws and ordinances designed in relation to the subject. His initiative has a double objective. The aim is to give the company the means to prosper in terms of financial resources and social stability on the one hand, and to give the employee the means to develop personally on the other. The effort has been long and the results have been deemed satisfactory.

Employee Stock Ownership in France: A Successful Bet

All the studies and surveys that have looked at the evaluation of the employee stock ownership experience in France, agree that it has been a notable success. Thus, according to the French Federation of Employee stock ownership (FAS), at the end of 1999 there were more than one million employee shareholders, for a total of 300 billion francs invested. More than 25,000 companies have opened their capital to their employees.

According to a large-scale study carried out in France by Trébucq in 2001, on behalf of the Observatoire de l'actionnariat salarié en Europe, the practice of employee stock ownership is far from being a marginal phenomenon. It varies according to the size, the sector of activity and the listing market of the companies concerned. The phenomenon tends to grow in listed companies, where the average percentage of capital held by employees is close to the objective initially set by the French legislator, i.e. 10% of the capital of any company subject to the obligation to open its capital to its employees;

Nevertheless, in order to reach the most meaningful evaluation of employee stock ownership in France, many specialists recommend that this evaluation be extended to unlisted companies, especially since listed companies represent only a small proportion of all companies concerned by employee ownership mechanisms. It oscillates around a thousand companies out of some 27,000 companies in which an employee share ownership plan has been adopted, i.e. about 4% of the total. Specialists add that it is not appropriate to reason only on the absolute percentage of the capital held by employees, but to consider this participation relatively to that of the other categories of shareholders (public, family shareholders, founders, financiers...), while taking into account the possible shareholders' Agreement.

The success achieved in France is obvious and is not in doubt. However, this should not obscure the fact that there are still a number of obstacles to which the legislator must find an appropriate solution. Among these obstacles, several studies and surveys emphasize the risk of mechanical dilution, particularly when the company concerned is content to carry out a few episodic operations, the difficulties of employee savings, the constraint of financial risk, the inadequacy of information, the still limited participation in decisions, a complex and sometimes unsuitable law of application... So many shortcomings that the legislator must address to resolve them. In this regard, the French Social Affairs Commission has developed a set of recommendations that are supposed to provide an adequate response to the shortcomings diagnosed. These are mainly 28 proposals of different natures: some are of a legislative nature, and others are of a regulatory nature, without forgetting the measures to be taken by the main actors, i.e. the company and its employees. Without pretending to be exhaustive, these proposals include: improving the information available on employee share ownership, encouraging the development of employee stock ownership operations within the company, ensuring better protection for employee stock ownership, strengthening the representation of employee stock ownership and their participation in the life of the company, and designing other forms of employee financial participation;

In any case, the assessment of the French experience in employee stock ownership allows us to deduce that, despite the persistence of some, this experience remains fruitful. Its success, at least relative, can be explained by the political will of the legislator, the almost total adhesion of all the partners on the basis of a significant number of advantages, of all kinds, which have been granted to them by the public authorities. In this way, the adoption of shareholding in France has resulted in the emergence of a stable and long-term shareholder base, the development of a dynamic of motivation and social cohesion, the achievement of economic performance and the consolidation of corporate governance. All these advantages make the French experience in this field an example to ponder. Can this model be applied in Morocco?

Outline of a Strategy to Promote Employee Ownership in Morocco

To the question of whether Morocco can transpose the French model and apply it to the Moroccan company and employee, it seems that the answer can only be negative. This negativity is due to the enormous difference between the French and Moroccan context and the need for Morocco to establish its own model and to forge its own experience in this area.

Drawing Inspiration From the French Model

The analysis of the French model which has instituted and developed employee stock ownership allows to deduce that it is an experience built from the particularities of the French society. Its conception is far from being fortuitous or the fruit of chance; it was built during a long process having integrated various aspects: economic, social and sociological, historical, cultural...

From an industrial point of view, France has an industrial anteriority which started with the industrial revolution at the end of the 18th century, which gave it the opportunity to develop an economic fabric of first importance. Its companies have reached an unprecedented level of development, which has led them to expand their activities beyond national borders; they are established throughout the world.

From an economic point of view, France presents itself as one of the main powers in the world, it is supposed to be a model of success that has only been achieved after a long period combining High and Low, peace and war. Its military power allowed it to expand beyond the European continent and to access new territories, which earned it an accession among the great powers.

From a cultural point of view, France has been able to develop its strengths especially after the great revolution where the French man freed himself from a set of negative values and attitudes long defended by the church. This revolution gave the French man the opportunity to adopt other values that advocate more freedom in property and expression.

From a cultural point of view, since the advent of classical economics, France has experienced a vast current of thought that makes private property and initiative a true engine of economic growth at both the micro and macro levels. Others have long emphasized the primacy of the firm as an economic agent that reserves the exclusive right to produce wealth. For this to happen, it must be in a good position and benefit from all the factors that guarantee it sufficient success in the exercise of its mission. Its social stability then becomes inevitable, which presupposes the reduction of conflicts within it that could break out between capital and labor. Shareholding can then be an effective means of achieving this.

Whatever the case, France is currently an economic and industrial power that stands out for a set of characteristics that make it strong. This is the logical result of a long evolution that has led to France's originality in all fields, including the field of work and production. The French economic system was built on the basis of the strengths and weaknesses of French society. Its tools and means were designed on the basis of its own characteristics. The development of employee ownership cannot be an exception. Its transposition to other countries seems inconceivable. Nevertheless, it can serve as a source of inspiration, on the sole condition that it must be a thoughtful inspiration. In this respect, Morocco can draw inspiration from the French experience in employee ownership. It must adapt it to the Moroccan context.

The Need for a Typically Moroccan Model

Trying to transpose the French experience in employee stock ownership and apply it to the Moroccan context does not seem to be a factor of success. Such a transposition is rather a factor of failure given that it is a model that has been built on the basis of a set of economic, historical, cultural and sociological data specific to the place of its application. The legislator, in his initiative, can refer to the model in order to be inspired by it, if only on the methodological level. The model that must serve the needs of the country must include the parameters that are specific to it in terms of resources, history, culture... It must take into account its strengths and weaknesses. The designer of the expected model must take into consideration that:

- Economically, the country has limited resources that do not allow the coverage of its basic needs. The consultation of the data relating to the general budget of the State is not likely to invalidate such an observation. Its economic fabric is constituted in a large proportion of SME suffering from a great fragility. These are family-owned and closed companies that tend not to be open, often run by people who value their independence, undercapitalized, with no strategic management... So many handicaps that are more present in Moroccan companies.
- Socially, a large layer of employees has only a limited purchasing power, which does not allow these employees to claim ownership of shares, especially since they often distrust the employer; they are not ready to risk their savings in a highly risky activity.
- On the industrial level, Morocco does not have a sufficient industrial history and the entrepreneurial spirit is still in its embryonic stage.
- On the institutional level, the absence of legislative texts which should allow the protection of each of the parties linked by a shareholding relationship. To this, one must add the deficiency of the judicial system which does not favour

in any way the setting up of a successful coalition between employee stock ownership and company directors. Its slowness, its complexity, its lack of transparency. So many factors that give rise to more mistrust.

In sum, the diagnosis of the economic and social situation of Morocco, the assessment of its companies, the nature of its entrepreneurs and employees, its socio-cultural values, its historical data, its political orientations ... allows us to deduce that the expected model must be forged on the basis of the above characteristics. However, it is possible to draw inspiration from the French experience, particularly from a methodological point of view. The methodology used must therefore be based on certain key ideas, including

- The elaboration of legal texts in conformity with the objectives sought, taking into account the particularity of its addressees, i.e. a reluctant manager, a distrustful employee, and a more restrictive environment. These texts must be constantly evaluated so that they are adaptable. In the current state of the environment, it seems that the revision of texts is the general rule, otherwise these texts become obsolete over time;
- A vast information movement aimed at both entrepreneurs and employees. The objective is to bring them to collaborate and to make the company a collective project. At this level, the road ahead will certainly be longer and more perilous. It requires more perseverance and patience. It is a long-term project that requires more resources and energy.
- The mobilization of all the public and private actors who must ensure the support of the project in terms of financing, advice, training and evaluation.
- The need for political will to make the success of the project a bet of the first kind not to be missed.

In conclusion, it seems that the development of employee ownership is a very important initiative whose design and successful implementation is far from being obvious. Its introduction implies the commitment of important efforts on several fronts and the mobilization of all the actors of the entrepreneurial sphere. So many elements that must be inserted in a harmonious way in a global system guaranteeing the convergence of all the efforts made without rushing about the expected result. This one is certainly not for tomorrow, it requires time and conviction.

REFERENCES

Amami, I., & Maalej, R. (2015). Actionnariat salarié et innovation: conception et interaction. *International Journal Economics & Strategic Management of Business Process,* 5, 43-47.

Aubert, N. (2009). *L'actionnariat salarié: Devenir actionnaire salarié. Aumage édition 2009*. F.A.S.

Aubert, N., Chassagnon, V., & Hollandts, X. (2016). Actionnariat salarié, gouvernance et performance de la firme. *Revue d'économie industrielle, 154*(2), 151-176.

Azzouzi, B., & Haoudi, A. (2020). Actionnariat familial et performance financière: le cas Marocain. *Revue du contrôle, de la comptabilité et de l'audit, 4*.

Desbrières, Ph. (1997). *« La participation financière des salariés et ses incidences sur la performance et l'organisation interne de l'entreprise » dans Le gouvernement des entreprises* (G. Charreaux, Ed.). Economica.

Desbrières, Ph. (2002, November-December). Les actionnaires salariés. *Revue Française de Gestion, 28*(141), 225–281.

Dondi, J. (1992). *Contribution à la connaissance de l'actionnariat salarié dans les entreprises françaises* (Thèse de doctorat en Sciences de Gestion). Université Bordeaux 1.

Elouadi S., (2015). Les effets attitudinaux de l'actionnariat salarié: une étude empirique dans le contexte des entreprises françaises du SBF 250. *Question (s) de Management*, (3), 11-24.

Elouadi, S., & Er rommani, H. (2021). Analyse des effets de l'actionnariat salarié sur la création de la valeur financière des entreprises marocaines cotées en bourse. *Revue du contrôle de la comptabilité et de l'audit, 5*(1), 65-88.

Elouadi, S., Noamene, T. B., & Chaher, D. (2016). Employee Ownership And Employee- Shareholders Satisfaction: An Analysis Of French Companies Listed On The SBF 250. *Journal of Applied Business Research, 32*(3), 981–994. doi:10.19030/jabr.v32i3.9647

FAS Fédération Française des Actionnaires Salariés et Anciens Salariés. (2006). *Guide de l'actionnaire salarié* (6th ed.). Author.

Garfatta Riadh. (2010). *Actionnariat salarié et création de valeur dans le cadre d'une gouvernance actionnariale et partenariale: application au contexte français* (Thèse de doctorat en science de gestion). Université de Bourgogne.

Guery, L., & Stevenot, A. (2014). Le lien entre l'actionnariat salarié et le climat social à l'épreuve des faits: le cas des entreprises françaises non cotées. *Revue française de gouvernance d'entreprise, 14*, 101-120.

Guery, L., & Stevenot, A. (2017). L'actionnariat salarié favorise-t-il la diffusion d'information aux salariés et leur participation aux décisions stratégiques? Une question de gouvernance d'entreprise. Revue management international, 21(4), 61-75.

Hollandts, X., & Guedri, Z. (2008). Les salariés capitalistes et la performance de l'entreprise. *Revue Française de Gestion, 34*(183), 35–50. doi:10.3166/rfg.183.35-50

Kovac, J., & Gaudemet-Toulemonde, L. G. (2020). Epargne salariale et actionnaire salarié. Frencis Lefebvre.

Law 17-95 on the Public Limited Company

Law 5-96 on the General Partnership, the Limited Partnership, the Limited Liability Company and the Joint Venture Company Law 39-89 authorizing the transfer of public enterprises to the private sector

Lieutier, J. P. (2012). *Le modèle de l'actionnariat salarié*. P. U. Aix-Marseille, Ed..

Ngongang, D. (2013). Actionnariat salarié comme levier de création de valeur ajoutée et de productivité dans les entreprises camerounaises. *La Revue Gestion et Organisation, 5*(5), 1–8. doi:10.1016/j.rgo.2013.10.001

Trébucq, S. (2001). Etat de l'actionnariat salarié en France au 31 décembre 2000: Premiers résultats statistiques. *Cahier de Recherche, IAE, Université Montesquieu Bordeaux, 4*.

Trébucq, S. (2002, December). L'actionnariat salarié dans les entreprises familiales: Un outil de création de valeur? *Finance Contrôle Stratégie, 5*(4), 107–135.

Vaughan-Whitehead, D. (1992). Intéressement, participation, actionnariat: Impacts économiques dans l'entreprise. *Economica.*

Waxin, T. (2011). *Salarié, performance et gouvernance des entreprises* (Thèse de doctorat en sciences de gestion). Université Paris Dauphine.

Chapter 9
Analysis of the Impact of Employee Share Ownership on the Quality of Governance:
Case of Listed Moroccan Companies

Wafae Nada Nejjar
University of Casablanca, Morocco

ABSTRACT

This research assesses the "positive or negative" effects of employee share ownership on good governance in Morocco. It focuses on a lagging but constantly evolving phenomenon in Morocco due, on the one hand, to the lack of awareness of its positive effects on both individual and organizational performance and, on the other hand, on the significant delay in Moroccan legislation regarding this subject. The authors propose an index to measure good governance that they use in order to test research hypotheses. The quantitative study examines all companies listed on the Casablanca Stock Exchange over an observation period from 2015 to 2020. Through this research, the authors demonstrate the favorable effects of employee share ownership on good governance.

INTRODUCTION

Corporate governance is a constantly evolving theme, both for practitioners and researchers. In recent years, Morocco has witnessed an evolution in the representation of employee shareholding. This category of shareholders becomes all the more interesting as it has a double dimension: a right of financial participation and a right

DOI: 10.4018/978-1-7998-8557-3.ch009

of participation in the decisions of the company. Even if employee share ownership is a common practice in several countries, since it allows the company to stabilize its capital, improve internal dialogue and reduce its refinancing costs. Employee share ownership notably allows employees "to build up a portfolio of securities and to acquire, often under advantageous conditions, shares in the company that employs them. » (Desbrières, 2002: 255).

In Morocco, it is starting to develop and the relationship of companies with their employees has started to change. In addition to multinationals and companies in the banking sector which are the most active in this area, other companies are increasingly looking for collaboration and greater cohesion with employees, especially now in these times of unprecedented health crisis, also marked. both by its nature and by the magnitude and gravity of its consequences.

Several studies have shown that employee share ownership has a direct impact on the quality of governance and on manager behavior. Employee shareholders can thus find themselves instrumentalized and manipulated by the latter. We will show that employee shareholding can modulate the agency relationship existing between shareholders and managers by starting from the disciplinary paradigm to the cognitive paradigm.

In this research, we formulate our research hypotheses following a review of the literature devoted to the effects of employee share ownership on corporate governance. We then present our sample, the data and the empirical approach followed as well as the results obtained. Finally, we conclude our article with a discussion of our results and the research perspectives offered.

EMPLOYEE SHAREHOLDER: HIS PLACE IN THE GOVERNANCE OF THE COMPANY

Attempts to define the concept of corporate governance date back to the twentieth century and refer to various mechanisms aimed at reducing transaction costs generated by the market.

Porta et al. (2000), define governance as: "the set of mechanisms that allow investors to protect themselves against the risk of expropriation on the part of managers and directors who are linked to managers". This idea is in line with the vision of Shleifer and Vishny (1997), who consider that "non-shareholder managers" are opportunistic and the system of governance must therefore protect investors from the risk of theft.

For Dionne-Proulx J. and Larochelle G. (2010), the concept of corporate governance covers the regulatory framework, the practices and mechanisms adopted by an organization and which govern the relations between managers and shareholders, or more broadly. between leaders and stakeholders.

The qualifier "good" was then added to the notion of governance in 1997, referring to a normative character of corporate governance. Indeed, this adjective refers to a need for the establishment of a regulatory framework and codes of good governance practices by the various national and international initiatives.

This is how international institutions have also presented attempts to define corporate governance. The organization for economic cooperation and development (OECD, 2015) proposes for its part a more extensive definition of corporate governance: "This concerns all the relationships between the management of a company, its board of directors. administration, its shareholders and various other stakeholders. It also determines the structure by which the objectives of a company are defined, as well as the means to achieve them and to monitor the results obtained. "

In the Moroccan context, the Moroccan Code of Good Practices in Corporate Governance of 2008 similarly defines corporate governance as being: "all relations between the directors of the company and its governance body, with the shareholders on the one hand and the other stakeholders on the other, with the objective of creating value for the company ".

The purpose of this first part is, first of all, to define employee shareholding and to present the Moroccan experience in the matter. Secondly, we will situate employee share ownership in financial theories, in this case the theory of property rights and agency theory.

Employee Shareholding: Let's Take Stock!

Employee shareholders represent a special category of shareholders. As shareholders, they are holders of legitimate rights of control and residual claims. This therefore places them, just like the shareholders, in a position of overhang in the contractual hierarchy of the company (Autenne,2005). As a result, employee shareholders become holders of a right of scrutiny, control and decision over the company which is able to find a real natural right to governance. Also, they are the only stakeholder to see themselves assuming a double risk.

In what follows, we will define employee shareholding and take stock of its development in Morocco.

Conceptual Approach of the Employee Owner

Employees are now key shareholders in the capital of companies, thus motivating them to work in the interests of the company. For companies, it offers many undeniable advantages by retaining and motivating employees while offering the advantage of better stabilizing capital and limiting the impact of stock market fluctuations on strategic decision-making. ESO offers employees the opportunity to fully share the resources of the company and to build up progressive savings on favorable terms.

Employee share ownership can take several forms such as multi-year savings plans, one-off subscription offers, option allocation plan or share subscription warrants, etc.)

These different shapes generally share two common characteristics.

- On the one hand, securities purchased by employees are blocked for a certain period to promote long-term value creation as well as employee loyalty.
- On the other hand, the securities are offered to employees at preferential conditions: either at a discounted price compared to the market price, or at the market price with an additional participation of the company;

The status of employee shareholder can be obtained by several means:

- During Employee Stock Purchase Plan, the decision is taken by the General Meeting of shareholders. The increase is open to all employees, if they wish to subscribe, subject to seniority conditions;
- When selling pre-existing shares, which will be paid into a special account or when allocating company shares as part of the participation;
- When distributing free shares, existing or to be issued, to employees and corporate officers of companies;
- When purchasing securities directly, on the market, when it is a listed company.

Unlike other types of shareholders, employee shareholders have the particularity of assuming a double risk: a first risk, which is that of their investment in human capital, and an additional risk, which is that of their financial capital. Starting from the logic of risk, employee shareholders should naturally be at the top of the shareholder hierarchy. The risk argument (Aglietta and Rebérioux, 2004) is classically used to fix the shareholder "hierarchy" of the company (Hollandts and Guedri, 2008).

Moroccan Experience of Employee Stock Ownership

In Morocco, employee share ownership is experiencing little growth compared to developed countries. It is almost reserved for companies in the banking sector, telecommunications and subsidiaries of foreign multinationals for which the use of employee savings is part of the culture of their parent companies.

Employee share ownership is still in the background and this is mainly due to two reasons. On the one hand, this is justified by the ignorance of the Moroccan public of the advantages of this type of shareholding both on the interests of the employee and on the performance of the company. On the other hand, Moroccan legislation still lags behind in this area. It should be noted that this practice dates back to the early 1990s and was driven by the state during the wave of privatizations. Even if the regime in Morocco did not yet benefit from the same tax advantages as in developed countries, these operations, from 2001, have multiplied over the years without much change in the regulatory framework. It was only during the last decade that the Plan Epargne Entreprise (PEE) was introduced by the 2013 Finance Act amending the general tax code, which introduced tax incentive provisions in favor of employees adhering to this plan. Before 2013, all operations related to employee owners were governed by the General Tax Code. The taxation of shares proposed under the Moroccan employee shareholding program is considered bleak. Indeed, the discount offered by the company, represented by the difference between the value of the share and the sale price to the employee, is exempt from GIT « General Income Taxe ». This discount must meet two major conditions:

- First, the discount cannot exceed 10% of the value of the share;
- Second, according to the 2001 Finance Law, the transfer of shares must not take place before a period of unavailability of 5 years from the date of grant of the option.

Employee Share Ownership: Between Financial Theories and Power Conflict

Financial theories set out to study how organizations actually work.

They focus on explaining organizational forms as a means of resolving power conflicts, drawing on several mechanisms. In what follows, we will present the contribution of property rights theory and agency theory to the analysis of the relationship of employee ownership and corporate governance.

THEORETICAL FRAMEWORK OF THE RESEARCH

Agency theory and property rights theory constitute the theoretical framework that will be mobilized in our research. These theories share the same vision of the neoclassical theory on the firm, perceived as being a knot of often incomplete contracts, resulting from a complex equilibrium and comparable to a market where the agents are rational. They will be used to understand the place of employee share ownership in corporate governance.

Contribution of the Theory of Property Rights

According to Alchian and Demsetz (1972), the theory of property rights is based on the fact that any exchange between agents can be considered as a contractual exchange of property rights.

This theory stipulates that all exchanges between individuals relate in reality to property rights, relating to goods and services, correspond to exchanges of property rights over objects, which must be clearly defined, transferable and exclusive.

Except that, human beings are in fact subjected to infinite desires, which can lead them to appropriate the goods possessed by other individuals. Likewise, the theory of property rights consists in showing the superiority of private property systems over collective property models, as well as the study of the impact that the attenuation of property rights can have on the efficiency of internal coordination of the organization.

The theory of property rights perfectly justifies the place occupied by employee ownership in corporate governance. Indeed, this theory helps explain how the securities held encourage, create, retain and enhance employee assets.

Contribution of Agency Theory

In 1976, Jensen and Meckling developed the agency theory which takes into account the multiplicity of categories of participants in the organization and the resulting divergence of interests. Shareholders, not having the necessary skills to manage their money, choose to delegate decision-making power to a manager. The problem with this situation lies in the divergence of interests between the two parties. In a context of information asymmetry, the manager can thus prioritize his objectives to the detriment of those of the shareholders. He may seek to maximize the growth of the company with the objective of increasing its own profit, reputation capital and value in the executive market.

The agency theory, Jensen and Meckling (1976), widely used in the literature on employee ownership, is based on two principles which are the divergence of interests and the costs that result from it. Several research studies have led to the conclusion that employee share ownership would reduce agency costs by aligning the interests of employees with those of shareholders (Desbrières, 1989, 1997a, 1997b, 2002; Gamble, Culpepper, & Blubaugh, 2002 ; Long, 1980). Thus, the challenge is to align the interests of employees with those of managers and with the objective of creating shareholder value (Pugh et al., 1999; Gamble, 2000). The idea is that the employee ownership aligns their interests with those of external shareholders and therefore constitutes an incentive mechanism contributing to achieving the objective of the firm, namely, the maximization of the value of the employees equity or shareholder value (Garfatta, 2010).

In this sense, the studies by Kruse et al. 2010 states that shared capitalism's modes of remuneration are widespread throughout the US economy, and that shared capitalism is linked to worker behavior that can increase productivity and profits, reduced turnover, and greater willingness to work hard.

This alignment of interests is also valid for analyzing the relationship between the non-executive employee shareholders of the firm and the shareholders external to the company, "employee shareholding, for its part, being analyzed as an incentive contract aimed at orienting the company. behavior of workers towards the creation of shareholder value, ie aiming to align the interests of workers with those of shareholders "(Autenne, 2005, p.232).

Likewise, Kruse et al. (2016), analyzed in their article the methods of remuneration of employee shareholders and their links with the performance of the company

Power at the Center of the Manager - Employee Relationship

Employee share ownership redefines the parts of the agency relationship. Employee shareholders suddenly play the role of principal. Hollandts X. et Guedri Z. (2008) they are also interested in how employee ownership could fit into the multiple agency relationships that we have just put into perspective. He points out that "the apparent singularity of being both a shareholder and an employee (therefore principal and agent) does not pose any real theoretical problems, except with regard to the relationship of employees to their managers" (p. 54).

According to Benartzi et al. (2007), The establishment of an employee shareholding mechanism is likely to facilitate the negative rooting of managers.

However, Hollandts (2007) continues his analysis by considering that "the fact of granting shares and property rights to employees leads to inefficiencies at three levels (…) which can manifest themselves in the framework of three types of agency relations: between employee shareholders and employees; between employee shareholders and external shareholders; between employee shareholders and managers "(p.54).

According to Guery and Stevenot (2017), employee shareholding would aim to reduce conflicts of interest between shareholders and employees and limit agency costs even if this implies sharing the annuity.

In this case, the agency relationship becomes conflictual in the event of a divergence of interests between the principal and the agent. The conflicts between managers and employees come fundamentally from the incompleteness of contracts and the propensity that each has to prioritize its own interests. In certain situations, employees can adopt behaviors such as absenteeism, reduced efforts ... which can be harmful for the company.

These conflicts can be mastered by a multitude of complementary mechanisms. Research works distinguish between:

- Employee incentive and control mechanisms such as audit procedures, remuneration formulas, participation in decision-making;
- Mechanisms to safeguard the interests of employees such as the terms of employment contracts, labor law and social law, membership of a trade union organization, etc.).

EMPLOYEE SHARE OWNERSHIP AND GOOD GOVERNANCE: DEVELOPMENT AND FORMULATION OF HYPOTHESES

The objective of what follows is to analyze employee share ownership according to the two paradigms. First the disciplinary paradigm, through the shareholder model and then the partnership model. Then, the cognitive paradigm and the role of employee ownership in reducing cognitive costs.

Subsequently, we will show the contribution of recent reflections related to the impact of employee share ownership on governance, part of the literature emphasizes the positive impact but is contrasted by another part of the literature which concludes that employee share ownership can also have negative effects.

Employee Shareholding: From the Disciplinary Paradigm to the Cognitive Paradigm

Initially, the disciplinary model refers to the purely shareholder or legal-financial current, which has long remained dominant, in which the relationship between manager (the agent) and shareholders (the principal) is central, making the shareholders the sole owners and including mechanisms intended to align the interests of managers with those of shareholders (Charreaux, 2012). The shareholder approach quickly demonstrated its limits and gave rise to a partnership approach that integrates all the other stakeholders in addition to the shareholders. In this sense, Germain and Lyon-Caen (2016) show that employee share ownership can be profitable because they hold private information which greatly limits the information asymmetry that can benefit managers.

Along with the disciplinary stream, the cognitive stream is interested in the process of creating value in business, which has been developed within the framework of the cognitive theories of the firm. From this perspective, certain cognitive biases (Charreaux and Wirtz, 2007; Charreaux, 2008, 2011) can be limited by employee shareholding and its involvement in governance bodies.

Employee Shareholding and the Creation of Shareholder Value Then Partnership

The shareholder model of governance finds its origin in the contractual theories of the firm. These are mainly property rights theories, transaction cost theory, and agency theory. This model looks at the capacity of governance mechanisms to limit the manager's latitude in order to best align the latter's interests with those of all of the company's shareholders of the company. This approach presents it as a particular system of contractual relationships, in the form of a "knot of contracts" between individuals in which the manager establishes agency relationships between the different stakeholders.

The objective of the various levers is to minimize agency and transaction costs across the entire node of contracts following possible opportunism from managers seeking to take advantage of information asymmetry. According to Charreaux (2012), this shareholder model has proven to be effective. However, its explanatory power remains limited to shareholder value alone, which has called it into question. This is how the partnership approach was born and constituted a theoretical extension of corporate governance. This model established the concept of partnership value which should allow a sustainable creation of wealth by the company (Hill C. et Jones M. 1992).

Unlike the shareholder view, limited to the interests of shareholders alone, the partnership view is extended to all stakeholders who then take on the status of residual creditors in the same way as shareholders. Charreaux (2012) binds the stakeholders together, making the firm a node of investments: a combination of assets and specialized people (Zingales, 1998; Rajan and Zingales, 2000). Thus, employee participation can influence the agency relationship by reducing the asymmetry of information between shareholders and managers but also between managers and employees and between actors in the company (Poulain-Rehm, 2007).

Employee shareholders tend to influence the creation of shareholder value (Faleye et al. 2006). for Ginglinger et al. (2011), several recent empirical studies highlight the overall negative impacts of a level of capital ownership by employees (Faleye et al. 2006; Kim and Ouimet, 2014).

In short, contractual theories essentially focus on resolving conflicts of interest between company stakeholders, ignoring the cognitive dimension. This gives rise to the need to analyze employee share ownership from a cognitive perspective.

Employee Shareholder and the Reduction of Cognitive Biases

In the context of the cognitive approach to governance, the efficiency of the company relates to its capacity to create specific knowledge and to its learning process. The maximization of the value created by the company depends here on the identification of skills and their development by the firm.

The cognitive approach to governance is based on business strategy theory.

The development of this theory dates back to the reflections of Penrose E. (1959), in his work, "The theory of the growth of the firm". Then came the famous article by B. Wernefelt published in 1984, entitled "Resource-Based View of the Firm" and which highlights the relevance of analyzing the resources and organizational capacities of the company, in order to define new strategic orientations.

In the cognitive approach, the company is considered as a set of resources and an entity of accumulation of knowledge guided by the vision of the leaders, following the experience they have acquired Parrat F. (2015). The objective is to improve the capacity for learning and knowledge influencing the creation of sustainable growth within the company.

According to Nikulina I.E.and Khomenko I. (2015), business management is done through tools affecting human cognitive capacities.

Gomez and Hollandts (2015), argue that from a cognitive point of view, the contribution of employee shareholders can be perceptible on three particular dimensions: the memory of the company, its internal knowledge and the defense of its sustainability. Due to their knowledge of the history of the company, its strategy, its successes, its failures ... employee shareholders appear to be internal experts. As such, they also appear as guarantkruseors of the sustainability of the company because it is obviously in their own interest (Germain and Lyon-Caen, 2016) but also in their collective interest (Roberts and Van den Steen, 2001; Thomsen et al, 2016).

Much of the literature highlights the positive impact of employee ownership on the quality of governance, such as Chang (1990), Mehran (1999), Balsi et al. (1996), Trébucq (2002), Kaarsemaker et al. (2010) et Kruse et al. (2010), Benartzi et al 2007, Rauh, Aubert et al 2004, Hollandts et al (2018).

They argue that this dual role of employee shareholders can lead to more involvement and more control in order to safeguard their interests and the interests of the company. They are doubly encouraged to participate by their financial investment and their investment in human capital (Desbrières, 2002). Regarding their participation in control bodies, Desbrières (1998), Mohat and Alidou (2019), Gardoni (2020), considers that it improves the effectiveness of their control and reduces the opportunism of managers, which makes it possible to align the interests of employees and those of other external shareholders of the company.

However, other researchers claim the negativity of the relationship, such as Scholes and Wolfson (1990), Scholes et al. (2002) and Autenne (2005). For these authors, employee shareholders have more power and leeway, and can more easily promote their interests. This could ultimately reinforce the harmful effects in terms of decision-making and governance.

The purpose of the following section is to justify and analyze the foundations of the two relationships.

Positive Influence of Employee Share Ownership on Governance

In 2016, authors such as O'Boyle et al. (2016) showed through a meta-analysis that employee ownership was likely to have a positive effect on company performance.

Pierce et al. (1991) advances the notion of "psychological ownership" which is based on the fact that, because of the monetary gains associated with the acquisition of stocks, employees would be all the more involved because they would thus feel associated with the capital. Several authors also consider that employee shareholding tends to reduce opportunistic behavior and free rider issues by reducing phenomena such as turnover, absenteeism, the probability of leaving the company Brown et al. (1999); Buchko, (1992); Wilson and Peel, (1991) and to increase the productivity and performance of the company (Ben-Ner and Jones, (1995); Jones and Kato, (1995); Desbrières, (2002); Robinson and Wilson (2006) ; Kaarsemaker et al. (2010). In addition, the famous model of Leland and Pyle (1977) indeed shows that the holding of shares by insiders can be considered as a good signal of the value of the company. Desbrières (2002) considers that this presence can enhance the disciplinary effectiveness of the board, thus improving the governance system by creating more value, whether analyzed from a disciplinary or cognitive perspective. It has also been shown that when the importance is attached to the production of human capital, this helps to give more weight to employees in the governance of the company (Roberts and Van den Steen, 2001) and to reduce the asymmetry of information between company (Poulain-Rehm, 2007). In this sense, the presence of employees on the board allows feature of reducing overall information asymmetry (Freeman and Lazear, 1995; Acharya et al, 2011). This better information also benefits other directors by allowing them to access information that they could not have obtained elsewhere (Mohat and Alidou, 2019).

In this perspective, several authors have asserted that the positive effects of employee share ownership on good governance through their presence on the board of directors. Even if historically, the council has always been a relatively secret place and reserved for an elite or even a caste (Burris, 2005) composed of similar profiles, this participation would be beneficial in several ways: in particular by allowing a transfer of effective information from the board of directors to employees so that employee representatives have precise information on the company's situation, which has the effect of mobilizing employees when the situation requires it (Freeman and Lazear, 1995) . Thus, employees, by virtue of their dual status, can play a productive role by constraining the actions of managers focused on their individual interests, by providing the board of directors with specific knowledge about the company (Acharya et al., 2011) . In this context, the participation of employee shareholders in the board of directors can however be a real asset for the governance of the companies concerned (Couret and Hirigoyen, 1990; Hirigoyen, 1997; Desbrières, 1997; Germain and Lyon-Caen, 2016) and promote the transfer of information to employees (Freeman and Lazear, 1995), between employees and board members (Acharya et al, 2011) leading to an alignment of the interests of employees, managers and shareholders (Ginglinger et al, 2011). It may appear favorable by being justified by their double investment which strongly encourages them to effectively exercise their mandate as director. They also have a direct incentive to exercise their mandate effectively. The smooth running of the business ensures them an income (Germain and Lyon-Caen, 2016) and allows them to develop their specific human capital (Morris et al, 2017; Coff and Raffiee, 2015). This is in line with what Desbrières (2002, p. 266 and p. 278) argued on the fact that this participation in the board introduces opportunities for employees to speak out, which promotes coalition stability, that is to say, the development of cooperation between the stakeholders of companies (shareholders, managers, executives, employees), and helps to give a preventive character to the system of governance and to discourage attempts of collusion between managers and external administrators.

We formulate the following hypothesis thus:

H1: Employee share ownership has a positive influence on corporate governance.

However, if several studies have shown the positive impact of employee shareholding, the literature also highlights the "hidden face" of employee shareholding, especially when employees are able to significantly influence the governance of their own. business. This negative relationship will be explained in the following section.

Negative Influence of Employee Share Ownership on Governance

Along with the positive aspects mentioned above, employee share ownership is likely to have negative effects. The large study by Faleye et al. (2006) investigated the influence of employee share ownership on company performance. These authors show that companies that display employee participation in capital and governance invest less, take less risk, develop more slowly, create fewer new jobs, and deviate more from the objective of maximizing profitability. shareholder value, and are less productive. The authors thus show that employee participation decreases shareholder value by 14.5% and that employee productivity is 21% lower for companies with high employee participation in capital. Employee share ownership entails a real risk of loss of competitiveness and corporate performance if the interests of employee (shareholders) are too favored (Kim and Ouimet, 2014; Guedri and Hollandts, 2008). Beyond the direct effects on governance, employee share ownership offers employees the political power necessary to influence strategic decisions in a direction that is favorable to them, such as salary increases at the expense of policies maximizing shareholder value or development. of the company (Faleye et al. 2006). Thus, it becomes susceptible to altering major strategic decisions. In addition, it grants residual claims to employees who traditionally seek to maximize the fixed part of their income (salaries) to the detriment of the “random” part represented by performance and dividends (Jensen and Meckling, 1979; Desbrières, 2002 ; Guedri and Hollandts, 2008; Aubert et al. 2014). In this sense, the empirical studies carried out on the impact of employee share ownership on company performance show different results. Livingston and Henry (1980) and Faleye et al. (2006) affirm the negativity of the relationship between ESO and the performance of the company. However, Guery (2018) noted limited and contrasting effects on the dissemination of information to employees and the participation in strategic decisions of employees or their representatives. Livingston and Henry (1980) and Faleye et al. (2006) explain the ineffectiveness of this mechanism by the “implicit contracts” that can take place between managers and certain senior executives (employee shareholders). These contracts often include benefits and promises related to job security, internal promotions, etc. (Charreaux. 1995 and 1997). Employee share ownership is analyzed in this case as a practice that promotes the desire for certain leaders to take root.

Indeed, several researchers such as Scholes and Wolfson (1990), Scholes et alii (2002) and Autenne (2005), identify two main motivations which push managers to establish and develop employee shareholding, namely:

- First of all, the benefit of tax provisions. The tax systems in force may encourage managers to favor this type of deferred “compensation” over salary increases.
- Then, a defensive mechanism and protection of the leaders from the risks of eviction or replacement.

In this sense, Rauh (2006) shows that an obvious and immediate objective for establishing employee ownership is to erect barriers to hostile takeovers. Generally speaking, employee share ownership can be seen as a “friendly” fraction of the shareholding for managers (Chaplinsky and Niehaus, 1994). This anti-takeover technique can also be considered to be more effective than other better known systems such as poison pills, golden parachutes, recapitalizations, leveraged buyouts or long-term investments. Chaplinsky and Niehaus, (1994).

In addition, Aubert et al. (2014) show, for example, that employee share ownership can be used as a rooting mechanism, in particular by "bad" leaders (underperforming) in order to serve their personal and strategic interests. The implementation of employee shareholding mechanisms is likely to facilitate negative entrenchment of managers (Jensen and Meckling, 1979; Chaplinsky and Niehaus, 1994; Gamble, 2000; Benartzi et al. 2007).

Regarding the participation of employee shareholders in governance bodies, the shareholder or disciplinary approach to governance offers the main arguments against employee representation. In line with the analysis of Alchian and Demsetz (1972) and Jensen and Meckling (1979), employee representation is related to a deviation from the optimal functioning of the board (Thomsen et al, 2016) whose disciplinary objective takes precedence over any other. Employee directors sometimes tend to consider that this function offers them an additional union forum, on top of the traditional forms of union expression. A climate of mistrust can thus exist between managers, directors and employee directors. This situation can negatively impact the functioning of the board and reduce the interest of employee representation.

From this perspective, the literature emphasizes that the proximity of employee directors to their managers can lead to "friendly" control by employees over managers (Desbrières, 2002), Pagano M. and Volpin (2005). In some situations, they are presented as alibi administrators who are unconditional supporters of leaders (Gomez and Hollandts, 2015).

In view of what we have exposed, we can formulate the following hypothesis:

H2: Employee share ownership negatively influences corporate governance.

EMPIRICAL ANALYSIS OF THE RELATIONSHIP BETWEEN EMPLOYEE SHARE OWNERSHIP AND CORPORATE GOVERNANCE

The hypotheses of this research work will be tested through the mobilization of two types of variables:

- The variable to be explained is the participation of employees in the capital of the company.
- The explanatory variable relates to good corporate governance.

- To assess this variable, we developed an index to measure the quality of the governance system of each company. We based ourselves on several elements, mainly:
- The regulatory framework governing corporate governance in the context of companies listed in Morocco, in particular the Moroccan code of good governance practices of 2008,
- Best practices provided by soft laws (Codes, reports and expert recommendations),
- The rating systems for the quality of the corporate governance system which are used by international credit risk rating agencies,
- The latest survey report conducted by the Moroccan Institute of Directors (IMA) on the governance practices of listed companies (October 2016 version).

We were able to identify 14 criteria for evaluating the quality of the governance system of the companies in the sample, giving rise to a Governance Score for each of these companies and allowing us to get an idea of the quality of the governance mechanisms adopted. by the latter;

The population targeted by this research work and which will be used to test our research hypotheses is made up of 76 companies listed on the Casablanca Stock Exchange, covering most sectors of the Moroccan economy and observed between the period 2015-2020. We have excluded:

- Public enterprises because of their specificities;
- Companies whose governance data is not communicated.

Proposal of an Index of Good Governance

First, we will build an index measuring both the informational aspect and the relationship of the quality of governance. Next, we will test the different items using validity and reliability tests.

Construction of the Index

We have chosen, through this index, to measure both the informational and relational aspect of the quality of governance. The informational aspect is represented by both a substantive criterion, which is transparency, and a formal criterion, which is intelligibility. The relational aspect, for its part, is measured by the criterion of proximity to shareholders first, and then to other stakeholders. The criteria we have selected will allow us to choose a set of items that we present later.

These different categories will be used to assess:

- The quality of the control bodies
- The quality of the relationship with the shareholders;
- The quality of financial and extra-financial information;
- The quality of the relationship with other stakeholders

This classification made it possible to distinguish 39 items which constitute the index that we propose in Appendix 1. They are distributed as follows

- Eighteen items relate to the quality of control bodies;
- Nine items assess the quality of the relationship with shareholders.
- Twelve items assess the quality of financial and extra-financial information.

Index Test

In order to validate our index, we sent the governance quality assessment grid (appendix 1) in the form of a questionnaire to several financial analysts. They were asked to assign a score to each item. The responses reached us from January 2021 until the end of April 2021. After several reminders, by mail and by phone, we obtained a response rate of 22%. This rate remains relatively higher compared to the studies carried out. The valuation is done on the basis of the Likert scale with five entries ranging from "not at all important", "not important", "moderately important", "important" and "very important". This scale provides a measure of attitude that can be termed a measure of the level of intervals. It is the first of the metric type which makes it possible to carry out parametric tests.

Before applying the index, it is essential to subject it to a number of validity and reliability tests. We will first submit our index to a validity test in order to take into account any non-response bias measured using the Oppenheim test (1966). Secondly, we will use Cronbach's alpha to measure the internal consistency of our index in order to confirm its reliability.

- **Validity Test**

In order to validate the proposed index, it is essential to ensure that the responses we received are representative of the population of financial analysts. In this sense, the Oppenheim test (1966) will aim to take into account possible non-response bias of respondents. This test is based on the principle that responses received late should not be taken into account. Oppenheim (1966, p. 34) points out that the last respondents are included as non-respondents. We thus systematically kept the return date of each questionnaire in order to check to what extent a bias was introduced by non-responses.

The results of the Oppenheim test (1966), obtained using SPSS software, which show the absence of non-response bias. The tests for differences of means on the different items of the index did not show any significant difference between the first five and the last five responses.

This test allows us to consider the answers we obtained as representative of the attitude of the population of financial analysts.

We therefore consider that our measure of the quality of governance is valid from this point of view.

- **Reliability Test**

After having tested the validity of our index, we will in what follows, measure its reliability using the methods most used and recommended by Churchill (1979), namely the calculation of Cronbach's alpha and the correlation inter-item.

Cronbach's alpha is a technique used to assess the homogeneity and internal consistency of a scale. By applying this test on our index, we obtain, using SPSS software, a Cronbach's alpha equal to 0.743. This result represents a certain weakness since the decision rule is to have an alpha between 0.7 and 0.9 (Kline, 1993). Likewise, Evrard, Roux and Pras (2000) believe that an alpha greater than 0.6 is quite suitable for exploratory research. For Nunnally (1978), an alpha that approaches 1, the scale has good internal consistency.

Concerning the second indicator, these are correlations between pairs of items (or the correlations between each item and the instrument as a whole), measuring the same variable, are sufficiently high. We obtain, using SPSS software, inter-item correlations of 0.331. In this sense, Bearden et al. (1993) state that correlations greater than 0.3 are quite satisfactory.

Thus, we consider our index to be reliable from the point of view of Cronbach's alpha and inter-item correlations.

Application of the Governance Quality Measurement Index

Sampling Procedure

In this part, we will apply the index we built to the companies in our sample. Thus, first of all, we will proceed to the rating of the governance and the scores obtained by all the companies. Next, we will distinguish between two samples. Finally, we will test our research hypotheses.

- Scoring and calculation of scores:

We begin by reading the annual reports and consulting the websites of the minutes of general meetings and boards of directors in order to highlight each of its constituent items. This assessment is made on the basis of the index presented in Appendix 1 and ends with the attribution of an additional score to each company.

The score and index calculation protocol is detailed in Appendix 2

Table 1.

Maximum Quality score	174.8
Minimum Quality score	82.7
Average quality score	112.1
Standard déviation	18.5
Maximum quality index	0.68
Minimum quality index	0.29
Average quality index	0.54
Standard déviation	0.09

- ***Distinction of the two samples***

The scoring and classification made it possible to distinguish two distinct samples:

- A first sample of companies with good governance quality.
- A second sample of companies with poor quality governance.

After we have noted and classified all the companies, we will only keep the first quartile and the last quartile. The first quartile which represents companies with good governance and the last quartile which represents companies with poor governance

By excluding thirty-eight companies, we obtain two distinct samples of 19 companies each, which gives more significance to our study. The lack of dispersion of the scores is evidenced by the low standard deviations. This shows a certain homogeneity in the two groups. The difference of means tests carried out confirm the high significance of the difference between the two samples as shown in the table 2.

Table 2.

	Echantillon1: QG+ Companies With Governance Quality	Echantillon 2: QG- Companies That Do Not Have Governance Quality
Minimum Index	0.29	0.71
Maximum Index	0.48	0.89
Average Index	0.31	0.79
Standard deviaton	0.022	0.011

Analysis and Discussion of the Results of the Empirical Study

The objective of this part is to conduct a univariate analysis in order to test the research hypotheses concerning the influence of employee share ownership on the quality of governance.

- QG +: Companies with governance quality
- QG -: Companies that do not have governance quality

Table 3.

Average Data	**ESO**
QG+	22.03
QG-	11.57
Median Data	**ESO**
QG+	25
QG-	11.7
Standard Deviation	**ESO**
QCM+	8.37
QCM-	5.02
Statistical Test Results	**ESO**
U de Man Whitney	Ns [1]
Kolmogorov-smirnoff	0.01
T de Student	ns

The univariate analysis shows, through the comparison of averages and medians, that shareholding increases with the quality of governance.

Hypothesis H1 is validated, thus rejecting hypothesis H2. This confirms the positive relationship between employee stock ownership and the quality of governance.

CONCLUSION

Employee ownership is a global phenomenon that is experiencing an unprecedented development in Morocco to the point of appearing as a major element of shareholder capitalism. We have demonstrated, through this research, the favorable effects of employee ownership on good governance.

Indeed, this practice makes it possible to modify the trade-offs between different governance mechanisms, allowing to limit the agency costs inherent to conflicts of interest (Kruse et al (1997, 2010, 2016), Guery and stevenot (2017), Mehran (1999), Balsi et al (1996), Trébucq (2002), Kaarsemaker et al (2010), Benartzi et al 2007, Rauh, Aubert et al 2004, Hollandts et al (2018)...).

Also, the development of this type of shareholding allows employees to participate in general meetings of shareholders and may lead them to sit on the board of directors or supervisory board.

Several avenues of future research are possible. Indeed, our research can be completed by integrating the "time" effect of employee ownership. Indeed, the duration of the presence of employee shareholders in the firm, as well as the distribution and share of employee ownership, can have a considerable influence on the quality of governance.

Similarly, it would be very interesting to analyze, in another research, an adjustment of the theoretical framework, i.e. the agency theory and the property rights theory, taking into account the Moroccan specificity. The mere existence of an alternative model of finance such as Islamic finance may call into question the foundations of these theories.

REFERENCES

Acharya, V., Myers, S. C., & Rajan, R. G. (2011). The internal governance of firms. *The Journal of Finance*, *66*(3), 689–720. doi:10.1111/j.1540-6261.2011.01649.x

Aglietta, M., & Reberioux, A. (2004). *Dérives du capitalisme financier*. Albin Michel Economie.

Alchian, A., & Demsetz, H. (1972). Production, Information Costs and Economic Organization. American Economic Review, 62(5), 777-795.

Aubert, N., Garnotel, G., Lapied, A., & Rousseau, P. (2014). Employee Ownership: A Theoretical and Empirical Investigation of Management Entrenchment vs. Reward Management. *Economic Modelling, 40*, 423–434. doi:10.1016/j.econmod.2013.12.011

Aubert, N., & Rapp, T. (2008). Les Salariés Actionnaires: Pourquoi Investissent-ils dans leur Entreprise? Finance Contrôle Stratégie. *Association FCS, 11*(4), 87–110.

Autenne, A. (2005). *Analyse économique du droit de l'actionnariat salarié, Bibliothèque de la Faculté de Droit de l'Université Catholique de Louvain*. Bruylant.

Bearden, W. (1993). Handbook of marketing scales: multi item measures for marketing and consumer behaviour research. Academic Press.

Ben-Ner, A., & Jones, D. C. (1995). Employee Participation, Ownership, and Productivity: A Theoretical Framework. *Industrial Relations, 34*(4), 532–554. doi:10.1111/j.1468-232X.1995.tb00387.x

Benartzi, S. (2007). Company Stock, Market Rationality, and Legal Reform. *The Journal of Law & Economics, 2*(50), 45–79. doi:10.1086/508312

Blair, M. (1999). Firm-Specific Human Capital and Theories of the Firm. In Employees & Corporate Governance. Brooking Institution Press.

Brown, S., Fakhfakh, F., & Sessions, J. G. (1999). Absenteeism and Employee Sharing: An Empirical Analysis Based On French Panel Data, 1981-1991. *Industrial & Labor Relations Review, 52*(2), 234–251.

Buchko, A. A. (1992). Employee Ownership, Attitudes, and Turnover: An Empirical Assessment. *Human Relations, 45*(7), 711–733. doi:10.1177/001872679204500704

Burris, V. (2005). Interlocking Directorates and Political Cohesion among Corporate Elites. *American Journal of Sociology, 111*(1), 249–283. doi:10.1086/428817

Cardoni, H. (2020). Contribution à la connaissance de l'impact de l'actionnariat salarié sur la gouvernance des entreprises. *Entreprise et société*, 147-176.

Chang, S. (1990). Employee Stock Ownership and Shareholder Wealth: An Empirical Investigation. *Financial Management, 19*(1), 48–58. doi:10.2307/3666036

Chaplinsky, S., & Niehaus, G. (1994). The Role of ESOPs in Takeover Contests. *The Journal of Finance, 49*(4), 1451–1470. doi:10.1111/j.1540-6261.1994.tb02461.x

Charreaux, G. (1997). Vers une théorie du gouvernement des entreprises. In Le Gouvernement des Entreprises. Economica.

Charreaux, G. (1997). *Le gouvernement des Entreprises: Corporate Governance. Théories et Faits*. Economica.

Charreaux, G. (1997). *Le gouvernement des Entreprises: Corporate Governance. Théories et Faits*. Economica.

Charreaux, G. (2008). À la recherche du lien perdu entre caractéristiques des dirigeants et performance de la firme: Gouvernance et latitude managériale. *Économies et sociétés*, *42*(10), 1831–1867.

Charreaux, G. (2011). *Quelle théorie pour la gouvernance? De la gouvernance actionnariale à la gouvernance cognitive et comportementale*. Working Papers CREGO, n°1110402.

Charreaux, G. (2012). Le gouvernement d'entreprise. In J. Allouche (Coord.), Encyclopédie des ressources Humaines. Théories, instruments, méthodes, auteurs. Paris: Vuibert.

Charreaux, G., & Desbrières, P. (1997). *Le point sur le gouvernement des entreprises*. Revue Banque & Marchés.

Charreaux, G., & Wirtz, P. (2007). *Discipline ou compétence? L'apport des perspectives cognitive et comportementale à la compréhension des mécanismes de gouvernance*. Document halshs-00260119.

Code Marocain des bonnes pratiques de gouvernance, 2008.

Coff, R., & Raffiee, J. (2015). Toward a Theory of Perceived Firm-Specific Human Capital. Academy of Management Perspectives, 29(3), 326–341. doi:10.5465/amp.2014.0112

Couret, A., & Hirigoyen, G. (1990). *L'actionnariat des salariés*. PUF.

Desbrières, P. (1997). Le rôle de l'actionnariat des salariés non-dirigeants dans le système de gouvernement de l'entreprise. Le gouvernement des entreprises. Economica.

Desbrières, P. (2000). *La rémunération des dirigeants sous forme d'actions et de stockoptions*. WorkingPapers CREGO 1001102. Université de Bourgogne - CREGO EA7317 Centre de recherches en gestion des organisations.

Desbrières, P. (2002). Les actionnaires salariés. *Revue Française de Gestion*, *141*(28), 255–281.

Dionne-Proulx, J., & Larochelle, G. (2010). Éthique et gouvernance d'entreprise. Management et Avenir, 2(32), 36-53.

Enquête sur les pratiques de gouvernance des sociétés cotées -Version 2015- INSTITUT MAROCAIN DES ADMINISTRATEURS.pdf.

Faleye, O., Mehrotra, V., & Morck, R. (2006). When labor has a voice in corporate governance. *Journal of Financial and Quantitative Analysis, 41*(3), 489–510. doi:10.1017/S0022109000002519

Faleye, O., Mehrotra, V., & Morck, R. (2006). When Labor Has A Voice In Corporate Governance. *Journal of Financial and Quantitative Analysis, 41*(3), 489–510.

Freeman, R. B., & Lazear, E. P. (1995). An economic analysis of works councils. In J. Rogers & W. Streeck (Eds.), *Works councils: Consultation, representation, and cooperation in industrial relations* (pp. 27–52). University of Chicago Press.

Gamble, J. E. (2000). Management Commitment to Innovation and ESOP Stock Concentration. *Journal of Business Venturing, 15*(5–6), 433–447. doi:10.1016/S0883-9026(99)00037-3

Garfatta, R. (2010). *Actionnariat salarié et création de la valeur dans le cadre de la gouvernance actionnariale et partenariale: application au contexte f*rancais (Thèse de Doctorat soutenue). l'université de Bourgogne.

Ginglinger, E., Megginson, W., & Waxin, T. (2011). Employee Ownership, Board Representation, and Corporate Financial Policies. *Journal of Corporate Finance, 17*(4), 868–887. doi:10.1016/j.jcorpfin.2011.03.005

Gomez, P.-Y., & Hollandts, X. (2015). La représentation des salariés au conseil d'administration. *Revue de Droit du Travail*, (7/8), 451–457.

Guedri, Z., & Hollandts, X. (2008). Beyond Dichotomy: The Curvilinear Impact of Employee Ownership on Firm Performance. *Corporate Governance, 16*(5), 460–474. doi:10.1111/j.1467-8683.2008.00703.x

Guery, L. (2018). L'actionnariat salarié: une autre conception de la place des salariés dans l'entreprise? Rémunération du travail.

Guery, L., & Stevenot, A. (2017). L'actionnariat salarié favorise-t-il la diffusion d'information aux salariés et leur participation aux décisions stratégiques? Une question de gouvernance d'entreprise. *Revue Management International, 21*(4), 61–75.

Hansmann, H. (1996). *The Ownership of Enterprise.* Belknap Press of Harvard University Press.

Hill, C. W. L., & Jones, T. M. (1992). Stakeholder-agency theory. *Journal of Management Studies, 29*(2), 131–154. doi:10.1111/j.1467-6486.1992.tb00657.x

Hirigoyen, G. (1997). *Salariés-actionnaires: le capital sans le pouvoir?* Pouvoir et Gestion.

Hollandts, X., & Guedri, Z. (2008). Les salariés capitalistes et la performance de l'entreprise. *Revue Française de Gestion, 3*(183), 35–50. doi:10.3166/rfg.183.35-50

Imane & Djaoudath. (2019). Does employee share ownership influence the level of remuneration of executives of French listed companies ? Empirical study of the SBF 120 Stock Market Index. *Finance, Contrôle, Stratégie, 22*(2-3).

Jensen, M., & Meckling, W. (1979). Rights and Production Functions: An Application to Labor-Managed Firms and Codetermination. *The Journal of Business, 52*(4), 469–506. doi:10.1086/296060

Jones, D. C., & Kato, T. (1995). The Productivity Effects of Employee Stock-Ownership Plans and Bonuses: Evidence from Japanese Panel Data. *The American Economic Review, 85*(3), 391–414.

Kaarsemaker, E., Pendleton, A., & Poutsma, E. (2010). Employee Shareownership. In A. Wilkinson, M. Marchington, P. Gollan, & D. Lewin (Eds.), *Oxford Handbook of Participation in Organisations*. Oxford University Press.

Kim, E.H., & Ouimet, P. (2014). Broad-Based Employee Stock Ownership: Motives and Outcomes. *Journal of Finance, 69*(3), 1273-1319.

Kruse, D. (2010). Shared Capitalism at Work: Employee Ownership, Profit and Gain Sharing, and Broad-Based Stock Options. University of Chicago Press. doi:10.7208/chicago/9780226056968.001.0001

Kruse, D., & Blasi, J. R. (1997). Employee ownership, employee attitudes and firm performance: a review of the evidence. In B. Mitchell, D. Lewin, & M. Zaidi (Eds.), *Handbook of Human Resource Management*. JAI Press.

Leland, H., & Pyle, D. (1977). Informational Asymmetries, Financial Structure, and Financial Intermediation. *The Journal of Finance, 32*(2), 371. doi:10.2307/2326770

Livingston, D. T., & Henry, J. B. (1980). The Effect of Employee Stock Ownership Plans on Corporate Profits. *The Journal of Risk and Insurance, 47*(3), 491–505. doi:10.2307/252634

Morris, S., Alvarez, S., Barney, J., & Molloy, J. (2017). Firm-specific Human Capital Investments as a Signal of General Value: Revisiting Assumptions about Human Capital and How it Is Managed. *Strategic Management Journal, 38*(4), 912–919.

Moskalu, V. (2012). *Une analyse socio-cognitive de l'impact de l'actionnariat salarié sur la création de valeur des entreprises françaises cotées.* Gestion et management. Thèse soutenue à l'Université de Lorraine

Nikulina, I. E., & Khomenko, I. (2014). Cognitive management: theory and practice in the organization. *International Conference on Research Paradigms Transformation in Social Sciences.*

Notat, N., & Sénard, J.-D. (2018). *L'entreprise, objet d'intérêt collectif.* Rapport remis au Ministre de l'Economie et des Finances.

Note sur le résultat du questionnaire mené par l'AMMC (ex CDVM) sur les pratiques de bonne gouvernance des sociétés cotées -2010-

O'Boyle, E., Patel, P., & Gonzales-Mulé, E. (2016). Employee Ownership and Firm Performance: A Meta-Analysis. *Human Resource Management Journal, 26*(4), 425–448.

OCDE. (2015). *Principes de gouvernance d'entreprise du G20 et de l'OCDE.* OECD.

Pagano, M., & Volpin, P. (2005). Managers, workers, and corporate control. *The Journal of Finance, 60*(2), 841–868.

Parrat, F. (2015). *Théories et pratiques de la gouvernance d'entreprise.* Maxima Laurent du Mesnil.

Pierce, J. L., Rubenfeld, S. A., & Morgan, S. (1991). Employee Ownership: A Conceptual Model of Process and Effects. *Academy of Management Review, 16*(1), 121–144.

Poulain-Rehm, T. (2007). *L'actionnariat des salariés en France, un facteur de création de valeur?* Academic Press.

Pugh, W., Jahera, J., & Oswald, S. (1999). ESOPs, Takeover Protection, and Corporate Decision Making. *Journal of Economics and Finance, 23*(2), 170–185.

Rajan, R., & Zingales, L. (1998). Power in a Theory of the Firm. *Quarterly Journal of Economics, 113*(2), 387-432.

Roberts, J., & Van den Steen, E. (2001). Human Capital and Corporate Governance. In H. Albach & J. Schwalbach (Eds.), *Corporate governance: Essays in Honor of Horst Albach* (pp. 128–144). Springer.

Robinson, A. M., & Wilson, N. (2006). Employee Financial Participation and Productivity: An Empirical Reappraisal. *British Journal of Industrial Relations, 44*(1), 31–50.

Scholes, M. (2002). *Taxes and Business Strategy: A Planning Approach*. Prentice Hall.

Scholes, M., & Wolfson, M. (1990). Employee stock ownership plans and corporate restructuring: Myths and realities. *Financial Management, 19*, 12–28.

Shleifer, A., & Vishny, R. (1986). Greenmail, white knights, and shareholders' interests, Rand. *Journal of Economics, 17*, 293–309.

Siessima, D. (2017). La face cachée de l'actionnariat salarié: Etude empirique sur l'indice SBF 120 (2000-2014). *Revue finance contrôle stratégie, 20*(1).

Thomsen, S., Rose, C., & Kronborg, D. (2016). Employee Representation and Board Size in the Nordic Countries. *European Journal of Law and Economics, 42*(3), 471–490.

Trébucq, S. (2002). *L'actionnariat salarié dans les entreprises familiales du SBF250: un outil de création de valeur?* Finance Contrôle Stratégie.

Wernerfelt, B. (1984). A resource based view of the firm. *Strategic Management Journal, 5*(2), 171–180.

Wilson, N., & Peel, M. J. (1991). The Impact on Absenteeism and Quits Of Profit-Sharing and Other Forms of Employee Participation. *Industrial & Labor Relations Review, 44*(3), 454–468.

Zingales, L. (1998). Corporate Governance. In P. Newman (Ed.), The New Palgrave, Dictionary of Economy. Academic Press.

ENDNOTE

1 Significant difference at the 5% level: **

APPENDIX 1

Table 4. Governance quality assessment grid

How important is the following information to you in assessing the quality of a company's governance?				
1	**2**	**3**	**4**	**5**
Not at all important	**Not important**	**Moderately important**	**Important**	**Very important**

Table 5. Quality of control

Composition of the Board of adminitrator	1	2	3	4	5
Operation of the Board of administrator	1	2	3	4	5
Séparation of the functions of CEO and PCA	1	2	3	4	5
Size of the Board of administrator	1	2	3	4	5
Acces to training for administrator	1	2	3	4	5
Acces to information for administrator	1	2	3	4	5
Femal representation for the Board of adminitrator	1	2	3	4	5
Share of independant director in the Board of adminitrator	1	2	3	4	5
Présence of employee representative on the Board of adminitrator	1	2	3	4	5
Composition and functionning of committees	1	2	3	4	5
Organisation and conduct of board meeting	1	2	3	4	5
Internal control procedure	1	2	3	4	5
Share of employee shareholders	1	2	3	4	5
Share of institutionnal shareholders	1	2	3	4	5
Share of indicvidual shareholders	1	2	3	4	5
Share of executive shareholders	1	2	3	4	5
Concentration of capital	1	2	3	4	5
Operation of general meeting	1	2	3	4	5

Table 6. Quality of relationship with shareholders

Regularity of information to shareholders	1	2	3	4	5
Permanence of transparency	1	2	3	4	5
Speed of the provision of supports.	1	2	3	4	5
Presentation and clarity of materials	1	2	3	4	5
Organization of meetings and assemblies	1	2	3	4	5
Coherence and continuity of discourse	1	2	3	4	5
Closeness and regularity of the relationship	1	2	3	4	5
Availability of managers	1	2	3	4	5
Responsiveness of managers	1	2	3	4	5

Table 7. Quality of financial and extra-financial information

Transparency of financial information	1	2	3	4	5
Quality of the annual report	1	2	3	4	5
Publication of profit warnings	1	2	3	4	5
Quality of the presentation of results	1	2	3	4	5
Quality of press releases	1	2	3	4	5
Compliance with regulatory rules regarding financial communication	1	2	3	4	5
Information on Research and Development	1	2	3	4	5
Equity Men and Women	1	2	3	4	5
Staff organization (remuneration policy, skills development, integration of disabled employees, etc.).	1	2	3	4	5
Societal commitment	1	2	3	4	5
Environmental commitment	1	2	3	4	5
Information on governance (executive compensation, activity of the board of directors…)	1	2	3	4	5

APPENDIX 2

Score and Index Calculation Protocol

Calculation of the Theorical Score

Given the sector of activity and particularity of each company, some items may not be applicable to all the companies in the sample. we need to calculate a theoretical score corresponding to the maximum score they could achieve. Specific for each firm, this theoretical score is calculated by excluding items that are not applicable to it.

$$\boldsymbol{TS}_J = \sum_{i=1}^{n} S_i$$

Avec $\boldsymbol{TS}_J$ = Theorical Score
n = Nomber of items
S_i = score of item i if published and 0 otherwise.

Calculation of the Actual Score

After applying the index, we get the real score of each company

$$\boldsymbol{AS}_J = \sum_{i=1}^{n} S_i$$

Avec $\boldsymbol{AS}$ = actual Score
n = number of items
S_i = score of item i if published and 0 otherwise.

Once the real score and the theoretical score, we can calculate the quality index according to the following formula:

$$\boldsymbol{Quality\ Index}_J = \frac{\boldsymbol{AS}_J}{\boldsymbol{TS}_J}$$

Avec $\boldsymbol{AS}_J$ = Actual Score de la firme J,
$\boldsymbol{TS}_J$ = Théorical Score de la firme J.

Conclusion

Employee share ownership is defined by the holding of one or more securities giving access to the capital of the company in which the employee works.

When we are interested in employee savings, we must distinguish the source of the sums paid to employees (profit-sharing, profit-sharing, etc.) from the form of investment intended to carry this savings over the long term. The sums paid to employees in the form of shares can be placed in individual accounts, in shares of company mutual funds (FCPE) or in shares of an employee shareholding company with variable capital (SICAV).

Employee shareholding can target all employees of the company or be reserved for some of them (managerial shareholding).

It allows employees to acquire shares under preferential conditions: discount on prices (rebate), supplement paid by the company (contribution) and substantial tax benefits. The benefit of these advantages is linked to the length of detention conditions.

Employee share ownership has many advantages, both for the company and for the employees.

It is a question of bringing liquidity to the cash flow of companies without going through bank indebtedness which makes it possible to improve financial ratios and strengthen shareholders' equity. Employee share ownership also makes it possible to involve employees more in the success of the company and helps to develop collective motivation; (Elouadi 2020)

Moreover, shareholding provides the company with a stable shareholder base and studies carried out during the Covid-19 crisis show the resistance of employee shareholders compared to external shareholders.

Despite all the positive effects of employee shareholding, the practice also has some drawbacks, which should be kept in mind to avoid disappointments. The most important disadvantage is the loss of confidentiality suffered by the company, this concerns especially family businesses which cultivate the culture of confidentiality and the preservation of family patrimony.

When the employee becomes a shareholder, he shares power with the directors and has the right to information. The fear of the dilution of capital is also a drawback linked to employee shareholding and can dissuade managerial families from opening up their capital to employees.

Moreover, employee share ownership is an internal control mechanism that provides employees with additional legitimacy for the control of rulers. However, some studies also see it as a means that fosters the entrenchment of leaders.

Despite its positive results on performance, employee share ownership can be used for instrumentalization purposes, especially to guard against takeovers that sanction bad results of managers.

Charreaux (1997) defines the system of corporate governance as follows:"... all the organizational mechanisms that have the effect of delimiting the powers and influence the decisions of leaders, in other words who govern their conduct and define their discretionary space".

The rooting theory which is part of the corporate governance framework, supposes that the control mechanisms are not always sufficient to constrain the management teams to manage the firm in accordance with the interests of shareholders (Alexandre and Paquerot 2000).

The entrenchment of leaders is generally perceived, by a number of authors, as a reaction to internal and external control of the firm. Starting from the assumption that external control mechanisms are triggered only if the internal control mechanisms are ineffective in controlling leaders (Walsh and Seward 1990), strategies rooting therefore aims, first of all, to neutralize internal control (the board administration, control of shareholders, control of employees) and also to neutralize the means of external control (and more precisely to avoid attempts to take control).

But seen from another angle, employee shareholders can play a capital role against the entrenchment of leaders, by controlling the pathways of impairment.

According to Fama (1980), employees exercise control over the manager's activity and have an interest in that the value of the firm is most positive. He adds that the intensity of the control increases with the increase in their specific investment.

Gharbi (2002) presents in his stydy, the different rooting strategies which aim to counter the main internal and external control mechanisms. The mechanism's control are: boards of directors, employees and the control of shareholders, in addition to external takeover attempts. According to his work, the strategies rooting of the leaders then have the objective of neutralizing in the first place, the internal control of board of directors, shareholders and employees and secondly, external control.

According to Fama (1980), employees are considered to be one of the internal control mechanisms in the firm. One of the ways to ensure the effectiveness of this control is to involve them in capital of the firm. The employee shareholders of the firm depend on the manager: he is, at the same time, their employer and their agent on behalf of the funds they have invested in their business.

French (1987) suggests that employees, who control a large proportion of company shares, would be better able to exert pressure on the managerial team in order to ensure better long term performance. Employee shareholding plans which aim to motivate and retain employees, allow them to acquire the status of shareholder of the firm. These plans should then facilitate more effective internal control since they allow them to combine the informational advantages due to the two statuses.

In this book we have analyzed the different issues of employee share ownership. The first section was devoted to the role played by employee share ownership in absorbing the negative effects of the crisis.

Chapter 1, entitled "Dealing With COVID-19 Through Employee Stock Ownership Plans: Saving Money and Losing Power to Live an Extra Day," presents the granting of shares to employees as a salutary measure to limit the damage of the crisis because it helps boost the company's liquidity and reinforce feelings of motivation, involvement and loyalty.

In Chapter 2, entitled "Employee Ownership or How to Anticipate Financial Crises Within a Company: The Case of the Coronavirus Pandemic," the authors conducted a qualitative survey on the role played by employee shareholding in overcoming the effects of the crisis. based on employee perceptions.

The second section was dedicated to international studies dealing with employee share ownership. Chapter 3, entitled "The Use of Employee Financial Participation in Lithuanian Companies," studies the effects of employee shareholding on Lithuanian companies. The author concludes that the practice of employee share ownership plans helps develop several positive behaviors such as loyalty, sense of belonging and motivation.

Chapter 4, entitled "Understanding Employee Ownership in the Context of French Family Firms," provides an exploratory study of the situation of employee ownership in French family businesses. The authors indicate that not all family businesses have the same opinion regarding employee shareholding. The results show that when the CEO is a member of the owner family, the latter is reluctant to open the capital to employees. On the other hand, when the CEO does not belong to the family, managers develop a positive attitude more favorable to employee shareholding.

Chapter 5, entitled "International Overview of Employee Share Ownership," provides a general and comparative assessment of the situation of employee share ownership in several countries such as Canada, Kenya, France or the United States. The authors conclude that employee share ownership is adopted as a business strategy for different reasons and it depends on the context. The authors also claim that laws differ widely from country to country. And the boom in employee share ownership is gradually increasing, but at different rates all over the world. Adopting the ESOP plans influences positively workplace behaviors and leads to fewer turnovers, more engagement, increased efficiency and eventually sustainable business performance.

The third section was devoted to the situation of employee shareholding in Morocco. The studies deal in particular with the expansion of the practice of employee ownership, its effects on attitudes at work, on the governance of Moroccan companies and the degree of openness of Moroccan legislation to the practice of ESOP.

Chapter 6, entitled "Analysis of the Effects of Employee Share Ownership on the Creation of Financial Value of Moroccan Companies Listed on the Stock Exchange," aims to describe the situation of employee ownership in Moroccan companies listed on the stock exchange. The authors question the impact of the presence of employee share ownership on the creation of financial value. Despite all the advantages of employee savings plans, the study concludes that there is no link between the presence of employee share ownership and the creation of financial value.

Chapter 7, entitled "Exploratory Study of the Attitudinal Effects of Employee Shareholding in Morocco," deals with the attitudinal effects of employee shareholding in Moroccan companies. The authors conducted a questionnaire survey to make a comparison in terms of organizational behavior between employee shareholders and non-shareholders. The results of structural equation modeling conclude that ownership improves facets of organizational involvement and the propensity to invest in shares of one's business and reduces initial intention.

Chapter 8, entitled "Employee Stock Ownership in Morocco: Between Legal Reality and Need for Evolution," deals with the legislative and legal situation of employee ownership in Morocco. The authors note the lack of legislative incentive in favor of employee shareholding and outline the advantages of French legislation. The chapter ends with recommendations to enrich the Moroccan legal framework.

Chapter 9, entitled "Analysis of the Impact of Employee Share Ownership on the Quality of Governance: Case of Listed Moroccan Companies," deals with the impact of employee ownership on the quality of corporate governance.

The author wonders if employee shareholding can increase the natural alliance already existing between employees and managers and can encourage the latter to enter into implicit contracts in return for a "friendly" control of employee shareholders, which weaken the quality of governance.

REFERENCES

Alexandre, H., & Paquerot, M. (2000). Efficacité des structures de contrôle et enracinement des dirigeants. *Finance Contrôle Stratégie*, *3*(2), 5–29.

Charreaux, G. (1997). *Le gouvernement des entreprises: Corporate Governance, théories et faits*. Economica.

Elouadi, S. (2020). The Effects of Employee Ownership on Organizational Commitment and Job Satisfaction: An Empirical Evidence From French Listed Companies. *Journal of Organizational Psychology*, *20*(6).

Fama, E. F. (1980). *Agency Problems and the Theory of the Firm. Journal of Political Economy*, *88*(2), 288–307.

French, J. L. (1987). Employee perspectives of stock ownership: Financial investment or mechanism of control. *Academy of Management Review*, *12*(3), 427–435. doi:10.2307/258510

Gharbi, H. (2002). *Enracinement des dirigeants: une revue de la littérature*. Working paper, Paris Dauphine.

Walsh, J. P., & Seward, J. K. (1990). On the efficiency of internal and external corporate control. *Academy of Management Review*, *15*(3), 421–450. doi:10.5465/amr.1990.4308826

Compilation of References

Abdallah, K., & Cheluget, J. (2020). Determinants of Participation in Employee Share Ownership Plans in the Banking Sector: A Case of Listed Commercial Banks in Kenya. *Journal of Human Resource & Leadership*, 60-75.

Abduali, I. A., & Shafiwu, A. B. (2014). Participatory Decision Making and Employee Productivity. A Case Study of Community Banks in the Upper East region of Ghana. *Business and Economics Journal*, 35-50.

Abdullah, M. I., Sarfraz, M., Qun, W., & Chaudhary, M. (2019). Ownership concentration impact on firm financial performance. *Logforum*, *15*(1), 107–118. doi:10.17270/J.LOG.2019.317

Acharya, V., Myers, S. C., & Rajan, R. G. (2011). The internal governance of firms. *The Journal of Finance*, *66*(3), 689–720. doi:10.1111/j.1540-6261.2011.01649.x

Agbontaen, O. O. (2019). Workplace Diversity and Inclusion Policies: Insights from a Foreign Firm in the Nigeria Banking Sector. In Diversity within Diversity Management (pp. 239-280). Emerald Publishing Limited. doi:10.1108/S1877-636120190000021013

Aglietta, M., & Reberioux, A. (2004). *Dérives du capitalisme financier*. Albin Michel Economie.

Agnihotri, A., & Bahttacharya, S. (2020). ESOPs and New Product Launch: Conditional Effects of Financial Slack and Ownership Concentration. *International Journal of Innovation Management*, 1022–1040.

Alchian, A., & Demsetz, H. (1972). Production, Information Costs and Economic Organization. American Economic Review, 62(5), 777-795.

Alimi, O., & Victor, T. (2019). L'actionnariat Salarié Et La Création De Valeur Partenariale. Dans Les Entreprises Au Cameroun. European Scientific Journal, 15(34), 250.

Alim, O. (2019). Employee ownership in companies in Cameroon. *Journal of Participation and Employee Ownership.*, *2*(2), 93–114. doi:10.1108/JPEO-05-2019-0012

Allouche, J., & Amann, B. (2000). L'entreprise familiale, un état de l'art. *Finance Contrôle Stratégie*, *3*(1), 33–79.

Amami, I., & Maalej, R. (2015). Actionnariat salarié et innovation: conception et interaction. *International Journal Economics & Strategic Management of Business Process,* 5, 43-47.

Anderson, J. C., & Gerbing, D. W. (1988). Structural equation modeling in practice: A review and recommended two-step approach. *Psychological Bulletin, 103*(3), 411–423. doi:10.1037/0033-2909.103.3.411

Anderson, R., Duru, A., & Reeb, D. (2009). Founders, heirs, and corporate opacity in the United States. *Journal of Financial Economics, 92*(2), 205–222. doi:10.1016/j.jfineco.2008.04.006

Anderson, R., & Reeb, D. (2003). Founding-family ownership and firm per-formance. *The Journal of Finance, 58*(3), 1301–1328. doi:10.1111/1540-6261.00567

Anderson, R., Reeb, D., & Zhao, W. (2012). Family-controlled firms and informedtrading: Evidence from short sales. *The Journal of Finance, 67*(1), 351–385. doi:10.1111/j.1540-6261.2011.01714.x

Appiah-Kubi, K. (2001). State-Owned Enterprises and Privatisation in Ghana. *The Journal of Modern African Studies*, 197–229.

Arrègle, J.-L., & Mari, I. (2010). Avantages ou désavantages des entreprises familiales? Principaux résultats des recherches et perspectives. *Revue Française de Gestion, 1*(200), 87–109. doi:10.3166/rfg.200.87-109

Astrachan, J. (2010). Strategy in family business: Toward a multidimen-sional research agenda. *Journal of Family Business Strategy, 1*(1), 6–14. doi:10.1016/j.jfbs.2010.02.001

Astrachan, J., & McConaughy, D. (2001). Venture capitalists and closelyheld IPOs: Lessons for family-controlled firms. *Family Business Review, 14*(4), 295–311. doi:10.1111/j.1741-6248.2001.00295.x

Aubert, N., & Cordova, M. (2020). Sharing the risk at expense of power: Paying wages in equity to face the COVID-19. *Notas Académicas*. https://repositorio.pucp.edu.pe/index/handle/123456789/173261

Aubert, N., & Cordova, M. (2021). How society's constraints would undermine ESPP adaption in Latin America: The Case of Peru. In R. Zuloaga & G. Hernandez (Eds.), ESO in the Americas. Academic Press.

Aubert, N., Chassagnon, V., & Hollandts, X. (2016). Actionnariat salarié, gouvernance et performance de la firme. *Revue d'économie industrielle, 154*(2), 151-176.

Aubert, N. (2009). *L'actionnariat salarié: Devenir actionnaire salarié. Aumage édition 2009.* F.A.S.

Aubert, N., Ben Ameur, H., Garnotel, G., & Prigent, J. L. (2018). Optimal Employee Ownership Contracts under Ambiguity Aversion. *Economic Inquiry, 56*(1), 238–251. doi:10.1111/ecin.12478

Aubert, N., Garnotel, G., Lapied, A., & Rousseau, P. (2014). Employee Ownership: A Theoretical and Empirical Investigation of Management Entrenchment vs. Reward Management. *Economic Modelling, 40,* 423–434. doi:10.1016/j.econmod.2013.12.011

Aubert, N., Grand, B., Lapied, A., & Rousseau, P. (2009). Is employee ownership so senseless. *Finance, 30*(2), 5–29. doi:10.3917/fina.302.0005

Aubert, N., Kern, A., & Hollandts, X. (2017). Employee stock ownership and the cost of capital. *Research in International Business and Finance*, 67–78.

Aubert, N., & Rapp, T. (2008). Les Salariés Actionnaires: Pourquoi Investissent-ils dans leur Entreprise? Finance Contrôle Stratégie. *Association FCS, 11*(4), 87–110.

Autenne, A. (2005). Quelle gouvernance des plans d'actionnariat employee ownership larié? *Revue internationale de droit économique, 1.*

Autenne, A. (2005). *Analyse économique du droit de l'actionnariat salarié, Bibliothèque de la Faculté de Droit de l'Université Catholique de Louvain.* Bruylant.

Ayugi, C., & Wanaju, E. U. (2018). *MMAN Advocates Website.* Retrieved from Creating a Bigger Pie or Golden Handcuffs? Employee Share Ownership Plans in Kenya: https://mman.co.ke/content/creating-bigger-pie-or-golden-handcuffs-employee-share-ownership-plans-kenya

Ayyagar, K. C. (2021). In the Human Resource Management and Compansation Strategies adopted adopted across IT and ITES Industries due to COVID-19 in India. *KC Ayyagar - International Journal of Modern Agriculture*, 1472 - 1482.

Azzouzi, B., & Haoudi, A. (2020). Actionnariat familial et performance financière: le cas Marocain. *Revue Du contrôle, De La Comptabilité Et De l'audit, 4*(2).

Azzouzi, B., & Haoudi, A. (2020). Actionnariat familial et performance financière: le cas Marocain. *Revue du contrôle, de la comptabilité et de l'audit, 4.*

Basterretxea, I., Heras-Saizarbitoria, I., & Lertxundi, A. (2019). Can employee ownership and human resource management policies clash in worker cooperatives? Lessons from a defunct cooperative. *Human Resource Management*, 585-601.

Basterretxea, I., & Storey, J. (2018). Do Employee-Owned Firms Produce More Positive Employee Behavioural Outcomes? If Not Why Not? A British-Spanish Comparative Analysis. *British Journal of Industrial Relations*, 292–319.

Basterretxea, I., & Storey, J. (2018). Do employee-owned firms produce more positive employee behavioural outcomes? If not why not? A British-Spanish comparative analysis. *British Journal of Industrial Relations, 56*(2), 292–319. doi:10.1111/bjir.12247

Bazerman, M. (1984). The relevance of Kahneman and Tversky's conceptof framing to organizational behavior. *Journal of Management, 10*(3), 333–343. doi:10.1177/014920638401000307

Bearden, W. (1993). Handbook of marketing scales: multi item measures for marketing and consumer behaviour research. Academic Press.

BEE Empowered. (2021). *The elements of the BEE Scorecard.* Retrieved from Bee Empowered Website: https://bempowered.net/information/the-elements-of-the-bee-scorecard/

Benartzi, S., Thaler, R. H., Utkus, S. P., & Sunstein, C. R. (2007). The law and economics of company stock in 401 (k) plans. *The Journal of Law & Economics*, *50*(1), 45–79. doi:10.1086/508312

Ben-Ner, A., & Jones, D. C. (1995). Employee Participation, Ownership, and Productivity: A Theoretical Framework. *Industrial Relations*, *34*(4), 532–554. doi:10.1111/j.1468-232X.1995.tb00387.x

Berrone, P., Cruz, C., & Gomez-Mejia, L. (2012). Socioemotional wealth infamily firms: Theoretical dimensions, assessment approaches, andagenda for future research. *Family Business Review*, *25*(3), 258–279. doi:10.1177/0894486511435355

Bhattacheryay, S. (2020). Multinational enterprises motivational factors in capitalizing emerging market opportunities and preparedness of India. *Journal of Financial Economic Policy*, 609-640.

Biswas, D., & Dey, C. (2021). *Entrepreneurship Development in India*. Routledge.

Blair, M. (1999). Firm-Specific Human Capital and Theories of the Firm. In Employees & Corporate Governance. Brooking Institution Press.

Blair, M., Kruse, D., & Blasi, J. (2000). Employee ownership: An unstableform or stabilizing force? In M. Blair & T. Kochan (Eds.), *The newrelationship: Human capital in the American corporation* (pp. 241–298). Brookings Institution. doi:10.2139srn.142146

Blasi, J. R., Conte, M., & Kruse, D. L. (1996). Employee stock ownership and corporate performance among public companies. *Industrial & Labor Relations Review*, *50*(1), 60–79. doi:10.1177/001979399605000104

Blasi, J. R., Freeman, R. B., & Kruse, D. L. (2013). *The citizen's share: Putting ownership back into democracy*. Yale University Press.

Blasi, J., Freeman, R., & Kruse, D. (2016). Do Broadbased Employee Ownership, Profit Sharing and Stock Options Help the Best Firms Do Even Better? *British Journal of Industrial Relations*, 55–82.

Blasi, J., & Kruse, D. (2019). *Building the Assets of Low and Moderate Income Workers and Their Families: The Role of Employee Ownership*. Institute for the Study of Employee Ownership and Profit Sharing, Rutgers University.

Block, J. (2012). R&D investments in family and founder firms: An agency perspective. *Journal of Business Venturing*, *27*(2), 248–265. doi:10.1016/j.jbusvent.2010.09.003

Bloom, S. (1986). *Employee Ownership and Firm Performance*. Harvard University Press.

Bogićević-Milikić, B., & Došenović, D. (2020). Moderators of the relationship between intrinsic rewards and job satisfaction: The evidence from the Republic of Srpska. *Sociologija*, 416–437.

Borstadt, L., & Zwirlein, T. (1995). ESOPs in Publicly Held Companies: Evidence on Productivity and Firm Performance. *Journal of Financial and Strategic Decision Making*, *8*(1), 1–13.

Bradley, K., Estrin, S., & Taylor, S. (1990). Employee Ownership and Company Performance. *Industrial Relations*, 385–402.

Brown, S., Fakhfakh, F., & Sessions, J. G. (1999). Absenteeism and Employee Sharing: An Empirical Analysis Based On French Panel Data, 1981-1991. *Industrial & Labor Relations Review*, *52*(2), 234–251.

Bryson, A., Clark, A., Freeman, R., & Green, C. (2016). Share Capitalism and Worker Wellbeing. *Labour Economics*, 151–158.

Buchko, A. (1992). Employee Ownership, Attitudes and Turnover: An Empirical Assessment. *Human Relations*, *45*(7), 711–733. doi:10.1177/001872679204500704

Buchko, A. (1993). The effects of employee ownership on employee attitudes: An integrated cauemployee ownership l model and path analysis. *Journal of Management Studies*, *30*, 633–657. doi:10.1111/j.1467-6486.1993.tb00319.x

Budjanovcanin, A. (2018). Actions speak louder than words: How employees mind the implementation gap. *International Journal of Human Resource Management*, *29*(22), 3136–3155. doi:10.1080/09585192.2018.1443959

Burke, E. (2021). *5 European countries with better stock options than the US*. Retrieved from https://www.siliconrepublic.com/start-ups/stock-options-europe-latvia-lithuania-estonia-france-uk

Burris, V. (2005). Interlocking Directorates and Political Cohesion among Corporate Elites. *American Journal of Sociology*, *111*(1), 249–283. doi:10.1086/428817

Caby, J., & Hirigoyen, G. (2001). *La création de valeur actionnariale*. Academic Press.

Cammann, C., Fichman, M., Jenkins, G. D., & Klesh, J. R. (1983). Assessing the attitudes and per-ceptions of organizational members. In S. E. Seashore, E. E. Lawler, P. H. Mirvis, & C. Cammann (Eds.), *Assessing organizational change: A guide to methods, measures, and practices* (pp. 71–138). John Wiley & Sons.

Caramelli, M. (2006). *Une étude des effets de l'actionnariat employee ownership larie dans le contexte de l'entreprise multinationale: une approche attitudinale interculturelle* (Doctorat en sciences de gestion). Montpellier: Université Montpellier II sciences et Techniques.

Carberry, E. (2011). Employee ownership and shared capitalism: Assessingthe experience, research, and policy implications. In E. Carberry (Ed.), *Employee ownership and shared capitalism: New directions in research*. Labor and Employment Relations Association Series.

Cardoni, H. (2020). Contribution à la connaissance de l'impact de l'actionnariat salarié sur la gouvernance des entreprises. *Entreprise et société*, 147-176.

Chandra, V. (2021). *Work-Life Balance in India: Policy, Practices and the Road Ahead -Work-Life Interface: Non-Western Perspectives*. Springer Nature.

Chang, S. (1990). Employee stock ownership plans and shareholder wealth: An empirical Investigation. *Financial Management, 19*(1), 48–58. doi:10.2307/3666036

Chang, S., & Mayers, D. (1992). Managerial Vote Ownership and Shareholder Wealth: Evidence from Employee Stock Ownership Plans. *Journal of Financial Economics, 32*(1), 103–131. doi:10.1016/0304-405X(92)90027-U

Chaplinsky, S., & Niehaus, G. (1994, September). The Role of ESOPs in Takeover Contests. *The Journal of Finance, XLIX*(4), 1451–1470. doi:10.1111/j.1540-6261.1994.tb02461.x

Charreaux, G. (1997). Vers une théorie du gouvernement des entreprises. In Le Gouvernement des Entreprises. Economica.

Charreaux, G. (2002). L'actionnaire comme apporteur de ressources cognitives. *Revue française de gestion*, (5), 77-107.

Charreaux, G. (2011). *Quelle théorie pour la gouvernance? De la gouvernance actionnariale à la gouvernance cognitive et comportementale*. Working Papers CREGO, n°1110402.

Charreaux, G. (2012). Le gouvernement d'entreprise. In J. Allouche (Coord.), Encyclopédie des ressources Humaines. Théories, instruments, méthodes, auteurs. Paris: Vuibert.

Charreaux, G., & Wirtz, P. (2007). *Discipline ou compétence? L'apport des perspectives cognitive et comportementale à la compréhension des mécanismes de gouvernance*. Document halshs-00260119.

Charreaux, G. (1997). *Le gouvernement des Entreprises: Corporate Governance. Théories et Faits*. Economica.

Charreaux, G. (1998). *La théorie positive de l'agence: lecture et relectures*. IAE DIJON -CREGO / LATEC.

Charreaux, G. (2000). La théorie positive de l'agence: Positionnement et apports. *Revue d'Economie Industrielle, 92*(1), 193–214. doi:10.3406/rei.2000.1046

Charreaux, G. (2008). À la recherche du lien perdu entre caractéristiques des dirigeants et performance de la firme: Gouvernance et latitude managériale. *Économies et sociétés, 42*(10), 1831–1867.

Charreaux, G., & Desbrières, P. (1997). *Le point sur le gouvernement des entreprises*. Revue Banque & Marchés.

Chua, J., Chrisman, J., & Sharma, P. (1999). Defining the family businessby behavior. *Entrepreneurship Theory and Practice, 23*(4), 19–40. doi:10.1177/104225879902300402

Churchill, G. A. Jr. (1979). A paradigm for developing better measures of marketing constructs. *JMR, Journal of Marketing Research, 16*(1), 64–73. doi:10.1177/002224377901600110

Code Marocain des bonnes pratiques de gouvernance, 2008.

Coff, R., & Raffiee, J. (2015). Toward a Theory of Perceived Firm-Specific Human Capital. Academy of Management Perspectives, 29(3), 326–341. doi:10.5465/amp.2014.0112

Conte, M. A., & Svejnar, J. (1988). Productivity Effects of Worker Participation in Management, Profit-Sharing. Worker Ownership of Assets and Unionization in U.S Firms. *International Journal of Industrial Organization*, *6*(1), 139–151. doi:10.1016/0167-7187(88)90011-2

Conte, M., & Tannenbaum, A. S. (1978). Employee-owned companies: Is the difference measurable. *Monthly Labor Review*, *101*, 23.

Cordova, M. (2018). The evolution of interlocking directorates studies – A global trend perspective. *AD-Minister*, *33*, 135–165. doi:10.17230/ad-minister.33.7

CordovaM. (2019). "That is OK, he is a good fellow": introducing the outcomes dichotomy for corporate networks of interlocking directorates. *RAN - Revista Academia & Negocios*, *5*(1), 123-134. Retrieved from https://ssrn.com/abstract=3432045

Couret, A., & Hirigoyen, G. (1990). *L'actionnariat des salariés*. PUF.

Degbey, W. Y., Rodgers, P., Kromah, M. D., & Weber, Y. (2020). The impact of psychological ownership on employee retention in mergers and acquisitions. *Human Resource Management Review*, *31*(3), 100745. doi:10.1016/j.hrmr.2020.100745

Derksen, R. (2020). *Employee share ownership and firm performance: The mediation effect of employee turnover*. Radboud University.

Desbrières, P. (1997). Le rôle de l'actionnariat des salariés non-dirigeants dans le système de gouvernement de l'entreprise. Le gouvernement des entreprises. Economica.

Desbrières, P. (2000). *La rémunération des dirigeants sous forme d'actions et de stockoptions*. WorkingPapers CREGO 1001102. Université de Bourgogne - CREGO EA7317 Centre de recherches en gestion des organisations.

Desbrières, Ph. (1997a), Le rôle de l'actionnariat des salariés non-dirigeants dans le système de gouvernement de l'entreprise. In Recherche en Gestion. Economica.

Desbrières, Ph. (2002). Les Actionnaires – Salariés. *Revue Française De Gestion, 141*.

Desbrières, P. (1997). Le rôle de lactionnariat des employee ownership lariés non-dirigeants dans le système de gouvernement de l'entreprise. In G. Charreaux (Ed.), *Le gouvernement des entreprises: Corporate Governance, theories et faits*. Economica.

Desbrières, P. (2002). Les actionnaires employee ownership lariés. *Revue Française de Gestion*, *141*, 255–281.

Desbrières, Ph. (1997). *« La participation financière des salariés et ses incidences sur la performance et l'organisation interne de l'entreprise » dans Le gouvernement des entreprises* (G. Charreaux, Ed.). Economica.

Desbrières, Ph. (2002, November-December). Les actionnaires salariés. *Revue Française de Gestion*, *28*(141), 225–281.

Dhar, S., & De, S. (2009). ESOP Accounting in India: Measurement and Disclosure issues. *Journal of Business and Economic Issues*, 45-61.

Dhillon, U. S., & Ramírez, G. G. (1994). Employee stock ownership and corporate control: An empirical study. *Journal of Banking & Finance*, 9–25.

DiMaggio, P. J., & Powell, W. W. (1983). The iron cage revisited: Institutional isomorphism and collective rationality in organizational fields. *American Sociological Review*, *48*(2), 147–160. doi:10.2307/2095101

Dionne-Proulx, J., & Larochelle, G. (2010). Éthique et gouvernance d'entreprise. Management et Avenir, 2(32), 36-53.

Dondi, J. (1992). *Contribution à la connaissance de l'actionnariat des salariés dans les entreprises françaises* (Doctoral dissertation). Bordeaux 1.

Dondi, J. (1992). *Contribution à la connaissance de l'actionnariat salarié dans les entreprises françaises* (Thèse de doctorat en Sciences de Gestion). Université Bordeaux 1.

Dondi, J. (1993). *L'Actionnariat des Employee ownership lariés dans les Entreprises Françaises: Résultats Empiriques. Travaux de Recherche n° I.9302*. IAE de Bordeaux.

Dondi, J. (1994). L'actionnariat des employee ownership laries dans les entreprises françaises: L'identification de son rôle à laide de résultats empiriques. *Personnel*, *347*, 56–64.

Durand, F. (2018). *Odebrecht: La empresa que capturaba gobiernos*. Fondo Editorial PUCP.

Durand, F. (2019). *La Captura del Estado en América Latina: Reflexiones Teóricas*. Fondo Editorial PUCP.

Economic Survey of Employee Share Ownership. (2020). *New progression in Europe*. European Federation of Employee Share Ownership.

Eisenhardt, K. (1989). Agency Theory. An Assessment and Review. *Academy of Management Review*, *14*(1), 57–74. doi:10.5465/amr.1989.4279003

Elouadi & Ben Noamene. (2017). Does Employee Ownership Reduce the Intention to Leave? In *Handbook of Research on Human Resources Strategies for the New Millennial Workforce*. IGI Global.

Elouadi S., (2015). Les effets attitudinaux de l'actionnariat salarié: une étude empirique dans le contexte des entreprises françaises du SBF 250. *Question (s) de Management*, (3), 11-24.

Elouadi, S. (2015). Les effets attitudinaux de l'actionnariat employee ownership larié: une étude empirique dans le contexte des entreprises françaises du SBF 250. *Question (s) de Management*, (3), 11-24.

Elouadi, S. (2015). Les effets attitudinaux de l'actionnariat salarié: une étude empirique dans le contexte des entreprises françaises du SBF 250. *Question (s) de Management*, (3), 11-24.

Elouadi, S. (2020). L'influence des variables incitatives sur la employee ownership tisfaction des actionnaires employee ownership lariés: une modéliemployee ownership tion par équations structurelles. *Question (s) de Management*, (2), 35-49.

Elouadi, S. (2020). L'influence des variables incitatives sur la satisfaction des actionnaires salariés: une modélisation par équations structurelles. *Question(s) de Management, 2*(2), 35-49. doi:10.3917/qdm.202.0035

Elouadi, S., & Er rommani, H. (2021). Analyse des effets de l'actionnariat salarié sur la création de la valeur financière des entreprises marocaines cotées en bourse. *Revue du contrôle de la comptabilité et de l'audit, 5*(1), 65-88.

Elouadi, S., Noamene, T. B., & Chaher, D. (2016). Employee Ownership And Employee-Shareholders Satisfaction: An Analysis Of French Companies Listed On The SBF 250. *Journal of Applied Business Research, 32*(3), 981–994. doi:10.19030/jabr.v32i3.9647

Enquête sur les pratiques de gouvernance des sociétés cotées -Version 2015- INSTITUT MAROCAIN DES ADMINISTRATEURS.pdf.

Erdal, D. (2014). Employee Ownership and Health: An Initial Study. In S. Novkovic & T. Webb (Eds.), *Co-Operatives in a Post-Growth Era: Creating Co-Operative Economics* (pp. 210–220). Zed Books.

ESMAP. (2003). *Ghana: Corporatization of Distribution Concessions through Capitalization.* ESMAP-Energy Sector Management Assistance Program.

Eurofound. (2020). *How does employee involvement in decision-making benefit organisations?* European Working Conditions Survey 2015 series, Publications Office of the European Union.

European Federation of Employee Share Ownership. (n.d.). *Employee share ownership against the crisis: An employee share ownership fund to help companies.* http://www.efesonline.org/CORONA/Proposal%20-%20An%20employee%20share%20ownership%20found%20to%20help%20companies.pdf

Faccio, M., & Lang, L. H. (2002). The ultimate ownership of Western European corporations. *Journal of Financial Economics*, 365–395.

Faleye, O., Mehrotra, V., & Morck, R. (2006). When Labor Has A Voice In Corporate Governance. *Journal of Financial and Quantitative Analysis, 41*(3), 489–510.

Faleye, O., Mehrotra, V., & Morck, R. (2006). When Labor Has a Voice in Corporate Governance. *Journal of Financial and Quantitative Analysis, 41*(3), 489–510. doi:10.1017/S0022109000002519

FAS Fédération Française des Actionnaires Salariés et Anciens Salariés. (2006). *Guide de l'actionnaire salarié* (6th ed.). Author.

Fitzroy, F. R., & Nolan, M. A. (2020). *Towards Economic Democracy and Social Justice: Profit Sharing, Co-Determination, and Employee Ownership.* IZA Discussion Paper No. 13238, 15-30.

FitzRoy, F. R., & Kraft, K. (1987). Cooperation, productivity, and profit sharing. *The Quarterly Journal of Economics, 102*(1), 23–35. doi:10.2307/1884678

Freeman, R. B., Kruse, D. L., & Blasi, J. R. (2010). Worker Responses to Shirking under Shared Capitalism. *Shared Capitalism at Work: Employee Ownership, Profit and Gain Sharing, and Broad-Based Stock Options*, 77.

Freeman, R. B., & Lazear, E. P. (1995). An economic analysis of works councils. In J. Rogers & W. Streeck (Eds.), *Works councils: Consultation, representation, and cooperation in industrial relations* (pp. 27–52). University of Chicago Press.

French, J. L., & Rosenstein, J. (1984). Employee ownership, work attitudes, and power relationships. *Academy of Management Journal, 27*(4), 861–869.

Frohlich, F., Godard, J., Oppenheimer, J. A., & Starke, F. A. (1998). Employee versus conventionally-owned and controlled firms: An experimental analysis. *Managerial and Decision Economics, 19*(4-5), 311–326. doi:10.1002/(SICI)1099-1468(199806/08)19:4/5<311::AID-MDE893>3.0.CO;2-I

Gamble, J. E. (2000). Management Commitment to Innovation and ESOP Stock Concentration. *Journal of Business Venturing, 15*(5–6), 433–447. doi:10.1016/S0883-9026(99)00037-3

Gamble, J. E. (2000). Management commitment to innovation and esop stock concentration. *Journal of Business Venturing*, 433–447.

Gamble, J., Culpepper, R., & Blubaugh, M. (2002). ESOPs and Employee Attitudes: The Importance of Empowerment and Financial Value. *Personnel Review, 31*(1), 9–26. doi:10.1108/00483480210412391

Garfatta Riadh. (2010). *Actionnariat salarié et création de valeur dans le cadre d'une gouvernance actionnariale et partenariale: application au contexte français* (Thèse de doctorat en science de gestion). Université de Bourgogne.

Garfatta, R. (2010). *Actionnariat employee ownership larié et création de valeur dans le cadre d'une gouvernance actionnariale et partenariale: application au contexte français* (Doctorat en sciences de gestion). Bourgogne: Université de Bourgogne.

Garfatta, R. (2010). *Actionnariat salarié et création de la valeur dans le cadre de la gouvernance actionnariale et partenariale: application au contexte f*rancais (Thèse de Doctorat soutenue). l'université de Bourgogne.

Garfatta, R. (2010). *Actionnariat salarié et création de valeur dans le cadre d'une gouvernance actionnariale et partenariale: application au contexte française*. Academic Press.

Ghana Stock Exchange. (2020). *MTN Ghana Limited (MTNGH) - Notice of Virtual Extraordinary General Meeting of Shareholders*. MTN Ghana.

Ginglinger, E., Megginson, W., & Waxin, T. (2011). Employee Ownership, Board Representation, and Corporate Financial Policies. *Journal of Corporate Finance*, *17*(4), 868–887. doi:10.1016/j.jcorpfin.2011.03.005

Gomez-Mejia, L., Haynes, K., Nunez-Nickel, M., Jacobson, K., & Moyano-Fuentes, J. (2007). Socioemotional wealth and business risks in family-controlled firms: Evidence from Spanish olive oil mills. *Administrative Science Quarterly*, *52*(1), 106–137. doi:10.2189/asqu.52.1.106

Gomez, P.-Y., & Hollandts, X. (2015). La représentation des salariés au conseil d'administration. *Revue de Droit du Travail*, (7/8), 451–457.

Gonzalez-Perez, M. A., Cordova, M., Hermans, M., Nava-Aguirre, K. M., Monje-Cueto, F., Mingo, S., Tobon, S., Rodriguez, C., Salvaj, E., & Floriani, D. (2021). Crises conducting stakeholder salience: Shifts in the evolution of private universities' governance in Latin America. *Corporate Governance*, *21*(6), 1194–1214. Advance online publication. doi:10.1108/CG-09-2020-0397

Gonza, T., & Ellerman, D. P. (2020). *Turning Platform Workers into Owners: ESOP-Type Buyouts for the Labor-Based Platforms*. University of Ljubljana.

Gordon, L. A., & Pound, J. (1990). ESOPs and corporate control. *Journal of Financial Economics*, 525–555.

Gordon, L., & Pound, J. (1990). ESOPs and Corporate Control. *Journal of Financial Economics*, *27*(2), 525–555. doi:10.1016/0304-405X(90)90066-9

Guedri, Z., & Hollandts, X. (2008). Beyond dichotomy: The curvilinear impact of employee ownership on firm performance. *Corporate Governance*, *16*(5), 460–474. doi:10.1111/j.1467-8683.2008.00703.x

Guery, L. (2018). L'actionnariat salarié: une autre conception de la place des salariés dans l'entreprise? Rémunération du travail.

Guery, L., & Stevenot, A. (2014). Le lien entre l'actionnariat salarié et le climat social à l'épreuve des faits: le cas des entreprises françaises non cotées. *Revue française de gouvernance d'entreprise, 14*, 101-120.

Guery, L., & Stevenot, A. (2017). L'actionnariat salarié favorise-t-il la diffusion d'information aux salariés et leur participation aux décisions stratégiques? Une question de gouvernance d'entreprise. Revue management international, 21(4), 61-75.

Guery, L., & Stevenot, A. (2017). L'actionnariat salarié favorise-t-il la diffusion d'information aux salariés et leur participation aux décisions stratégiques? Une question de gouvernance d'entreprise. *Revue Management International, 21*(4), 61–75.

Gupta, P., & Mittal, P. (2020). Corporate Governance and Risk Bundling: Evidence from Indian Compannies. *European Journal of Science & Technology*, 37-52.

Hair, J. F. (2006). *Multivariate Data Analysis*. Auflage.

Hallock, D. (2003). A Research Model to Investigate the Organiemployee ownership tional Impact of an ESOP. *The International Journal of Sociology and Social Policy*, *12*(23), 47–63. doi:10.1108/01443330310790390

Hallock, D. E., Salazar, R. J., & Venneman, S. (2004). Demographic and Attitudinal Correlates of Employee Satisfaction with an ESOP. *British Journal of Management*, 78–99.

Hammer, T. H., & Stern, R. N. (1980, March). Employee Ownership: Implications for the organisational distribution of power. *Academy of Management Journal*, *23*(1), 78–100.

Hansmann, H. (1996). *The Ownership of Enterprise*. Belknap Press of Harvard University Press.

Hansmann, H. (1996). *The ownership of enterprise*. Harvard University Press.

Haw, I., Hu, B., Wu, D., & Zhang, X. (2018). Having a Finger in the Pie: Labor Power and Corporate Payout Policy. *Financial Management*, *47*(4), 993–1027. doi:10.1111/fima.12211

Hewitt Associates. (2002, Mar. 25). L'actionnariat salarié divise les entreprises patrimoniales. *La Tribune*.

Hieu, T. P. (2020). Effectiveness of policy measures to promote employee share ownership programs in banks. *Université de Limoges*, 100-125.

Hieu, P. H. (2018). *The determinants of employee stock ownership plans (ESOPs)*. Université de Limoges.

Higgins, R. C. (1977). How Much Growth Can a Firm Afford? *Financial Management*, 7–16.

Hill, C. W. L., & Jones, T. M. (1992). Stakeholder-agency theory. *Journal of Management Studies*, *29*(2), 131–154. doi:10.1111/j.1467-6486.1992.tb00657.x

Hinkin, T. R. (1995). A review of scale development practices in the study of organizations. *Journal of Management*, *21*(5), 967–988. doi:10.1177/014920639502100509

Hirigoyen, G. (1997). *Salariés-actionnaires: le capital sans le pouvoir?* Pouvoir et Gestion.

Hoehn-Velasco, L., Silverio-Murillo, A., & Balmori de la Miyar, J. R. (2021). The long downturn: The impact of the great lockdown on formal employment. *Journal of Economics and Business*, *115*, 105983. Advance online publication. doi:10.1016/j.jeconbus.2021.105983

Holgersen, H., Jia, Z., & Svenkerud, S. (2021). Who and how many can work from home? Evidence from task descriptions. *Journal for Labour Market Research*, *55*(1), 4. Advance online publication. doi:10.118612651-021-00287-z PMID:33681696

Hollandts, X. & Guedri, Z. (2008). Les salariés capitalistes et la performance de l'entreprise. *Revue Française de Gestion, 183*(3), 35-50.

Hollandts, X. (2007). *Les effets de participation des employee ownership lariés sur la performance de l'entreprise*. Doctorat en sciences de gestion.

Hollandts, X., & Guedri, Z. (2008). Les salariés capitalistes et la performance de l'entreprise. *Revue Française de Gestion*, *34*(183), 35–50. doi:10.3166/rfg.183.35-50

Imane & Djaoudath. (2019). Does employee share ownership influence the level of remuneration of executives of French listed companies ? Empirical study of the SBF 120 Stock Market Index. *Finance, Contrôle, Stratégie, 22*(2-3).

Industrial Development Corporation. (2021). *Broad-based Black Economic Empowerment (BBBEE)*. Industrial Development Corporation.

IndustriALL Global Union. (2009). *ESOP Accord reached Between Ghana Mineworkers and AngloGold, Averting Industrial Actions*. Retrieved from IndustriALL Global Union Web Site: http://www.industriall-union.org/

IRS. (2021a). *Employee Stock Ownership Plans (ESOPs)*. Retrieved from Internal Revenue Service-Government: https://www.irs.gov/retirement-plans/employee-stock-ownership-plans-esops

IRS. (2021b). *Stocks (Options, Splits, Traders)*. Retrieved from IRS Web site: https://www.irs.gov/faqs/capital-gains-losses-and-sale-of-home/stocks-options-splits-traders

Jan, D., & Fabo, B. (2016). The Platform Economy and the Disruption of the Employment Relationship. *Social Science Research Network*, 35-53.

Jay, W. (2016). Civil Society's Role in a Public Health Crisis. *Issues in Science and Technology*, *32*(4), 43–48.

Jensen, M. C., & Et Meckling, W. H. (1976). Theory of The Firm: Managerial Behavior, Agency Costs and Ownership Structure. *Journal of Financial Economics*, *3*(10), 305–360. doi:10.1016/0304-405X(76)90026-X

Jensen, M., & Meckling, W. (1979). Rights and Production Functions: An Application to Labor-Managed Firms and Codetermination. *The Journal of Business*, *52*(4), 469–506. doi:10.1086/296060

Jessri, M., Kosmidou, V., & Ahuja, M. K. (2020). Employees' decision to participate in corporate venturing: A conjoint experiment of financial and non-financial motivations. *Journal of Business Venturing Insights*, *13*, e00161. doi:10.1016/j.jbvi.2020.e00161

Johnson, R. E., Pratt, R. T., & Stewart, S. S. (1982). The Economic Consequences of ESOPs. *Journal of Financial Research*, 75–83.

Jones, D. C., & Kato, T. (1993). The scope, nature, and effects of employee stock ownership plans in Japan. *Industrial & Labor Relations Review*, *46*(2), 352–367. doi:10.1177/001979399304600209

Jones, D. C., & Kato, T. (1995). The productivity effects of employee stock ownership plans and bonuses: Evidence from Japanese panel data. *The American Economic Review*, *3*, 391–414.

Jones, D. C., & Kato, T. (1995). The Productivity Effects of Employee Stock-Ownership Plans and Bonuses: Evidence from Japanese Panel Data. *The American Economic Review*, *85*(3), 391–414.

Kaarsemaker, E. C., & Poutsma, E. (2006). The fit of employee ownership with other human resource management practices: Theoretical and empirical suggestions regarding the existence of an ownership high-performance work system. *Economic and Industrial Democracy*, 669–685.

Kaarsemaker, E., Pendleton, A., & Poutsma, E. (2010). Employee Shareownership. In A. Wilkinson, M. Marchington, P. Gollan, & D. Lewin (Eds.), *Oxford Handbook of Participation in Organisations*. Oxford University Press.

Kaplan, J., & Ludwig, R. (1985). *ESOP*. Tax Management.

Katoch, R. (2017). Accounting Mechanism of Employee Stock Options in India: A Case Study of Wipro Limited, an IT Service Provider Company in India. *International Journal of Management, IT & Engineering*, 433-553.

Kenyan Wall Street. (2016). *CMA Approves ARM Cement to give employees 21Million shares via ESOP*. Hisa Technologies Ltd.

Kim, E.H., & Ouimet, P. (2014). Broad-Based Employee Stock Ownership: Motives and Outcomes. *Journal of Finance, 69*(3), 1273-1319.

Kim, A., & Han, K. (2019). All for one and one for all: A mechanism through which broad-based employee stock ownership and employee-perceived involvement practice create a productive workforce. *Human Resource Management*, 571–584.

Kim, E. H., & Ouimet, P. (2014). Broad-Based Employee Stock Ownership: Motives and Outcomes. *The Journal of Finance*, 1273–1319.

Kim, E., & Ouimet, P. (2014). Broad-based employee stock ownership: Motives and outcomes. *The Journal of Finance*, *69*(3), 1273–1319. doi:10.1111/jofi.12150

Kim, K. Y., & Patel, P. C. (2020). A multilevel contingency model of employee ownership and firm productivity: The moderating roles of industry growth and instability. *Organization Science*, 1–25.

Klein, K. (1987). Employee Stock Ownership and Employee Attitudes: A Test of Three Models. *The Journal of Applied Psychology*, *72*(2), 319–332. doi:10.1037/0021-9010.72.2.319 PMID:3583982

Kolitz, D. (2020). *Why Don't Workers Get Paid in Equity Like CEOs Do?* Giz Asks. Retrieved from https://gizmodo.com/why-don-t-regular-workers-get-paid-in-equity-like-ceos-1843749588

Kovac, J., & Gaudemet-Toulemonde, L. G. (2020). Epargne salariale et actionnaire salarié. Frencis Lefebvre.

Kramer, B. (2010). Employee ownership and participation effects on out-comes in firms majority employee-owned through employee stockownership plans in the US. *Economic and Industrial Democracy*, *31*(4), 449–476. doi:10.1177/0143831X10365574

Kruse, D. (2010). Shared Capitalism at Work: Employee Ownership, Profit and Gain Sharing, and Broad-Based Stock Options. University of Chicago Press. doi:10.7208/chicago/9780226056968.001.0001

Kruse, D. L., Blasi, J., Weltmann, D., Kang, S., Kim, J. O., & Castellano, W. (2019). *Do Employee Share Owners Face Too Much Financial Risk?* IZA Discussion Paper No. 12303.

Kruse, D., Freeman, R., & Blasi, J. (2010). Shared Capitalism at Work: Employee Ownership, Profit and Gain Sharing, and Broad-based Stock Options. National Bureau of Economic Research, 257-289.

Kruse, D. (1984). *Employee ownership and employee attitudes: Two case studies*. Norwood Editions.

Kruse, D., & Blasi, J. R. (1997). Employee ownership, employee attitudes and firm performance: a review of the evidence. In B. Mitchell, D. Lewin, & M. Zaidi (Eds.), *Handbook of Human Resource Management*. JAI Press.

Kumbhakar, S. C., & Dunbar, A. E. (1993). The elusive ESOP—Productivity link: Evidence from US firm-level data. *Journal of Public Economics*, *52*(2), 273–283. doi:10.1016/0047-2727(93)90024-N

Kurtulus, F. A., & Kruse, D. L. (2017). *How Did Employee Ownership Firms Weather the Last Two Recessions?: Employee Ownership, Employment Stability, and Firm Survival: 1999-2011*. WE Upjohn Institute.

Kuvaas, B. (2003). Employee ownership and affective organizational commitment: Employees' perceptions of fairness and their preference for company shares over cash. *Scandinavian Journal of Management*, 193–212.

Lamberg, J.-A., Savage, G. T., & Pajunen, K. (2003). Strategic stakeholder perspective to ESOP negotiations: The case of United Airlines. *Management Decision*, 383–393.

Lampel, J., Bhalla, A., & Jha, P. P. (2012). The Employee Owned Business Model During Growth and Adversity: How Well Does it Hold Up? *European Business Review*, 20–25.

Law 17-95 on the Public Limited Company

Law 5-96 on the General Partnership, the Limited Partnership, the Limited Liability Company and the Joint Venture Company Law 39-89 authorizing the transfer of public enterprises to the private sector

Lawler, E. E. (1977). Job and work satisfaction. In W. C. Hamner & F. L. Schmidt (Eds.), *Comtemporary problems in personnel*. St. Clair Press.

Le Breton-Miller, I., & Miller, D. (2006). Why do some family businessesout-compete? Governance, long-term orientations, and sustainablecapability. *Entrepreneurship Theory and Practice*, *30*(6), 731–746.

Le Breton-Miller, I., & Miller, D. (2013). Socioemotional wealth across thefamily firm life cycle: A commentary on "Family Business Survival and theRole of Boards.". *Entrepreneurship Theory and Practice*, *37*(6), 1391–1397.

Lee, J. (2006). Family firm performance: Further evidence. *Family Business Review*, *19*(2), 103–114. doi:10.1111/j.1741-6248.2006.00060.x

Leitterstorf, M., & Rau, S. (2014). Socioemotional wealth and IPO under-pricing of family firms. *Strategic Management Journal*, *35*(5), 751–760. doi:10.1002mj.2236

Leland, H., & Pyle, D. (1977). Informational Asymmetries, Financial Structure, and Financial Intermediation. *The Journal of Finance*, *32*(2), 371. doi:10.2307/2326770

Lieutier, J. P. (2012). *Le modèle de l'actionnariat salarié*. P. U. Aix-Marseille, Ed..

Livingston, D., & Henry, J. (1980). The effects of employee stock ownership on corporate profits. *The Journal of Risk and Insurance*, *47*(3), 491–505. doi:10.2307/252634

Long, R. J. (1978). The Relative Effects of Share Ownership Versus Control on Job Attitudes in An Employee-Owned Company. *Human Relations*, *31*(9), 753–763. doi:10.1177/001872677803100901

Long, R. J. (1978a). The effects of employee ownership on organizational identification, employee attitudes, and organizational performance: A tentative framework and empirical findings. *Human Relations*, *31*(1), 29–38. doi:10.1177/001872677803100102

Long, R. J. (1980). Job Attitudes and Organizational Performance under Employee Ownership. *Academy of Management Journal*, *23*(4).

Long, R. J. (1980). Job attitudes and organizational performance under employee ownership. *Academy of Management Journal*, *23*, 726–737.

Long, R. J. (1982). Worker ownership and job attitudes: A field study. *Industrial Relations*, *21*(2), 196–215. doi:10.1111/j.1468-232X.1982.tb00228.x

Mackin, C. (2021, October 6). *Toward an economic democracy*. The New Republic. Retrieved from https://newrepublic.com/article/157055/toward-economic-democracy

Majumdar, R. (2021). *Paytm Expands ESOP Scheme To $604 Mn, Largest Among Indian Startups*. New Delhi: inc42.

Markowitz, H. M., Blasi, J. R., & Kruse, D. L. (2010). Employee stock ownership and diversification. *Annals of Operations Research*, *176*(1), 95–107. doi:10.100710479-009-0544-1

Martechseries. (2021). *Insights*. Retrieved from Martechseries Web Site: https://martechseries.com/mts-insights/staff-writers/top-tech-companies-successful-esop-processes-plans/

Mathieu, M. (2020). *Annual Economic Survey of Employee Share Ownership in European Countries*. European Federation of Share Ownership.

McDaniel, W. R., Madura, J., & Wiant, J. K. (1995). Performance following ESOP formations by publicly-held corporations. *Journal of Economics and Finance*, 147–169.

Megginson, W., Nash, R., & Randenborgh, M. V. (1994). The financial and operatingperformance of newly privatized firms: An international empirical analysis. *The Journal of Finance*, 122–145.

Meyer, J., & Allen, N. (1997). *Commitment in the Workplace: Theory, Research, and Application.* Employee Ownership ge Publications.

Meyer, J., Allen, N., & Smith, C. (1993). Commitment to organizations and occupations: Extension and test of a three-component conceptualization. *The Journal of Applied Psychology, 78*(4), 538–551. doi:10.1037/0021-9010.78.4.538

Miller, D., Le Breton-Miller, I., Lester, R. H., & Cannella, A. A. Jr. (2007). Are familyfirms really superior performers? *Journal of Corporate Finance, 13*(5), 829–858. doi:10.1016/j.jcorpfin.2007.03.004

Mooney, A. (2020, August 22). The Great Dividend Reset: Is there a new normal for investors? *Financial Times.* Retrieved from https://www.ft.com/content/b0873571-b4f4-4c9e-aa18-318cb7589e7f

Morris, S., Alvarez, S., Barney, J., & Molloy, J. (2017). Firm-specific Human Capital Investments as a Signal of General Value: Revisiting Assumptions about Human Capital and How it Is Managed. *Strategic Management Journal, 38*(4), 912–919.

Moskalu, V. (2012). *Une analyse socio-cognitive de l'impact de l'actionnariat salarié sur la création de valeur des entreprises françaises cotées.* Gestion et management. Thèse soutenue à l'Université de Lorraine

Mowday, R., Steers, R., & Porter, L. (1979). The measurement of organizational commitment. *Journal of Vocational Behavior, 14*(2), 224–247. doi:10.1016/0001-8791(79)90072-1

Mullins, F. (2018). A Piece of the Pie? TheEffects of Familial Control Enhancements on the Use of Broad-Based Employee Ownership Programs in Family Firms. *Hum Resour Manage., 57,* 979–992. doi:10.1002/hrm.21828

Mullins, F. (2018). A piece of the pie? The effects of familial control enhancements on the use of broad-based employee ownership programs in family firms. *Human Resource Management,* 979–992.

Naím, M. (2015). The End of Power. Basic Books.

National Center for Employee Ownership. (2019). *A Statistical Profile of Employee Ownership.* National Center for Employee Ownership.

NCEO. (2020, July 5). *Publications.* Retrieved from NCEO Web Site: https://www.nceo.org/articles/employee-ownership-100

Ngongang, D. (2013). Actionnariat salarié comme levier de création de valeur ajoutée et de productivité dans les entreprises camerounaises. *La Revue Gestion et Organisation, 5*(1), 1–8. doi:10.1016/j.rgo.2013.10.001

Nikulina, I. E., & Khomenko, I. (2014). Cognitive management: theory and practice in the organization. *International Conference on Research Paradigms Transformation in Social Sciences.*

Nomafu, Z. (2018). *Why Companies Need to Support ESOP Initiatives*. Dadelane Wastewater Solutions.

Notat, N., & Sénard, J.-D. (2018). *L'entreprise, objet d'intérêt collectif*. Rapport remis au Ministre de l'Economie et des Finances.

Note sur le résultat du questionnaire mené par l'AMMC (ex CDVM) sur les pratiques de bonne gouvernance des sociétés cotées -2010-

O'Boyle, E. H., Patel, P. C., & Gonzalez-Mulé, E. (2016). Employee ownership and firm performance: A meta-analysis. *Human Resource Management Journal*, *26*(4), 425–448. doi:10.1111/1748-8583.12115

O'Boyle, E., Patel, P., & Gonzales-Mulé, E. (2016). Employee Ownership and Firm Performance: A Meta-Analysis. *Human Resource Management Journal*, *26*(4), 425–448.

OCDE. (2015). *Principes de gouvernance d'entreprise du G20 et de l'OCDE*. OECD.

October is employee ownership month. (n.d.). *NCEO*. Retrieved from https://www.nceo.org/

OECD. (2020a). *COVID-19 and international trade: Issues and actions*. Retrieved from https://www.oecd.org/coronavirus/policy-responses/covid-19-and-international-trade-issues-and-actions-494da2fa/

OECD. (2020b). *Supporting businesses in financial distress to avoid insolvency during the COVID-19 crisis*. https://www.oecd.org/coronavirus/policy-responses/supporting-businesses-in-financial-distress-to-avoid-insolvency-during-thecovid-19-crisis-b4154a8b/

OECD. (2020c). *COVID-19 Government Financing Support Programmes for Businesses*. www.oecd.org/finance/COVID-19-Government-Financing-Support-Programmes-for-Businesses.pdf

OECD. (2020d). *Global Financial Markets Policy Responses to COVID-19*. https://www.oecd.org/coronavirus/policy-responses/global-financial-markets-policy-responses-to-covid-19-2d98c7e0/

Pagano, M., & Volpin, P. F. (2005). Managers, workers, and corporate control. *The Journal of Finance*, *60*(2), 841–868. doi:10.1111/j.1540-6261.2005.00748.x

Palmer, M., Mawad, M., & Treyz, C. (2020). Europe loosens rules on stock options, but employees are still sceptical. *Financial Times*. Retrieved from https://sifted.eu/articles/stock-option-changes-europe/

Palmer, T. B., & Wiseman, R. M. (1999). Decoupling risk taking from income stream uncertainty: A holistic model of risk. *Strategic Management Journal*, 1037–1062.

Pan, H. (2021). Core-Staff-Based ESOPs: a new concept of employee share ownership in China. Lorraine: University of Lorraine: European Centre for Research in Financial Economics and Business Management.

Park, S., & Song, M. H. (1995). Employee Stock Ownership Plans, Firm Performance and Monitoring by Outside Blockholders. *Financial Management*, *24*(4), 52–65. doi:10.2307/3665950

Parrat, F. (2015). *Théories et pratiques de la gouvernance d'entreprise*. Maxima Laurent du Mesnil.

Paterson, T. A., & Welbourne, T. M. (2019). I am therefore I own: Implications of organization-based identity for employee stock ownership. *Human Resource Management*, 175–183.

Pendleton, A. (2001). Employee ownership, participation and governance: a study of ESOPs in the UK. Routledge.

Pendleton, A. (2006). Incentives, Monitoring and Employee Stock Ownership Plans: New *Industrial Relations*. Academic Press.

Pendleton, A., Wilson, N., & Wright, M. (1998). The Perception and Effects of Share Ownership: Empirical Evidence from Employee Buy-Outs. *British Journal of Industrial Relations*, *36*(1), 99–123. doi:10.1111/1467-8543.00082

Pendleton, A., Wilson, N., & Wright, M. (1998). The Perception and Effects of Share Ownership: Empirical Evidence from Employee Buy-Outs. *British Journal of Industrial Relations*, 99–123.

Peng, M. W., Sun, S. L., Pinkham, B., & Chen, H. (2009). The institution-based view as a third leg for a strategy tripod. *The Academy of Management Perspectives*, *23*(3), 63–81. doi:10.5465/amp.2009.43479264

Pettigrew, A. M. (1992). On studying managerial elites. *Strategic Management Journal*, *13*(S2), 163–182. doi:10.1002mj.4250130911

Pfeffer, J. (2010). *Power: Why some people have it – and others don't* (1st ed.). HarperCollins Publishers.

Philip, K. (2003). *Co-operatives in South Africa: Their Role in Job Creation and Poverty Reduction*. South African Foundation.

Pierce, J. L., Rubenfeld, S. A., & Morgan, S. (1991). *Employee ownership: A conceptual model of process and effects*. Academic Press.

Pierce, J. L., Rubenfeld, S. A., & Morgan, S. (1991). Employee Ownership: A Conceptual Model of Process and Effects. *Academy of Management Review*, *16*(1), 121–144.

Policy responses to covid19. (n.d.). *IMF*. Retrieved from https://www.imf.org/en/Topics/imf-and-covid19/Policy-Responses-to-COVID-19#U

Poulain-Rehm, T. (2006), *L'actionnariat des salariés en France, un facteur de création de valeur?* Note de recherche, www.iae.Univpoitiers.Fr/affi2006/coms/130.pdf

Poulain-Rehm, T. (2007). *L'actionnariat des salariés en France, un facteur de création de valeur?* Academic Press.

Poulain-Rehm, T. (2006). Qu'est-ce qu'une entreprise familiale? *La Revue des Sciences de Gestion*, *219*(3), 77–88. doi:10.3917/rsg.219.0077

Poulain-Rehm, T. (2007). L'actionnariat des employee ownership lariés en France, un facteur de création de valeur. *Bankers Markets and Investors*, *88*, 25–36.

Poulain-Rehm, T., & Lepers, X. (2013). Does employee ownership benefit value creation? The case of France (2001–2005). *Journal of Business Ethics*, *112*(2), 325–340. doi:10.100710551-012-1255-0

Poutsma, F., Ligthart, P. E., & Poutsma, E. (2017). *Sharing in the Company: Determinants, Processes and Outcomes of Employee Participation*. Emerald Group Publishing Limited.

Public-Private Infrastructure Advisory Facility (PPIAF). (2021). *Key Elements of a Labor Program*. Retrieved from Public-Private Infrastructure Advisory Facility (PPIAF) Website: https://ppiaf.org/sites/ppiaf.org/files/documents/toolkits/LaborToolkit/Toolkit/module5/employee.html

Pugh, W., Jahera, J., & Oswald, S. (1999). ESOPs, Takeover Protection, and Corporate Decision Making. *Journal of Economics and Finance*, *23*(2), 170–185.

Rajan, R., & Zingales, L. (1998). Power in a Theory of the Firm. *Quarterly Journal of Economics*, *113*(2), 387-432.

Ramchandani, S. B., & Pandya, H. B. (2019). *Evaluating the Effect of Employee Stock Option Plans on the Financial Performance of Indian Construction & Infrastructure Companies*. Academic Press.

Ren, T., Xiao, Y., Yang, H., & Liu, S. (2019). Employee ownership heterogeneity and firm performance in China. *Human Resource Management*, 621–639.

Riaz, F., Razzaq, A., & Waqar, A. (2017). Effect of Employee Stock Ownership Plans (ESOPs) on the performance of Small business in Karachi. *International Journal of Applied Business and Management Studies*, 1-16.

Roberts, J., & Van den Steen, E. (2001). Human Capital and Corporate Governance. In H. Albach & J. Schwalbach (Eds.), *Corporate governance: Essays in Honor of Horst Albach* (pp. 128–144). Springer.

Robinson, A. M., & Wilson, N. (2006). Employee Financial Participation and Productivity: An Empirical Reappraisal. *British Journal of Industrial Relations*, *44*(1), 31–50.

Rosen, C., & Rodrick, S. (2005). *The ESOP reader: A primer on employeestock ownership plans* (4th ed.). National Center for Employee Ownership.

Rosen, C., & Rodrick, S. (2013). *Understanding ESOPs*. National Center for Employee Ownership.

Rotondi, T. Jr. (1975). Organizational identification: Issues and implications. *Organizational Performance and Human Behavior*, *13*(1), 95–109. doi:10.1016/0030-5073(75)90007-0

Rottenberg, S. (1962). Property in work. *Industrial & Labor Relations Review*, *15*(3), 402–405. doi:10.1177/001979396201500306

Roussel, P. (1996). *Rémunération, motivation et employee ownership tisfaction au travail*. Editions Economica.

Roussel, P., Durieu, F., Campoy, E., & El Akremi, A. (2002). *Méthodes d'équations structurelles: recherche et applications en gestion*. Économica.

Roux, H. L. (2005). Esops emerging as key to broad-based empowerment. *Engineering News*. Retrieved from https://www.engineeringnews.co.za/article/esops-emerging-as-key-to-broadbased-empowerment-2005-06-06/rep_id:4136

Russell, R., Hochner, A., & Perry, S. (1979). Participation, influence, and worker ownership. *Industrial Relations*, *3*(3), 330–341. doi:10.1111/j.1468-232X.1997.tb00932.x

Sagan, A., Thomas, S., McKee, M., Karanikolos, M., Azzopardi-Muscat, N., De La Mata, I., & Figueras, J. (2020). *COVID-19 and health systems resilience: Lessons going forwards*. World Health Organization. https://apps.who.int/iris/bitstream/handle/10665/336290/Eurohealth-26-2-20-24-eng.pdf

Samah, I. H. A., Shamsuddin, A. S., Rashid, I. M. A., & Amlus, M. H. (2019). Mediating effect of employee empowerment in the relationship between communication and retention. *International Journal of Scientific and Technology Research*, *8*(12), 3457–3459. http://www.ijstr.org/final-print/dec2019/Mediating-Effect-Of-Employee-Empowerment-In-The-Relationship-Between-Communication-And-Retention-.pdf

Samantara, R., & Dhawan, S. (2020). Corporate social responsibility in India: Issues and challenges. *IIMS Journal of Management Science*, 91-103.

Schneider, N. (2020). Broad-Based Stakeholder Ownership in Journalism: Co-ops, ESOPs, Blockchains. *Media Industries Journal*, 123-140.

Schneider, B. R. (2013). *Hierarchical capitalism in Latin America. Business, labor, and the challenges of equitable development* (1st ed.). Cambridge University Press. doi:10.1017/CBO9781107300446

Scholes, M. (2002). *Taxes and Business Strategy: A Planning Approach*. Prentice Hall.

Scholes, M., & Wolfson, M. (1990). Employee stock ownership plans and corporate restructuring: Myths and realities. *Financial Management*, *19*, 12–28.

Shleifer, A., & Vishny, R. (1986). Greenmail, white knights, and shareholders' interests, Rand. *Journal of Economics*, *17*, 293–309.

Siessima, D. (2017). La face cachée de l'actionnariat salarié: Etude empirique sur l'indice SBF 120 (2000-2014). *Revue finance contrôle stratégie, 20*(1).

Sinenhlanhla, S. (2019). *Unpacking Employee Share Ownership Plans ESOPs*. Sam Tambni Research Institute.

South African Government. (2021). *Broad-based Black Economic Empowerment Act 53 of 2003*. Retrieved from South African Government Website: https://www.gov.za/documents/broad-based-black-economic-empowerment-act

Taylor, T. (2017). ESOPs Help Some CPA Firms with Retention, Succession: Employee Stock Ownership Plans Can Boost a Firm's Productivity and Growth. *Journal of Accountancy, 223*(5), 51.

Teoh, K. B., Cordova, M., Hor, S. N., Lim, Ch. H., Yeoh, L. K., Madhu, A., Warrier, U., Chan, J. J., Kee, D. M. H., Tan, F. E., Chia, J. X., & Chuah, Y. J. (2021). The Factors of Employee Performance: A Study of SearchNEasy. *Asia Pacific Journal of Management and Education, 4*(1), 82–96. doi:10.32535/apjme.v4i1.1053

The Catholic University of Brussels. (2000). *A company perspective on financial participation in the European Union: objectives and obstacles*. The Catholic University of Brussels.

The European Commission. (2003). *The legal and administrative environment for Employee*. The European Commission.

The European Commission. (2014). *The Promotion of Employee Ownership and Participation*. The European Commission.

The European Union. (2020). *Employee Involvement - Employment, Social Affairs & Inclusion - European Commission*. Brussels: The European Union.

The European Union. (2021). *Start Up Europe*. Brussels: The European Union.

The World Bank. (2020a). *The Global Economic Outlook During the COVID-19 Pandemic: A Changed World*. https://www.worldbank.org/en/news/feature/2020/06/08/the-global-economic-outlook-during-the-covid-19-pandemic-a-changed-world

The World Bank. (2020b). *Tackling the impact of job displacement through public policies*. https://www.worldbank.org/en/news/feature/2020/10/20/tackling-the-impact-of-job-displacement-through-public-policies

Thomsen, S., Rose, C., & Kronborg, D. (2016). Employee Representation and Board Size in the Nordic Countries. *European Journal of Law and Economics, 42*(3), 471–490.

Tiscini, R., & Raoli, E. (2013). Stock option plan practices in family firms:The idiosyncratic private benefits approach. *Journal of Family Business Strategy, 4*(2), 93–105. doi:10.1016/j.jfbs.2013.03.001

Transcend. (2021, July 5). *Our Clients*. Retrieved from Transcend Web Site: https://www.transcend.co.za

Trébucq, S. (2001). Etat de l'actionnariat salarié en France au 31 décembre 2000: Premiers résultats statistiques. *Cahier de Recherche, IAE, Université Montesquieu Bordeaux, 4*.

Trébucq, S. (2002). L'actionnariat salarié dans les entreprises familiales du SBF 250: Un outil de création de valeur Revue Finance, Contrôle. *Stratégie, 5*(4), 107–135.

Trébucq, S. (2002). *L'actionnariat salarié dans les entreprises familiales du SBF250: un outil de création de valeur?* Finance Contrôle Stratégie.

Trébucq, S. (2002, December). L'actionnariat salarié dans les entreprises familiales: Un outil de création de valeur? *Finance Contrôle Stratégie*, *5*(4), 107–135.

Tucker, J., Nock, S., & Toscano, D. (1989). Employee ownership and perceptions of work. *Work and Occupations*, *16*(1), 26–42. doi:10.1177/0730888489016001002

UNCTAD. (2020). *Impact of the Covid-19 Pandemic on Global FDI and GVCs*. Global Investment Trends Monitor No. 35 (Special Issue March 2020). Geneva: UNCTAD. Retrieved from https://unctad.org/en/PublicationsLibrary/diaeiainf2020d3_en.pdf

UNIDO. (2020). *COVID-19 and the global contraction in FDI*. Retrieved from https://iap.unido.org/articles/covid-19-and-global-contraction-fdi

Useem, M. (1984). *The inner circle. Large corporations and the rise of business political activity in the U.S. and U.K.* Oxford University Press.

Vandenberg, R. J., & Lance, C. E. (2000). *A Review and Synthesis of the Measurement Invariance Literature: Suggestions, Practices, and Recommendations for Organizational Research*. Organizational Research Methods.

Vaughan-Whitehead, D. (1992). *Interessement, participation, actionnariat: impacts économiques dans l'entreprise*. Economica.

Vaughan-Whitehead, D. (1992). Intéressement, participation, actionnariat: Impacts économiques dans l'entreprise. *Economica*.

Vaughan-Whitehead, D., & Barre, R., & Barre, R. (1992). Intéressement, participation, actionnariat: Impacts économiques dans l'entreprise. *Economica*.

Villalonga, B., & Amit, R. (2006). How do family ownership, control and man-agement affect firm value? *Journal of Financial Economics*, *80*(2), 385–417. doi:10.1016/j.jfineco.2004.12.005

Villalonga, B., & Amit, R. (2009). How are U.S. family firms controlled? *Review of Financial Studies*, *22*(8), 3047–3091. doi:10.1093/rfs/hhn080

Villalonga, B., & Amit, R. (2010). Family control of firms and industries. *Financial Management*, *39*(3), 863–904. doi:10.1111/j.1755-053X.2010.01098.x

Wagner, I., & Rosen, C. (1985). Employee ownership: Its effects on corporate performance. *Employment Relations Today*, *12*(1), 77–82.

Wang, H. C., He, J., & Mahoney, J. T. (2009). Firm-specific knowledge resources and competitive advantage: The roles of economic-and relationship-based employee governance mechanisms. *Strategic Management*, 1265–1285.

Wanjiku, R. (2008, June 4). Kenya's Safaricom IPO disappoints small investors. *Ntework World*, p. 1. Retrieved May 25, 2021, from https://www.networkworld.com/article/2280772/kenya-s-safaricom-ipo-disappoints-small-investors.html

Waxin, T. (2011). *Salarié, performance et gouvernance des entreprises* (Thèse de doctorat en sciences de gestion). Université Paris Dauphine.

Weber, M., & Newhouse, D. (2021). *Developing countries introduced an unprecedented social protection and jobs policy response to mitigate the effects of the pandemic*. World Bank Blogs. https://blogs.worldbank.org/jobs/developing-countries-introduced-unprecedented-social-protection-and-jobs-policy-response

Weiser, J., Brody, F., & Quarrey, M. (1988). Family businesses and employee ownership. *Family Business Review*, *1*(1), 23–35. doi:10.1111/j.1741-6248.1988.00023.x

Weitzman, M., & Kruse, D. (1990). *Profit sharing and productivity*. Academic Press.

Welbourne, T., & Cyr, L. (1999). Using ownership as an incentive. *Group & Organization Management*, *24*(4), 438–460. doi:10.1177/1059601199244003

Wen, X., Li, Z., Zhang, Y., & Shen, S. (2021). ESOP and Corporate Sustainable Growth. *Web of Conferences*, 1-6.

Wernerfelt, B. (1984). A resource based view of the firm. *Strategic Management Journal*, *5*(2), 171–180.

Weyher, H., & Knott, H. (1985). *The employee stock ownership plan*. Commerce Clearinghouse.

Whitfield, K., Pendleton, A., Sengupta, S., & Huxley, K. (2017). Employee share ownership and organizational performance: A tentative opening of the black box. *Personnel Review*, 123–140.

WHO. (2020). *Coronavirus disease 2019 (COVID-19)*. Situation Report 51. Retrieved from https://www.who.int/docs/default-source/coronaviruse/situation-reports/20200311-sitrep-51-covid-19.pdf?sfvrsn=1ba62e57_10

Whyte, W. F. (1978). In support of voluntary employee ownership. *Society*, *15*(6), 73–82. doi:10.1007/BF02697780

Wilson, N., & Peel, M. J. (1991). The Impact on Absenteeism and Quits Of Profit-Sharing and Other Forms of Employee Participation. *Industrial & Labor Relations Review*, *44*(3), 454–468.

Yale Law Journal Company, Inc. (1990). When Does Worker Ownership Work? ESOPs, Law Firms, Codetermination, and Economic Democracy. *The Yale Law Journal*, 1749–1816.

Yoon, Y., & Sengupta, S. (2019). Employee share ownership, training, and early promotion policy as a bundle in enhancing labor productivity: A test of the three-way interaction effect. *Human Resource Management*, 603–620.

Zellweger, T., & Astrachan, J. (2008). On the emotional value of owning afirm. *Family Business Review*, *21*(4), 347–363. doi:10.1177/08944865080210040106

Zellweger, T., Nason, R., Nordqvist, M., & Brush, C. (2011). Why do family firms strive for non-financial goals? An organizational identity perspec-tive. *Entrepreneurship Theory and Practice*, *37*(2), 222–249.

Zhou, D., Huang, J., & Zhao, Y. (2019). Employee Stock Ownership Plans and Corporate Innovation. *Journal of Accounting Research*, 63–70.

Zingales, L. (1998). Corporate Governance. In P. Newman (Ed.), The New Palgrave, Dictionary of Economy. Academic Press.

Related References

To continue our tradition of advancing information science and technology research, we have compiled a list of recommended IGI Global readings. These references will provide additional information and guidance to further enrich your knowledge and assist you with your own research and future publications.

Abtahi, M. S., Behboudi, L., & Hasanabad, H. M. (2017). Factors Affecting Internet Advertising Adoption in Ad Agencies. *International Journal of Innovation in the Digital Economy*, *8*(4), 18–29. doi:10.4018/IJIDE.2017100102

Agrawal, S. (2017). The Impact of Emerging Technologies and Social Media on Different Business(es): Marketing and Management. In O. Rishi & A. Sharma (Eds.), *Maximizing Business Performance and Efficiency Through Intelligent Systems* (pp. 37–49). Hershey, PA: IGI Global. doi:10.4018/978-1-5225-2234-8.ch002

Alnoukari, M., Razouk, R., & Hanano, A. (2016). BSC-SI: A Framework for Integrating Strategic Intelligence in Corporate Strategic Management. *International Journal of Social and Organizational Dynamics in IT*, *5*(2), 1–14. doi:10.4018/IJSODIT.2016070101

Alnoukari, M., Razouk, R., & Hanano, A. (2016). BSC-SI, A Framework for Integrating Strategic Intelligence in Corporate Strategic Management. *International Journal of Strategic Information Technology and Applications*, *7*(1), 32–44. doi:10.4018/IJSITA.2016010103

Altındağ, E. (2016). Current Approaches in Change Management. In A. Goksoy (Ed.), *Organizational Change Management Strategies in Modern Business* (pp. 24–51). Hershey, PA: IGI Global. doi:10.4018/978-1-4666-9533-7.ch002

Alvarez-Dionisi, L. E., Turner, R., & Mittra, M. (2016). Global Project Management Trends. *International Journal of Information Technology Project Management, 7*(3), 54–73. doi:10.4018/IJITPM.2016070104

Anantharaman, R. N., Rajeswari, K. S., Angusamy, A., & Kuppusamy, J. (2017). Role of Self-Efficacy and Collective Efficacy as Moderators of Occupational Stress Among Software Development Professionals. *International Journal of Human Capital and Information Technology Professionals, 8*(2), 45–58. doi:10.4018/IJHCITP.2017040103

Aninze, F., El-Gohary, H., & Hussain, J. (2018). The Role of Microfinance to Empower Women: The Case of Developing Countries. *International Journal of Customer Relationship Marketing and Management, 9*(1), 54–78. doi:10.4018/IJCRMM.2018010104

Arsenijević, O. M., Orčić, D., & Kastratović, E. (2017). Development of an Optimization Tool for Intangibles in SMEs: A Case Study from Serbia with a Pilot Research in the Prestige by Milka Company. In M. Vemić (Ed.), *Optimal Management Strategies in Small and Medium Enterprises* (pp. 320–347). Hershey, PA: IGI Global. doi:10.4018/978-1-5225-1949-2.ch015

Aryanto, V. D., Wismantoro, Y., & Widyatmoko, K. (2018). Implementing Eco-Innovation by Utilizing the Internet to Enhance Firm's Marketing Performance: Study of Green Batik Small and Medium Enterprises in Indonesia. *International Journal of E-Business Research, 14*(1), 21–36. doi:10.4018/IJEBR.2018010102

Atiku, S. O., & Fields, Z. (2017). Multicultural Orientations for 21st Century Global Leadership. In N. Baporikar (Ed.), *Management Education for Global Leadership* (pp. 28–51). Hershey, PA: IGI Global. doi:10.4018/978-1-5225-1013-0.ch002

Atiku, S. O., & Fields, Z. (2018). Organisational Learning Dimensions and Talent Retention Strategies for the Service Industries. In N. Baporikar (Ed.), *Global Practices in Knowledge Management for Societal and Organizational Development* (pp. 358–381). Hershey, PA: IGI Global. doi:10.4018/978-1-5225-3009-1.ch017

Ávila, L., & Teixeira, L. (2018). The Main Concepts Behind the Dematerialization of Business Processes. In M. Khosrow-Pour, D.B.A. (Ed.), Encyclopedia of Information Science and Technology, Fourth Edition (pp. 888-898). Hershey, PA: IGI Global. doi:10.4018/978-1-5225-2255-3.ch076

Bartens, Y., Chunpir, H. I., Schulte, F., & Voß, S. (2017). Business/IT Alignment in Two-Sided Markets: A COBIT 5 Analysis for Media Streaming Business Models. In S. De Haes & W. Van Grembergen (Eds.), *Strategic IT Governance and Alignment in Business Settings* (pp. 82–111). Hershey, PA: IGI Global. doi:10.4018/978-1-5225-0861-8.ch004

Bashayreh, A. M. (2018). Organizational Culture and Organizational Performance. In W. Lee & F. Sabetzadeh (Eds.), *Contemporary Knowledge and Systems Science* (pp. 50–69). Hershey, PA: IGI Global. doi:10.4018/978-1-5225-5655-8.ch003

Bedford, D. A. (2018). Sustainable Knowledge Management Strategies: Aligning Business Capabilities and Knowledge Management Goals. In N. Baporikar (Ed.), *Global Practices in Knowledge Management for Societal and Organizational Development* (pp. 46–73). Hershey, PA: IGI Global. doi:10.4018/978-1-5225-3009-1.ch003

Benmoussa, F., Nakara, W. A., & Jaouen, A. (2016). The Use of Social Media by SMEs in the Tourism Industry. In I. Lee (Ed.), *Encyclopedia of E-Commerce Development, Implementation, and Management* (pp. 2159–2170). Hershey, PA: IGI Global. doi:10.4018/978-1-4666-9787-4.ch155

Berger, R. (2016). Indigenous Management and Bottom of Pyramid Countries: The Role of National Institutions. In U. Aung & P. Ordoñez de Pablos (Eds.), *Managerial Strategies and Practice in the Asian Business Sector* (pp. 107–123). Hershey, PA: IGI Global. doi:10.4018/978-1-4666-9758-4.ch007

Bharwani, S., & Musunuri, D. (2018). Reflection as a Process From Theory to Practice. In M. Khosrow-Pour, D.B.A. (Ed.), Encyclopedia of Information Science and Technology, Fourth Edition (pp. 1529-1539). Hershey, PA: IGI Global. doi:10.4018/978-1-5225-2255-3.ch132

Bhatt, G. D., Wang, Z., & Rodger, J. A. (2017). Information Systems Capabilities and Their Effects on Competitive Advantages: A Study of Chinese Companies. *Information Resources Management Journal, 30*(3), 41–57. doi:10.4018/IRMJ.2017070103

Bhushan, M., & Yadav, A. (2017). Concept of Cloud Computing in ESB. In R. Bhadoria, N. Chaudhari, G. Tomar, & S. Singh (Eds.), *Exploring Enterprise Service Bus in the Service-Oriented Architecture Paradigm* (pp. 116–127). Hershey, PA: IGI Global. doi:10.4018/978-1-5225-2157-0.ch008

Bhushan, S. (2017). System Dynamics Base-Model of Humanitarian Supply Chain (HSCM) in Disaster Prone Eco-Communities of India: A Discussion on Simulation and Scenario Results. *International Journal of System Dynamics Applications, 6*(3), 20–37. doi:10.4018/IJSDA.2017070102

Biswas, A., & De, A. K. (2017). On Development of a Fuzzy Stochastic Programming Model with Its Application to Business Management. In S. Trivedi, S. Dey, A. Kumar, & T. Panda (Eds.), *Handbook of Research on Advanced Data Mining Techniques and Applications for Business Intelligence* (pp. 353–378). Hershey, PA: IGI Global. doi:10.4018/978-1-5225-2031-3.ch021

Bücker, J., & Ernste, K. (2018). Use of Brand Heroes in Strategic Reputation Management: The Case of Bacardi, Adidas, and Daimler. In A. Erdemir (Ed.), *Reputation Management Techniques in Public Relations* (pp. 126–150). Hershey, PA: IGI Global. doi:10.4018/978-1-5225-3619-2.ch007

Bureš, V. (2018). Industry 4.0 From the Systems Engineering Perspective: Alternative Holistic Framework Development. In R. Brunet-Thornton & F. Martinez (Eds.), *Analyzing the Impacts of Industry 4.0 in Modern Business Environments* (pp. 199–223). Hershey, PA: IGI Global. doi:10.4018/978-1-5225-3468-6.ch011

Buzady, Z. (2017). Resolving the Magic Cube of Effective Case Teaching: Benchmarking Case Teaching Practices in Emerging Markets – Insights from the Central European University Business School, Hungary. In D. Latusek (Ed.), *Case Studies as a Teaching Tool in Management Education* (pp. 79–103). Hershey, PA: IGI Global. doi:10.4018/978-1-5225-0770-3.ch005

Campatelli, G., Richter, A., & Stocker, A. (2016). Participative Knowledge Management to Empower Manufacturing Workers. *International Journal of Knowledge Management, 12*(4), 37–50. doi:10.4018/IJKM.2016100103

Căpusneanu, S., & Topor, D. I. (2018). Business Ethics and Cost Management in SMEs: Theories of Business Ethics and Cost Management Ethos. In I. Oncioiu (Ed.), *Ethics and Decision-Making for Sustainable Business Practices* (pp. 109–127). Hershey, PA: IGI Global. doi:10.4018/978-1-5225-3773-1.ch007

Carneiro, A. (2016). Maturity in Health Organization Information Systems: Metrics and Privacy Perspectives. *International Journal of Privacy and Health Information Management, 4*(2), 1–18. doi:10.4018/IJPHIM.2016070101

Chan, R. L., Mo, P. L., & Moon, K. K. (2018). Strategic and Tactical Measures in Managing Enterprise Risks: A Study of the Textile and Apparel Industry. In K. Strang, M. Korstanje, & N. Vajjhala (Eds.), *Research, Practices, and Innovations in Global Risk and Contingency Management* (pp. 1–19). Hershey, PA: IGI Global. doi:10.4018/978-1-5225-4754-9.ch001

Chandan, H. C. (2016). Motivations and Challenges of Female Entrepreneurship in Developed and Developing Economies. In N. Baporikar (Ed.), *Handbook of Research on Entrepreneurship in the Contemporary Knowledge-Based Global Economy* (pp. 260–286). Hershey, PA: IGI Global. doi:10.4018/978-1-4666-8798-1.ch012

Charlier, S. D., Burke-Smalley, L. A., & Fisher, S. L. (2018). Undergraduate Programs in the U.S: A Contextual and Content-Based Analysis. In J. Mendy (Ed.), *Teaching Human Resources and Organizational Behavior at the College Level* (pp. 26–57). Hershey, PA: IGI Global. doi:10.4018/978-1-5225-2820-3.ch002

Chaudhuri, S. (2016). Application of Web-Based Geographical Information System (GIS) in E-Business. In U. Panwar, R. Kumar, & N. Ray (Eds.), *Handbook of Research on Promotional Strategies and Consumer Influence in the Service Sector* (pp. 389–405). Hershey, PA: IGI Global. doi:10.4018/978-1-5225-0143-5.ch023

Choudhuri, P. S. (2016). An Empirical Study on the Quality of Services Offered by the Private Life Insurers in Burdwan. In U. Panwar, R. Kumar, & N. Ray (Eds.), *Handbook of Research on Promotional Strategies and Consumer Influence in the Service Sector* (pp. 31–55). Hershey, PA: IGI Global. doi:10.4018/978-1-5225-0143-5.ch002

Dahlberg, T., Kivijärvi, H., & Saarinen, T. (2017). IT Investment Consistency and Other Factors Influencing the Success of IT Performance. In S. De Haes & W. Van Grembergen (Eds.), *Strategic IT Governance and Alignment in Business Settings* (pp. 176–208). Hershey, PA: IGI Global. doi:10.4018/978-1-5225-0861-8.ch007

Damnjanović, A. M. (2017). Knowledge Management Optimization through IT and E-Business Utilization: A Qualitative Study on Serbian SMEs. In M. Vemić (Ed.), *Optimal Management Strategies in Small and Medium Enterprises* (pp. 249–267). Hershey, PA: IGI Global. doi:10.4018/978-1-5225-1949-2.ch012

Daneshpour, H. (2017). Integrating Sustainable Development into Project Portfolio Management through Application of Open Innovation. In M. Vemić (Ed.), *Optimal Management Strategies in Small and Medium Enterprises* (pp. 370–387). Hershey, PA: IGI Global. doi:10.4018/978-1-5225-1949-2.ch017

Daniel, A. D., & Reis de Castro, V. (2018). Entrepreneurship Education: How to Measure the Impact on Nascent Entrepreneurs. In A. Carrizo Moreira, J. Guilherme Leitão Dantas, & F. Manuel Valente (Eds.), *Nascent Entrepreneurship and Successful New Venture Creation* (pp. 85–110). Hershey, PA: IGI Global. doi:10.4018/978-1-5225-2936-1.ch004

David, F., van der Sijde, P., & van den Besselaar, P. (2016). Enterpreneurial Incentives, Obstacles, and Management in University-Business Co-Operation: The Case of Indonesia. In J. Saiz-Álvarez (Ed.), *Handbook of Research on Social Entrepreneurship and Solidarity Economics* (pp. 499–518). Hershey, PA: IGI Global. doi:10.4018/978-1-5225-0097-1.ch024

David, R., Swami, B. N., & Tangirala, S. (2018). Ethics Impact on Knowledge Management in Organizational Development: A Case Study. In N. Baporikar (Ed.), *Global Practices in Knowledge Management for Societal and Organizational Development* (pp. 19–45). Hershey, PA: IGI Global. doi:10.4018/978-1-5225-3009-1.ch002

Delias, P., & Lakiotaki, K. (2018). Discovering Process Horizontal Boundaries to Facilitate Process Comprehension. *International Journal of Operations Research and Information Systems, 9*(2), 1–31. doi:10.4018/IJORIS.2018040101

Denholm, J., & Lee-Davies, L. (2018). Success Factors for Games in Business and Project Management. In *Enhancing Education and Training Initiatives Through Serious Games* (pp. 34–68). Hershey, PA: IGI Global. doi:10.4018/978-1-5225-3689-5.ch002

Deshpande, M. (2017). Best Practices in Management Institutions for Global Leadership: Policy Aspects. In N. Baporikar (Ed.), *Management Education for Global Leadership* (pp. 1–27). Hershey, PA: IGI Global. doi:10.4018/978-1-5225-1013-0.ch001

Deshpande, M. (2018). Policy Perspectives for SMEs Knowledge Management. In N. Baporikar (Ed.), *Knowledge Integration Strategies for Entrepreneurship and Sustainability* (pp. 23–46). Hershey, PA: IGI Global. doi:10.4018/978-1-5225-5115-7.ch002

Dezdar, S. (2017). ERP Implementation Projects in Asian Countries: A Comparative Study on Iran and China. *International Journal of Information Technology Project Management, 8*(3), 52–68. doi:10.4018/IJITPM.2017070104

Domingos, D., Martinho, R., & Varajão, J. (2016). Controlled Flexibility in Healthcare Processes: A BPMN-Extension Approach. In M. Cruz-Cunha, I. Miranda, R. Martinho, & R. Rijo (Eds.), *Encyclopedia of E-Health and Telemedicine* (pp. 521–535). Hershey, PA: IGI Global. doi:10.4018/978-1-4666-9978-6.ch040

Domingos, D., Respício, A., & Martinho, R. (2017). Reliability of IoT-Aware BPMN Healthcare Processes. In C. Reis & M. Maximiano (Eds.), *Internet of Things and Advanced Application in Healthcare* (pp. 214–248). Hershey, PA: IGI Global. doi:10.4018/978-1-5225-1820-4.ch008

Dosumu, O., Hussain, J., & El-Gohary, H. (2017). An Exploratory Study of the Impact of Government Policies on the Development of Small and Medium Enterprises in Developing Countries: The Case of Nigeria. *International Journal of Customer Relationship Marketing and Management*, *8*(4), 51–62. doi:10.4018/IJCRMM.2017100104

Durst, S., Bruns, G., & Edvardsson, I. R. (2017). Retaining Knowledge in Smaller Building and Construction Firms. *International Journal of Knowledge and Systems Science*, *8*(3), 1–12. doi:10.4018/IJKSS.2017070101

Edvardsson, I. R., & Durst, S. (2017). Outsourcing, Knowledge, and Learning: A Critical Review. *International Journal of Knowledge-Based Organizations*, *7*(2), 13–26. doi:10.4018/IJKBO.2017040102

Edwards, J. S. (2018). Integrating Knowledge Management and Business Processes. In M. Khosrow-Pour, D.B.A. (Ed.), Encyclopedia of Information Science and Technology, Fourth Edition (pp. 5046-5055). Hershey, PA: IGI Global. doi:10.4018/978-1-5225-2255-3.ch437

Ejiogu, A. O. (2018). Economics of Farm Management. In *Agricultural Finance and Opportunities for Investment and Expansion* (pp. 56–72). Hershey, PA: IGI Global. doi:10.4018/978-1-5225-3059-6.ch003

Ekanem, I., & Abiade, G. E. (2018). Factors Influencing the Use of E-Commerce by Small Enterprises in Nigeria. *International Journal of ICT Research in Africa and the Middle East*, *7*(1), 37–53. doi:10.4018/IJICTRAME.2018010103

Ekanem, I., & Alrossais, L. A. (2017). Succession Challenges Facing Family Businesses in Saudi Arabia. In P. Zgheib (Ed.), *Entrepreneurship and Business Innovation in the Middle East* (pp. 122–146). Hershey, PA: IGI Global. doi:10.4018/978-1-5225-2066-5.ch007

El Faquih, L., & Fredj, M. (2017). Ontology-Based Framework for Quality in Configurable Process Models. *Journal of Electronic Commerce in Organizations*, *15*(2), 48–60. doi:10.4018/JECO.2017040104

El-Gohary, H., & El-Gohary, Z. (2016). An Attempt to Explore Electronic Marketing Adoption and Implementation Aspects in Developing Countries: The Case of Egypt. *International Journal of Customer Relationship Marketing and Management*, *7*(4), 1–26. doi:10.4018/IJCRMM.2016100101

Entico, G. J. (2016). Knowledge Management and the Medical Health Librarians: A Perception Study. In J. Yap, M. Perez, M. Ayson, & G. Entico (Eds.), *Special Library Administration, Standardization and Technological Integration* (pp. 52–77). Hershey, PA: IGI Global. doi:10.4018/978-1-4666-9542-9.ch003

Faisal, M. N., & Talib, F. (2017). Building Ambidextrous Supply Chains in SMEs: How to Tackle the Barriers? *International Journal of Information Systems and Supply Chain Management, 10*(4), 80–100. doi:10.4018/IJISSCM.2017100105

Fernandes, T. M., Gomes, J., & Romão, M. (2017). Investments in E-Government: A Benefit Management Case Study. *International Journal of Electronic Government Research, 13*(3), 1–17. doi:10.4018/IJEGR.2017070101

Fouda, F. A. (2016). A Suggested Curriculum in Career Education to Develop Business Secondary Schools Students' Career Knowledge Management Domains and Professional Thinking. *International Journal of Technology Diffusion, 7*(2), 42–62. doi:10.4018/IJTD.2016040103

Gallardo-Vázquez, D., & Pajuelo-Moreno, M. L. (2016). How Spanish Universities are Promoting Entrepreneurship through Your Own Lines of Teaching and Research? In L. Carvalho (Ed.), *Handbook of Research on Entrepreneurial Success and its Impact on Regional Development* (pp. 431–454). Hershey, PA: IGI Global. doi:10.4018/978-1-4666-9567-2.ch019

Gao, S. S., Oreal, S., & Zhang, J. (2018). Contemporary Financial Risk Management Perceptions and Practices of Small-Sized Chinese Businesses. In I. Management Association (Ed.), Global Business Expansion: Concepts, Methodologies, Tools, and Applications (pp. 917-931). Hershey, PA: IGI Global. doi:10.4018/978-1-5225-5481-3.ch041

Garg, R., & Berning, S. C. (2017). Indigenous Chinese Management Philosophies: Key Concepts and Relevance for Modern Chinese Firms. In B. Christiansen & G. Koc (Eds.), *Transcontinental Strategies for Industrial Development and Economic Growth* (pp. 43–57). Hershey, PA: IGI Global. doi:10.4018/978-1-5225-2160-0.ch003

Gencer, Y. G. (2017). Supply Chain Management in Retailing Business. In U. Akkucuk (Ed.), *Ethics and Sustainability in Global Supply Chain Management* (pp. 197–210). Hershey, PA: IGI Global. doi:10.4018/978-1-5225-2036-8.ch011

Giacosa, E. (2016). Innovation in Luxury Fashion Businesses as a Means for the Regional Development. In L. Carvalho (Ed.), *Handbook of Research on Entrepreneurial Success and its Impact on Regional Development* (pp. 206–222). Hershey, PA: IGI Global. doi:10.4018/978-1-4666-9567-2.ch010

Giacosa, E. (2018). The Increasing of the Regional Development Thanks to the Luxury Business Innovation. In L. Carvalho (Ed.), *Handbook of Research on Entrepreneurial Ecosystems and Social Dynamics in a Globalized World* (pp. 260–273). Hershey, PA: IGI Global. doi:10.4018/978-1-5225-3525-6.ch011

Gianni, M., & Gotzamani, K. (2016). Integrated Management Systems and Information Management Systems: Common Threads. In P. Papajorgji, F. Pinet, A. Guimarães, & J. Papathanasiou (Eds.), *Automated Enterprise Systems for Maximizing Business Performance* (pp. 195–214). Hershey, PA: IGI Global. doi:10.4018/978-1-4666-8841-4.ch011

Gianni, M., Gotzamani, K., & Linden, I. (2016). How a BI-wise Responsible Integrated Management System May Support Food Traceability. *International Journal of Decision Support System Technology*, *8*(2), 1–17. doi:10.4018/IJDSST.2016040101

Glykas, M., & George, J. (2017). Quality and Process Management Systems in the UAE Maritime Industry. *International Journal of Productivity Management and Assessment Technologies*, *5*(1), 20–39. doi:10.4018/IJPMAT.2017010102

Glykas, M., Valiris, G., Kokkinaki, A., & Koutsoukou, Z. (2018). Banking Business Process Management Implementation. *International Journal of Productivity Management and Assessment Technologies*, *6*(1), 50–69. doi:10.4018/IJPMAT.2018010104

Gomes, J., & Romão, M. (2017). The Balanced Scorecard: Keeping Updated and Aligned with Today's Business Trends. *International Journal of Productivity Management and Assessment Technologies*, *5*(2), 1–15. doi:10.4018/IJPMAT.2017070101

Gomes, J., & Romão, M. (2017). Aligning Information Systems and Technology with Benefit Management and Balanced Scorecard. In S. De Haes & W. Van Grembergen (Eds.), *Strategic IT Governance and Alignment in Business Settings* (pp. 112–131). Hershey, PA: IGI Global. doi:10.4018/978-1-5225-0861-8.ch005

Grefen, P., & Turetken, O. (2017). Advanced Business Process Management in Networked E-Business Scenarios. *International Journal of E-Business Research*, *13*(4), 70–104. doi:10.4018/IJEBR.2017100105

Haider, A., & Saetang, S. (2017). Strategic IT Alignment in Service Sector. In S. Rozenes & Y. Cohen (Eds.), *Handbook of Research on Strategic Alliances and Value Co-Creation in the Service Industry* (pp. 231–258). Hershey, PA: IGI Global. doi:10.4018/978-1-5225-2084-9.ch012

Haider, A., & Tang, S. S. (2016). Maximising Value Through IT and Business Alignment: A Case of IT Governance Institutionalisation at a Thai Bank. *International Journal of Technology Diffusion*, *7*(3), 33–58. doi:10.4018/IJTD.2016070104

Hajilari, A. B., Ghadaksaz, M., & Fasghandis, G. S. (2017). Assessing Organizational Readiness for Implementing ERP System Using Fuzzy Expert System Approach. *International Journal of Enterprise Information Systems*, *13*(1), 67–85. doi:10.4018/IJEIS.2017010105

Haldorai, A., Ramu, A., & Murugan, S. (2018). Social Aware Cognitive Radio Networks: Effectiveness of Social Networks as a Strategic Tool for Organizational Business Management. In H. Bansal, G. Shrivastava, G. Nguyen, & L. Stanciu (Eds.), *Social Network Analytics for Contemporary Business Organizations* (pp. 188–202). Hershey, PA: IGI Global. doi:10.4018/978-1-5225-5097-6.ch010

Hall, O. P. Jr. (2017). Social Media Driven Management Education. *International Journal of Knowledge-Based Organizations*, *7*(2), 43–59. doi:10.4018/IJKBO.2017040104

Hanifah, H., Halim, H. A., Ahmad, N. H., & Vafaei-Zadeh, A. (2017). Innovation Culture as a Mediator Between Specific Human Capital and Innovation Performance Among Bumiputera SMEs in Malaysia. In N. Ahmad, T. Ramayah, H. Halim, & S. Rahman (Eds.), *Handbook of Research on Small and Medium Enterprises in Developing Countries* (pp. 261–279). Hershey, PA: IGI Global. doi:10.4018/978-1-5225-2165-5.ch012

Hartlieb, S., & Silvius, G. (2017). Handling Uncertainty in Project Management and Business Development: Similarities and Differences. In Y. Raydugin (Ed.), *Handbook of Research on Leveraging Risk and Uncertainties for Effective Project Management* (pp. 337–362). Hershey, PA: IGI Global. doi:10.4018/978-1-5225-1790-0.ch016

Hass, K. B. (2017). Living on the Edge: Managing Project Complexity. In Y. Raydugin (Ed.), *Handbook of Research on Leveraging Risk and Uncertainties for Effective Project Management* (pp. 177–201). Hershey, PA: IGI Global. doi:10.4018/978-1-5225-1790-0.ch009

Hassan, A., & Privitera, D. S. (2016). Google AdSense as a Mobile Technology in Education. In J. Holland (Ed.), *Wearable Technology and Mobile Innovations for Next-Generation Education* (pp. 200–223). Hershey, PA: IGI Global. doi:10.4018/978-1-5225-0069-8.ch011

Hassan, A., & Rahimi, R. (2016). Consuming "Innovation" in Tourism: Augmented Reality as an Innovation Tool in Digital Tourism Marketing. In N. Pappas & I. Bregoli (Eds.), *Global Dynamics in Travel, Tourism, and Hospitality* (pp. 130–147). Hershey, PA: IGI Global. doi:10.4018/978-1-5225-0201-2.ch008

Hawking, P., & Carmine Sellitto, C. (2017). Developing an Effective Strategy for Organizational Business Intelligence. In M. Tavana (Ed.), *Enterprise Information Systems and the Digitalization of Business Functions* (pp. 222–237). Hershey, PA: IGI Global. doi:10.4018/978-1-5225-2382-6.ch010

Hawking, P., & Sellitto, C. (2017). A Fast-Moving Consumer Goods Company and Business Intelligence Strategy Development. *International Journal of Enterprise Information Systems, 13*(2), 22–33. doi:10.4018/IJEIS.2017040102

Hawking, P., & Sellitto, C. (2017). Business Intelligence Strategy: Two Case Studies. *International Journal of Business Intelligence Research, 8*(2), 17–30. doi:10.4018/IJBIR.2017070102

Haynes, J. D., Arockiasamy, S., Al Rashdi, M., & Al Rashdi, S. (2016). Business and E Business Strategies for Coopetition and Thematic Management as a Sustained Basis for Ethics and Social Responsibility in Emerging Markets. In M. Al-Shammari & H. Masri (Eds.), *Ethical and Social Perspectives on Global Business Interaction in Emerging Markets* (pp. 25–39). Hershey, PA: IGI Global. doi:10.4018/978-1-4666-9864-2.ch002

Hee, W. J., Jalleh, G., Lai, H., & Lin, C. (2017). E-Commerce and IT Projects: Evaluation and Management Issues in Australian and Taiwanese Hospitals. *International Journal of Public Health Management and Ethics, 2*(1), 69–90. doi:10.4018/IJPHME.2017010104

Hernandez, A. A. (2018). Exploring the Factors to Green IT Adoption of SMEs in the Philippines. *Journal of Cases on Information Technology, 20*(2), 49–66. doi:10.4018/JCIT.2018040104

Hernandez, A. A., & Ona, S. E. (2016). Green IT Adoption: Lessons from the Philippines Business Process Outsourcing Industry. *International Journal of Social Ecology and Sustainable Development, 7*(1), 1–34. doi:10.4018/IJSESD.2016010101

Hollman, A., Bickford, S., & Hollman, T. (2017). Cyber InSecurity: A Post-Mortem Attempt to Assess Cyber Problems from IT and Business Management Perspectives. *Journal of Cases on Information Technology, 19*(3), 42–70. doi:10.4018/JCIT.2017070104

Igbinakhase, I. (2017). Responsible and Sustainable Management Practices in Developing and Developed Business Environments. In Z. Fields (Ed.), *Collective Creativity for Responsible and Sustainable Business Practice* (pp. 180–207). Hershey, PA: IGI Global. doi:10.4018/978-1-5225-1823-5.ch010

Ilahi, L., Ghannouchi, S. A., & Martinho, R. (2016). A Business Process Management Approach to Home Healthcare Processes: On the Gap between Intention and Reality. In M. Cruz-Cunha, I. Miranda, R. Martinho, & R. Rijo (Eds.), *Encyclopedia of E-Health and Telemedicine* (pp. 439–457). Hershey, PA: IGI Global. doi:10.4018/978-1-4666-9978-6.ch035

Iwata, J. J., & Hoskins, R. G. (2017). Managing Indigenous Knowledge in Tanzania: A Business Perspective. In P. Jain & N. Mnjama (Eds.), *Managing Knowledge Resources and Records in Modern Organizations* (pp. 198–214). Hershey, PA: IGI Global. doi:10.4018/978-1-5225-1965-2.ch012

Jabeen, F., Ahmad, S. Z., & Alkaabi, S. (2016). The Internationalization Decision-Making of United Arab Emirates Family Businesses. In N. Zakaria, A. Abdul-Talib, & N. Osman (Eds.), *Handbook of Research on Impacts of International Business and Political Affairs on the Global Economy* (pp. 1–22). Hershey, PA: IGI Global. doi:10.4018/978-1-4666-9806-2.ch001

Jain, P. (2017). Ethical and Legal Issues in Knowledge Management Life-Cycle in Business. In P. Jain & N. Mnjama (Eds.), *Managing Knowledge Resources and Records in Modern Organizations* (pp. 82–101). Hershey, PA: IGI Global. doi:10.4018/978-1-5225-1965-2.ch006

Jamali, D., Abdallah, H., & Matar, F. (2016). Opportunities and Challenges for CSR Mainstreaming in Business Schools. *International Journal of Technology and Educational Marketing*, *6*(2), 1–29. doi:10.4018/IJTEM.2016070101

James, S., & Hauli, E. (2017). Holistic Management Education at Tanzanian Rural Development Planning Institute. In N. Baporikar (Ed.), *Management Education for Global Leadership* (pp. 112–136). Hershey, PA: IGI Global. doi:10.4018/978-1-5225-1013-0.ch006

Janošková, M., Csikósová, A., & Čulková, K. (2018). Measurement of Company Performance as Part of Its Strategic Management. In R. Leon (Ed.), *Managerial Strategies for Business Sustainability During Turbulent Times* (pp. 309–335). Hershey, PA: IGI Global. doi:10.4018/978-1-5225-2716-9.ch017

Jean-Vasile, A., & Alecu, A. (2017). Theoretical and Practical Approaches in Understanding the Influences of Cost-Productivity-Profit Trinomial in Contemporary Enterprises. In A. Jean Vasile & D. Nicolò (Eds.), *Sustainable Entrepreneurship and Investments in the Green Economy* (pp. 28–62). Hershey, PA: IGI Global. doi:10.4018/978-1-5225-2075-7.ch002

Jha, D. G. (2016). Preparing for Information Technology Driven Changes. In S. Tiwari & L. Nafees (Eds.), *Innovative Management Education Pedagogies for Preparing Next-Generation Leaders* (pp. 258–274). Hershey, PA: IGI Global. doi:10.4018/978-1-4666-9691-4.ch015

Joia, L. A., & Correia, J. C. (2018). CIO Competencies From the IT Professional Perspective: Insights From Brazil. *Journal of Global Information Management, 26*(2), 74–103. doi:10.4018/JGIM.2018040104

Juma, A., & Mzera, N. (2017). Knowledge Management and Records Management and Competitive Advantage in Business. In P. Jain & N. Mnjama (Eds.), *Managing Knowledge Resources and Records in Modern Organizations* (pp. 15–28). Hershey, PA: IGI Global. doi:10.4018/978-1-5225-1965-2.ch002

K., I., & A, V. (2018). Monitoring and Auditing in the Cloud. In K. Munir (Ed.), *Cloud Computing Technologies for Green Enterprises* (pp. 318-350). Hershey, PA: IGI Global. doi:10.4018/978-1-5225-3038-1.ch013

Kabra, G., Ghosh, V., & Ramesh, A. (2018). Enterprise Integrated Business Process Management and Business Intelligence Framework for Business Process Sustainability. In A. Paul, D. Bhattacharyya, & S. Anand (Eds.), *Green Initiatives for Business Sustainability and Value Creation* (pp. 228–238). Hershey, PA: IGI Global. doi:10.4018/978-1-5225-2662-9.ch010

Kaoud, M. (2017). Investigation of Customer Knowledge Management: A Case Study Research. *International Journal of Service Science, Management, Engineering, and Technology, 8*(2), 12–22. doi:10.4018/IJSSMET.2017040102

Kara, M. E., & Fırat, S. Ü. (2016). Sustainability, Risk, and Business Intelligence in Supply Chains. In M. Erdoğdu, T. Arun, & I. Ahmad (Eds.), *Handbook of Research on Green Economic Development Initiatives and Strategies* (pp. 501–538). Hershey, PA: IGI Global. doi:10.4018/978-1-5225-0440-5.ch022

Katuu, S. (2018). A Comparative Assessment of Enterprise Content Management Maturity Models. In N. Gwangwava & M. Mutingi (Eds.), *E-Manufacturing and E-Service Strategies in Contemporary Organizations* (pp. 93–118). Hershey, PA: IGI Global. doi:10.4018/978-1-5225-3628-4.ch005

Khan, M. A. (2016). MNEs Management Strategies in Developing Countries: Establishing the Context. In M. Khan (Ed.), *Multinational Enterprise Management Strategies in Developing Countries* (pp. 1–33). Hershey, PA: IGI Global. doi:10.4018/978-1-5225-0276-0.ch001

Khan, M. A. (2016). Operational Approaches in Organizational Structure: A Case for MNEs in Developing Countries. In M. Khan (Ed.), *Multinational Enterprise Management Strategies in Developing Countries* (pp. 129–151). Hershey, PA: IGI Global. doi:10.4018/978-1-5225-0276-0.ch007

Kinnunen, S., Ylä-Kujala, A., Marttonen-Arola, S., Kärri, T., & Baglee, D. (2018). Internet of Things in Asset Management: Insights from Industrial Professionals and Academia. *International Journal of Service Science, Management, Engineering, and Technology*, *9*(2), 104–119. doi:10.4018/IJSSMET.2018040105

Klein, A. Z., Sabino de Freitas, A., Machado, L., Freitas, J. C. Jr, Graziola, P. G. Jr, & Schlemmer, E. (2017). Virtual Worlds Applications for Management Education. In L. Tomei (Ed.), *Exploring the New Era of Technology-Infused Education* (pp. 279–299). Hershey, PA: IGI Global. doi:10.4018/978-1-5225-1709-2.ch017

Kożuch, B., & Jabłoński, A. (2017). Adopting the Concept of Business Models in Public Management. In M. Lewandowski & B. Kożuch (Eds.), *Public Sector Entrepreneurship and the Integration of Innovative Business Models* (pp. 10–46). Hershey, PA: IGI Global. doi:10.4018/978-1-5225-2215-7.ch002

Kumar, J., Adhikary, A., & Jha, A. (2017). Small Active Investors' Perceptions and Preferences Towards Tax Saving Mutual Fund Schemes in Eastern India: An Empirical Note. *International Journal of Asian Business and Information Management*, *8*(2), 35–45. doi:10.4018/IJABIM.2017040103

Lassoued, Y., Bouzguenda, L., & Mahmoud, T. (2016). Context-Aware Business Process Versions Management. *International Journal of e-Collaboration*, *12*(3), 7–33. doi:10.4018/IJeC.2016070102

Lavassani, K. M., & Movahedi, B. (2017). Applications Driven Information Systems: Beyond Networks toward Business Ecosystems. *International Journal of Innovation in the Digital Economy*, *8*(1), 61–75. doi:10.4018/IJIDE.2017010104

Lazzareschi, V. H., & Brito, M. S. (2017). Strategic Information Management: Proposal of Business Project Model. In G. Jamil, A. Soares, & C. Pessoa (Eds.), *Handbook of Research on Information Management for Effective Logistics and Supply Chains* (pp. 59–88). Hershey, PA: IGI Global. doi:10.4018/978-1-5225-0973-8.ch004

Lederer, M., Kurz, M., & Lazarov, P. (2017). Usage and Suitability of Methods for Strategic Business Process Initiatives: A Multi Case Study Research. *International Journal of Productivity Management and Assessment Technologies, 5*(1), 40–51. doi:10.4018/IJPMAT.2017010103

Lee, I. (2017). A Social Enterprise Business Model and a Case Study of Pacific Community Ventures (PCV). In V. Potocan, M. Üngan, & Z. Nedelko (Eds.), *Handbook of Research on Managerial Solutions in Non-Profit Organizations* (pp. 182–204). Hershey, PA: IGI Global. doi:10.4018/978-1-5225-0731-4.ch009

Lee, L. J., & Leu, J. (2016). Exploring the Effectiveness of IT Application and Value Method in the Innovation Performance of Enterprise. *International Journal of Enterprise Information Systems, 12*(2), 47–65. doi:10.4018/IJEIS.2016040104

Lee, Y. (2016). Alignment Effect of Entrepreneurial Orientation and Marketing Orientation on Firm Performance. *International Journal of Customer Relationship Marketing and Management, 7*(4), 58–69. doi:10.4018/IJCRMM.2016100104

Leon, L. A., Seal, K. C., Przasnyski, Z. H., & Wiedenman, I. (2017). Skills and Competencies Required for Jobs in Business Analytics: A Content Analysis of Job Advertisements Using Text Mining. *International Journal of Business Intelligence Research, 8*(1), 1–25. doi:10.4018/IJBIR.2017010101

Leu, J., Lee, L. J., & Krischke, A. (2016). Value Engineering-Based Method for Implementing the ISO14001 System in the Green Supply Chains. *International Journal of Strategic Decision Sciences, 7*(4), 1–20. doi:10.4018/IJSDS.2016100101

Levy, C. L., & Elias, N. I. (2017). SOHO Users' Perceptions of Reliability and Continuity of Cloud-Based Services. In M. Moore (Ed.), *Cybersecurity Breaches and Issues Surrounding Online Threat Protection* (pp. 248–287). Hershey, PA: IGI Global. doi:10.4018/978-1-5225-1941-6.ch011

Levy, M. (2018). Change Management Serving Knowledge Management and Organizational Development: Reflections and Review. In N. Baporikar (Ed.), *Global Practices in Knowledge Management for Societal and Organizational Development* (pp. 256–270). Hershey, PA: IGI Global. doi:10.4018/978-1-5225-3009-1.ch012

Lewandowski, M. (2017). Public Organizations and Business Model Innovation: The Role of Public Service Design. In M. Lewandowski & B. Kożuch (Eds.), *Public Sector Entrepreneurship and the Integration of Innovative Business Models* (pp. 47–72). Hershey, PA: IGI Global. doi:10.4018/978-1-5225-2215-7.ch003

Lhannaoui, H., Kabbaj, M. I., & Bakkoury, Z. (2017). A Survey of Risk-Aware Business Process Modelling. *International Journal of Risk and Contingency Management, 6*(3), 14–26. doi:10.4018/IJRCM.2017070102

Li, J., Sun, W., Jiang, W., Yang, H., & Zhang, L. (2017). How the Nature of Exogenous Shocks and Crises Impact Company Performance?: The Effects of Industry Characteristics. *International Journal of Risk and Contingency Management, 6*(4), 40–55. doi:10.4018/IJRCM.2017100103

Lu, C., & Liu, S. (2016). Cultural Tourism O2O Business Model Innovation-A Case Study of CTrip. *Journal of Electronic Commerce in Organizations, 14*(2), 16–31. doi:10.4018/JECO.2016040102

Machen, B., Hosseini, M. R., Wood, A., & Bakhshi, J. (2016). An Investigation into using SAP-PS as a Multidimensional Project Control System (MPCS). *International Journal of Enterprise Information Systems, 12*(2), 66–81. doi:10.4018/IJEIS.2016040105

Malega, P. (2017). Small and Medium Enterprises in the Slovak Republic: Status and Competitiveness of SMEs in the Global Markets and Possibilities of Optimization. In M. Vemić (Ed.), *Optimal Management Strategies in Small and Medium Enterprises* (pp. 102–124). Hershey, PA: IGI Global. doi:10.4018/978-1-5225-1949-2.ch006

Malewska, K. M. (2017). Intuition in Decision-Making on the Example of a Non-Profit Organization. In V. Potocan, M. Ünğan, & Z. Nedelko (Eds.), *Handbook of Research on Managerial Solutions in Non-Profit Organizations* (pp. 378–399). Hershey, PA: IGI Global. doi:10.4018/978-1-5225-0731-4.ch018

Maroofi, F. (2017). Entrepreneurial Orientation and Organizational Learning Ability Analysis for Innovation and Firm Performance. In N. Baporikar (Ed.), *Innovation and Shifting Perspectives in Management Education* (pp. 144–165). Hershey, PA: IGI Global. doi:10.4018/978-1-5225-1019-2.ch007

Martins, P. V., & Zacarias, M. (2017). A Web-based Tool for Business Process Improvement. *International Journal of Web Portals, 9*(2), 68–84. doi:10.4018/IJWP.2017070104

Matthies, B., & Coners, A. (2017). Exploring the Conceptual Nature of e-Business Projects. *Journal of Electronic Commerce in Organizations, 15*(3), 33–63. doi:10.4018/JECO.2017070103

McKee, J. (2018). Architecture as a Tool to Solve Business Planning Problems. In M. Khosrow-Pour, D.B.A. (Ed.), Encyclopedia of Information Science and Technology, Fourth Edition (pp. 573-586). Hershey, PA: IGI Global. doi:10.4018/978-1-5225-2255-3.ch050

McMurray, A. J., Cross, J., & Caponecchia, C. (2018). The Risk Management Profession in Australia: Business Continuity Plan Practices. In N. Bajgoric (Ed.), *Always-On Enterprise Information Systems for Modern Organizations* (pp. 112–129). Hershey, PA: IGI Global. doi:10.4018/978-1-5225-3704-5.ch006

Meddah, I. H., & Belkadi, K. (2018). Mining Patterns Using Business Process Management. In R. Hamou (Ed.), *Handbook of Research on Biomimicry in Information Retrieval and Knowledge Management* (pp. 78–89). Hershey, PA: IGI Global. doi:10.4018/978-1-5225-3004-6.ch005

Mendes, L. (2017). TQM and Knowledge Management: An Integrated Approach Towards Tacit Knowledge Management. In D. Jaziri-Bouagina & G. Jamil (Eds.), *Handbook of Research on Tacit Knowledge Management for Organizational Success* (pp. 236–263). Hershey, PA: IGI Global. doi:10.4018/978-1-5225-2394-9.ch009

Mnjama, N. M. (2017). Preservation of Recorded Information in Public and Private Sector Organizations. In P. Jain & N. Mnjama (Eds.), *Managing Knowledge Resources and Records in Modern Organizations* (pp. 149–167). Hershey, PA: IGI Global. doi:10.4018/978-1-5225-1965-2.ch009

Mokoqama, M., & Fields, Z. (2017). Principles of Responsible Management Education (PRME): Call for Responsible Management Education. In Z. Fields (Ed.), *Collective Creativity for Responsible and Sustainable Business Practice* (pp. 229–241). Hershey, PA: IGI Global. doi:10.4018/978-1-5225-1823-5.ch012

Muniapan, B. (2017). Philosophy and Management: The Relevance of Vedanta in Management. In P. Ordóñez de Pablos (Ed.), *Managerial Strategies and Solutions for Business Success in Asia* (pp. 124–139). Hershey, PA: IGI Global. doi:10.4018/978-1-5225-1886-0.ch007

Muniapan, B., Gregory, M. L., & Ling, L. A. (2016). Marketing Education in Sarawak: Looking at It from the Employers' Viewpoint. In B. Smith & A. Porath (Eds.), *Global Perspectives on Contemporary Marketing Education* (pp. 112–130). Hershey, PA: IGI Global. doi:10.4018/978-1-4666-9784-3.ch008

Murad, S. E., & Dowaji, S. (2017). Using Value-Based Approach for Managing Cloud-Based Services. In A. Turuk, B. Sahoo, & S. Addya (Eds.), *Resource Management and Efficiency in Cloud Computing Environments* (pp. 33–60). Hershey, PA: IGI Global. doi:10.4018/978-1-5225-1721-4.ch002

Mutahar, A. M., Daud, N. M., Thurasamy, R., Isaac, O., & Abdulsalam, R. (2018). The Mediating of Perceived Usefulness and Perceived Ease of Use: The Case of Mobile Banking in Yemen. *International Journal of Technology Diffusion*, *9*(2), 21–40. doi:10.4018/IJTD.2018040102

Naidoo, V. (2017). E-Learning and Management Education at African Universities. In N. Baporikar (Ed.), *Management Education for Global Leadership* (pp. 181–201). Hershey, PA: IGI Global. doi:10.4018/978-1-5225-1013-0.ch009

Naidoo, V., & Igbinakhase, I. (2018). Opportunities and Challenges of Knowledge Retention in SMEs. In N. Baporikar (Ed.), *Knowledge Integration Strategies for Entrepreneurship and Sustainability* (pp. 70–94). Hershey, PA: IGI Global. doi:10.4018/978-1-5225-5115-7.ch004

Nayak, S., & Prabhu, N. (2017). Paradigm Shift in Management Education: Need for a Cross Functional Perspective. In N. Baporikar (Ed.), *Management Education for Global Leadership* (pp. 241–255). Hershey, PA: IGI Global. doi:10.4018/978-1-5225-1013-0.ch012

Ndede-Amadi, A. A. (2016). Student Interest in the IS Specialization as Predictor of the Success Potential of New Information Systems Programmes within the Schools of Business in Kenyan Public Universities. *International Journal of Information Systems and Social Change*, *7*(2), 63–79. doi:10.4018/IJISSC.2016040104

Nedelko, Z., & Potocan, V. (2016). Management Practices for Processes Optimization: Case of Slovenia. In G. Alor-Hernández, C. Sánchez-Ramírez, & J. García-Alcaraz (Eds.), *Handbook of Research on Managerial Strategies for Achieving Optimal Performance in Industrial Processes* (pp. 545–561). Hershey, PA: IGI Global. doi:10.4018/978-1-5225-0130-5.ch025

Nedelko, Z., & Potocan, V. (2017). Management Solutions in Non-Profit Organizations: Case of Slovenia. In V. Potocan, M. Üngan, & Z. Nedelko (Eds.), *Handbook of Research on Managerial Solutions in Non-Profit Organizations* (pp. 1–22). Hershey, PA: IGI Global. doi:10.4018/978-1-5225-0731-4.ch001

Nedelko, Z., & Potocan, V. (2017). Priority of Management Tools Utilization among Managers: International Comparison. In V. Wang (Ed.), *Encyclopedia of Strategic Leadership and Management* (pp. 1083–1094). Hershey, PA: IGI Global. doi:10.4018/978-1-5225-1049-9.ch075

Nedelko, Z., Raudeliūnienė, J., & Črešnar, R. (2018). Knowledge Dynamics in Supply Chain Management. In N. Baporikar (Ed.), *Knowledge Integration Strategies for Entrepreneurship and Sustainability* (pp. 150–166). Hershey, PA: IGI Global. doi:10.4018/978-1-5225-5115-7.ch008

Nguyen, H. T., & Hipsher, S. A. (2018). Innovation and Creativity Used by Private Sector Firms in a Resources-Constrained Environment. In S. Hipsher (Ed.), *Examining the Private Sector's Role in Wealth Creation and Poverty Reduction* (pp. 219–238). Hershey, PA: IGI Global. doi:10.4018/978-1-5225-3117-3.ch010

Nycz, M., & Pólkowski, Z. (2016). Business Intelligence as a Modern IT Supporting Management of Local Government Units in Poland. *International Journal of Knowledge and Systems Science*, *7*(4), 1–18. doi:10.4018/IJKSS.2016100101

Obaji, N. O., Senin, A. A., & Olugu, M. U. (2016). Supportive Government Policy as a Mechanism for Business Incubation Performance in Nigeria. *International Journal of Information Systems and Social Change*, *7*(4), 52–66. doi:10.4018/IJISSC.2016100103

Obicci, P. A. (2017). Risk Sharing in a Partnership. In *Risk Management Strategies in Public-Private Partnerships* (pp. 115–152). Hershey, PA: IGI Global. doi:10.4018/978-1-5225-2503-5.ch004

Obidallah, W. J., & Raahemi, B. (2017). Managing Changes in Service Oriented Virtual Organizations: A Structural and Procedural Framework to Facilitate the Process of Change. *Journal of Electronic Commerce in Organizations*, *15*(1), 59–83. doi:10.4018/JECO.2017010104

Ojasalo, J., & Ojasalo, K. (2016). Service Logic Business Model Canvas for Lean Development of SMEs and Start-Ups. In N. Baporikar (Ed.), *Handbook of Research on Entrepreneurship in the Contemporary Knowledge-Based Global Economy* (pp. 217–243). Hershey, PA: IGI Global. doi:10.4018/978-1-4666-8798-1.ch010

Ojo, O. (2017). Impact of Innovation on the Entrepreneurial Success in Selected Business Enterprises in South-West Nigeria. *International Journal of Innovation in the Digital Economy*, *8*(2), 29–38. doi:10.4018/IJIDE.2017040103

Okdinawati, L., Simatupang, T. M., & Sunitiyoso, Y. (2017). Multi-Agent Reinforcement Learning for Value Co-Creation of Collaborative Transportation Management (CTM). *International Journal of Information Systems and Supply Chain Management*, *10*(3), 84–95. doi:10.4018/IJISSCM.2017070105

Ortner, E., Mevius, M., Wiedmann, P., & Kurz, F. (2016). Design of Interactional Decision Support Applications for E-Participation in Smart Cities. *International Journal of Electronic Government Research*, *12*(2), 18–38. doi:10.4018/IJEGR.2016040102

Pal, K. (2018). Building High Quality Big Data-Based Applications in Supply Chains. In A. Kumar & S. Saurav (Eds.), *Supply Chain Management Strategies and Risk Assessment in Retail Environments* (pp. 1–24). Hershey, PA: IGI Global. doi:10.4018/978-1-5225-3056-5.ch001

Palos-Sanchez, P. R., & Correia, M. B. (2018). Perspectives of the Adoption of Cloud Computing in the Tourism Sector. In J. Rodrigues, C. Ramos, P. Cardoso, & C. Henriques (Eds.), *Handbook of Research on Technological Developments for Cultural Heritage and eTourism Applications* (pp. 377–400). Hershey, PA: IGI Global. doi:10.4018/978-1-5225-2927-9.ch018

Parry, V. K., & Lind, M. L. (2016). Alignment of Business Strategy and Information Technology Considering Information Technology Governance, Project Portfolio Control, and Risk Management. *International Journal of Information Technology Project Management*, *7*(4), 21–37. doi:10.4018/IJITPM.2016100102

Pashkova, N., Trujillo-Barrera, A., Apostolakis, G., Van Dijk, G., Drakos, P. D., & Baourakis, G. (2016). Business Management Models of Microfinance Institutions (MFIs) in Africa: A Study into Their Enabling Environments. *International Journal of Food and Beverage Manufacturing and Business Models*, *1*(2), 63–82. doi:10.4018/IJFBMBM.2016070105

Patiño, B. E. (2017). New Generation Management by Convergence and Individual Identity: A Systemic and Human-Oriented Approach. In N. Baporikar (Ed.), *Innovation and Shifting Perspectives in Management Education* (pp. 119–143). Hershey, PA: IGI Global. doi:10.4018/978-1-5225-1019-2.ch006

Pawliczek, A., & Rössler, M. (2017). Knowledge of Management Tools and Systems in SMEs: Knowledge Transfer in Management. In A. Bencsik (Ed.), *Knowledge Management Initiatives and Strategies in Small and Medium Enterprises* (pp. 180–203). Hershey, PA: IGI Global. doi:10.4018/978-1-5225-1642-2.ch009

Pejic-Bach, M., Omazic, M. A., Aleksic, A., & Zoroja, J. (2018). Knowledge-Based Decision Making: A Multi-Case Analysis. In R. Leon (Ed.), *Managerial Strategies for Business Sustainability During Turbulent Times* (pp. 160–184). Hershey, PA: IGI Global. doi:10.4018/978-1-5225-2716-9.ch009

Perano, M., Hysa, X., & Calabrese, M. (2018). Strategic Planning, Cultural Context, and Business Continuity Management: Business Cases in the City of Shkoder. In A. Presenza & L. Sheehan (Eds.), *Geopolitics and Strategic Management in the Global Economy* (pp. 57–77). Hershey, PA: IGI Global. doi:10.4018/978-1-5225-2673-5.ch004

Pereira, R., Mira da Silva, M., & Lapão, L. V. (2017). IT Governance Maturity Patterns in Portuguese Healthcare. In S. De Haes & W. Van Grembergen (Eds.), *Strategic IT Governance and Alignment in Business Settings* (pp. 24–52). Hershey, PA: IGI Global. doi:10.4018/978-1-5225-0861-8.ch002

Perez-Uribe, R., & Ocampo-Guzman, D. (2016). Conflict within Colombian Family Owned SMEs: An Explosive Blend between Feelings and Business. In J. Saiz-Álvarez (Ed.), *Handbook of Research on Social Entrepreneurship and Solidarity Economics* (pp. 329–354). Hershey, PA: IGI Global. doi:10.4018/978-1-5225-0097-1.ch017

Pérez-Uribe, R. I., Torres, D. A., Jurado, S. P., & Prada, D. M. (2018). Cloud Tools for the Development of Project Management in SMEs. In R. Perez-Uribe, C. Salcedo-Perez, & D. Ocampo-Guzman (Eds.), *Handbook of Research on Intrapreneurship and Organizational Sustainability in SMEs* (pp. 95–120). Hershey, PA: IGI Global. doi:10.4018/978-1-5225-3543-0.ch005

Petrisor, I., & Cozmiuc, D. (2017). Global Supply Chain Management Organization at Siemens in the Advent of Industry 4.0. In L. Saglietto & C. Cezanne (Eds.), *Global Intermediation and Logistics Service Providers* (pp. 123–142). Hershey, PA: IGI Global. doi:10.4018/978-1-5225-2133-4.ch007

Pierce, J. M., Velliaris, D. M., & Edwards, J. (2017). A Living Case Study: A Journey Not a Destination. In N. Silton (Ed.), *Exploring the Benefits of Creativity in Education, Media, and the Arts* (pp. 158–178). Hershey, PA: IGI Global. doi:10.4018/978-1-5225-0504-4.ch008

Radosavljevic, M., & Andjelkovic, A. (2017). Multi-Criteria Decision Making Approach for Choosing Business Process for the Improvement: Upgrading of the Six Sigma Methodology. In J. Stanković, P. Delias, S. Marinković, & S. Rochhia (Eds.), *Tools and Techniques for Economic Decision Analysis* (pp. 225–247). Hershey, PA: IGI Global. doi:10.4018/978-1-5225-0959-2.ch011

Radovic, V. M. (2017). Corporate Sustainability and Responsibility and Disaster Risk Reduction: A Serbian Overview. In M. Camilleri (Ed.), *CSR 2.0 and the New Era of Corporate Citizenship* (pp. 147–164). Hershey, PA: IGI Global. doi:10.4018/978-1-5225-1842-6.ch008

Raghunath, K. M., Devi, S. L., & Patro, C. S. (2018). Impact of Risk Assessment Models on Risk Factors: A Holistic Outlook. In K. Strang, M. Korstanje, & N. Vajjhala (Eds.), *Research, Practices, and Innovations in Global Risk and Contingency Management* (pp. 134–153). Hershey, PA: IGI Global. doi:10.4018/978-1-5225-4754-9.ch008

Raman, A., & Goyal, D. P. (2017). Extending IMPLEMENT Framework for Enterprise Information Systems Implementation to Information System Innovation. In M. Tavana (Ed.), *Enterprise Information Systems and the Digitalization of Business Functions* (pp. 137–177). Hershey, PA: IGI Global. doi:10.4018/978-1-5225-2382-6.ch007

Rao, Y., & Zhang, Y. (2017). The Construction and Development of Academic Library Digital Special Subject Databases. In L. Ruan, Q. Zhu, & Y. Ye (Eds.), *Academic Library Development and Administration in China* (pp. 163–183). Hershey, PA: IGI Global. doi:10.4018/978-1-5225-0550-1.ch010

Ravasan, A. Z., Mohammadi, M. M., & Hamidi, H. (2018). An Investigation Into the Critical Success Factors of Implementing Information Technology Service Management Frameworks. In K. Jakobs (Ed.), *Corporate and Global Standardization Initiatives in Contemporary Society* (pp. 200–218). Hershey, PA: IGI Global. doi:10.4018/978-1-5225-5320-5.ch009

Renna, P., Izzo, C., & Romaniello, T. (2016). The Business Process Management Systems to Support Continuous Improvements. In W. Nuninger & J. Châtelet (Eds.), *Handbook of Research on Quality Assurance and Value Management in Higher Education* (pp. 237–256). Hershey, PA: IGI Global. doi:10.4018/978-1-5225-0024-7.ch009

Rezaie, S., Mirabedini, S. J., & Abtahi, A. (2018). Designing a Model for Implementation of Business Intelligence in the Banking Industry. *International Journal of Enterprise Information Systems, 14*(1), 77–103. doi:10.4018/IJEIS.2018010105

Riccò, R. (2016). Diversity Management: Bringing Equality, Equity, and Inclusion in the Workplace. In J. Prescott (Ed.), *Handbook of Research on Race, Gender, and the Fight for Equality* (pp. 335–359). Hershey, PA: IGI Global. doi:10.4018/978-1-5225-0047-6.ch015

Romano, L., Grimaldi, R., & Colasuonno, F. S. (2017). Demand Management as a Success Factor in Project Portfolio Management. In L. Romano (Ed.), *Project Portfolio Management Strategies for Effective Organizational Operations* (pp. 202–219). Hershey, PA: IGI Global. doi:10.4018/978-1-5225-2151-8.ch008

Rostek, K. B. (2016). Risk Management: Role and Importance in Business Organization. In D. Jakóbczak (Ed.), *Analyzing Risk through Probabilistic Modeling in Operations Research* (pp. 149–178). Hershey, PA: IGI Global. doi:10.4018/978-1-4666-9458-3.ch007

Rouhani, S., & Savoji, S. R. (2016). A Success Assessment Model for BI Tools Implementation: An Empirical Study of Banking Industry. *International Journal of Business Intelligence Research, 7*(1), 25–44. doi:10.4018/IJBIR.2016010103

Ruan, Z. (2016). A Corpus-Based Functional Analysis of Complex Nominal Groups in Written Business Discourse: The Case of "Business". *International Journal of Computer-Assisted Language Learning and Teaching*, *6*(2), 74–90. doi:10.4018/IJCALLT.2016040105

Ruhi, U. (2018). Towards an Interdisciplinary Socio-Technical Definition of Virtual Communities. In M. Khosrow-Pour, D.B.A. (Ed.), Encyclopedia of Information Science and Technology, Fourth Edition (pp. 4278-4295). Hershey, PA: IGI Global. doi:10.4018/978-1-5225-2255-3.ch371

Ryan, J., Doster, B., Daily, S., & Lewis, C. (2016). A Case Study Perspective for Balanced Perioperative Workflow Achievement through Data-Driven Process Improvement. *International Journal of Healthcare Information Systems and Informatics*, *11*(3), 19–41. doi:10.4018/IJHISI.2016070102

Safari, M. R., & Jiang, Q. (2018). The Theory and Practice of IT Governance Maturity and Strategies Alignment: Evidence From Banking Industry. *Journal of Global Information Management*, *26*(2), 127–146. doi:10.4018/JGIM.2018040106

Sahoo, J., Pati, B., & Mohanty, B. (2017). Knowledge Management as an Academic Discipline: An Assessment. In B. Gunjal (Ed.), *Managing Knowledge and Scholarly Assets in Academic Libraries* (pp. 99–126). Hershey, PA: IGI Global. doi:10.4018/978-1-5225-1741-2.ch005

Saini, D. (2017). Relevance of Teaching Values and Ethics in Management Education. In N. Baporikar (Ed.), *Management Education for Global Leadership* (pp. 90–111). Hershey, PA: IGI Global. doi:10.4018/978-1-5225-1013-0.ch005

Sambhanthan, A. (2017). Assessing and Benchmarking Sustainability in Organisations: An Integrated Conceptual Model. *International Journal of Systems and Service-Oriented Engineering*, *7*(4), 22–43. doi:10.4018/IJSSOE.2017100102

Sambhanthan, A., & Potdar, V. (2017). A Study of the Parameters Impacting Sustainability in Information Technology Organizations. *International Journal of Knowledge-Based Organizations*, *7*(3), 27–39. doi:10.4018/IJKBO.2017070103

Sánchez-Fernández, M. D., & Manríquez, M. R. (2018). The Entrepreneurial Spirit Based on Social Values: The Digital Generation. In P. Isaias & L. Carvalho (Eds.), *User Innovation and the Entrepreneurship Phenomenon in the Digital Economy* (pp. 173–193). Hershey, PA: IGI Global. doi:10.4018/978-1-5225-2826-5.ch009

Sanchez-Ruiz, L., & Blanco, B. (2017). Process Management for SMEs: Barriers, Enablers, and Benefits. In M. Vemić (Ed.), *Optimal Management Strategies in Small and Medium Enterprises* (pp. 293–319). Hershey, PA: IGI Global. doi:10.4018/978-1-5225-1949-2.ch014

Sanz, L. F., Gómez-Pérez, J., & Castillo-Martinez, A. (2018). Analysis of the European ICT Competence Frameworks. In V. Ahuja & S. Rathore (Eds.), *Multidisciplinary Perspectives on Human Capital and Information Technology Professionals* (pp. 225–245). Hershey, PA: IGI Global. doi:10.4018/978-1-5225-5297-0.ch012

Sarvepalli, A., & Godin, J. (2017). Business Process Management in the Classroom. *Journal of Cases on Information Technology*, *19*(2), 17–28. doi:10.4018/JCIT.2017040102

Satpathy, B., & Muniapan, B. (2016). Ancient Wisdom for Transformational Leadership and Its Insights from the Bhagavad-Gita. In U. Aung & P. Ordoñez de Pablos (Eds.), *Managerial Strategies and Practice in the Asian Business Sector* (pp. 1–10). Hershey, PA: IGI Global. doi:10.4018/978-1-4666-9758-4.ch001

Saygili, E. E., Ozturkoglu, Y., & Kocakulah, M. C. (2017). End Users' Perceptions of Critical Success Factors in ERP Applications. *International Journal of Enterprise Information Systems*, *13*(4), 58–75. doi:10.4018/IJEIS.2017100104

Saygili, E. E., & Saygili, A. T. (2017). Contemporary Issues in Enterprise Information Systems: A Critical Review of CSFs in ERP Implementations. In M. Tavana (Ed.), *Enterprise Information Systems and the Digitalization of Business Functions* (pp. 120–136). Hershey, PA: IGI Global. doi:10.4018/978-1-5225-2382-6.ch006

Seidenstricker, S., & Antonino, A. (2018). Business Model Innovation-Oriented Technology Management for Emergent Technologies. In M. Khosrow-Pour, D.B.A. (Ed.), Encyclopedia of Information Science and Technology, Fourth Edition (pp. 4560-4569). Hershey, PA: IGI Global. doi:10.4018/978-1-5225-2255-3.ch396

Senaratne, S., & Gunarathne, A. D. (2017). Excellence Perspective for Management Education from a Global Accountants' Hub in Asia. In N. Baporikar (Ed.), *Management Education for Global Leadership* (pp. 158–180). Hershey, PA: IGI Global. doi:10.4018/978-1-5225-1013-0.ch008

Sensuse, D. I., & Cahyaningsih, E. (2018). Knowledge Management Models: A Summative Review. *International Journal of Information Systems in the Service Sector*, *10*(1), 71–100. doi:10.4018/IJISSS.2018010105

Sensuse, D. I., Wibowo, W. C., & Cahyaningsih, E. (2016). Indonesian Government Knowledge Management Model: A Theoretical Model. *Information Resources Management Journal, 29*(1), 91–108. doi:10.4018/irmj.2016010106

Seth, M., Goyal, D., & Kiran, R. (2017). Diminution of Impediments in Implementation of Supply Chain Management Information System for Enhancing its Effectiveness in Indian Automobile Industry. *Journal of Global Information Management, 25*(3), 1–20. doi:10.4018/JGIM.2017070101

Seyal, A. H., & Rahman, M. N. (2017). Investigating Impact of Inter-Organizational Factors in Measuring ERP Systems Success: Bruneian Perspectives. In M. Tavana (Ed.), *Enterprise Information Systems and the Digitalization of Business Functions* (pp. 178–204). Hershey, PA: IGI Global. doi:10.4018/978-1-5225-2382-6.ch008

Shaikh, A. A., & Karjaluoto, H. (2016). On Some Misconceptions Concerning Digital Banking and Alternative Delivery Channels. *International Journal of E-Business Research, 12*(3), 1–16. doi:10.4018/IJEBR.2016070101

Shams, S. M. (2016). Stakeholder Relationship Management in Online Business and Competitive Value Propositions: Evidence from the Sports Industry. *International Journal of Online Marketing, 6*(2), 1–17. doi:10.4018/IJOM.2016040101

Shamsuzzoha, A. (2016). Management of Risk and Resilience within Collaborative Business Network. In R. Addo-Tenkorang, J. Kantola, P. Helo, & A. Shamsuzzoha (Eds.), *Supply Chain Strategies and the Engineer-to-Order Approach* (pp. 143–159). Hershey, PA: IGI Global. doi:10.4018/978-1-5225-0021-6.ch008

Shaqrah, A. A. (2018). Analyzing Business Intelligence Systems Based on 7s Model of McKinsey. *International Journal of Business Intelligence Research, 9*(1), 53–63. doi:10.4018/IJBIR.2018010104

Sharma, A. J. (2017). Enhancing Sustainability through Experiential Learning in Management Education. In N. Baporikar (Ed.), *Management Education for Global Leadership* (pp. 256–274). Hershey, PA: IGI Global. doi:10.4018/978-1-5225-1013-0.ch013

Shetty, K. P. (2017). Responsible Global Leadership: Ethical Challenges in Management Education. In N. Baporikar (Ed.), *Innovation and Shifting Perspectives in Management Education* (pp. 194–223). Hershey, PA: IGI Global. doi:10.4018/978-1-5225-1019-2.ch009

Sinthupundaja, J., & Kohda, Y. (2017). Effects of Corporate Social Responsibility and Creating Shared Value on Sustainability. *International Journal of Sustainable Entrepreneurship and Corporate Social Responsibility*, *2*(1), 27–38. doi:10.4018/IJSECSR.2017010103

Škarica, I., & Hrgović, A. V. (2018). Implementation of Total Quality Management Principles in Public Health Institutes in the Republic of Croatia. *International Journal of Productivity Management and Assessment Technologies*, *6*(1), 1–16. doi:10.4018/IJPMAT.2018010101

Smuts, H., Kotzé, P., Van der Merwe, A., & Loock, M. (2017). Framework for Managing Shared Knowledge in an Information Systems Outsourcing Context. *International Journal of Knowledge Management*, *13*(4), 1–30. doi:10.4018/IJKM.2017100101

Soares, E. R., & Zaidan, F. H. (2016). Information Architecture and Business Modeling in Modern Organizations of Information Technology: Professional Career Plan in Organizations IT. In G. Jamil, J. Poças Rascão, F. Ribeiro, & A. Malheiro da Silva (Eds.), *Handbook of Research on Information Architecture and Management in Modern Organizations* (pp. 439–457). Hershey, PA: IGI Global. doi:10.4018/978-1-4666-8637-3.ch020

Sousa, M. J., Cruz, R., Dias, I., & Caracol, C. (2017). Information Management Systems in the Supply Chain. In G. Jamil, A. Soares, & C. Pessoa (Eds.), *Handbook of Research on Information Management for Effective Logistics and Supply Chains* (pp. 469–485). Hershey, PA: IGI Global. doi:10.4018/978-1-5225-0973-8.ch025

Spremic, M., Turulja, L., & Bajgoric, N. (2018). Two Approaches in Assessing Business Continuity Management Attitudes in the Organizational Context. In N. Bajgoric (Ed.), *Always-On Enterprise Information Systems for Modern Organizations* (pp. 159–183). Hershey, PA: IGI Global. doi:10.4018/978-1-5225-3704-5.ch008

Steenkamp, A. L. (2018). Some Insights in Computer Science and Information Technology. In *Examining the Changing Role of Supervision in Doctoral Research Projects: Emerging Research and Opportunities* (pp. 113–133). Hershey, PA: IGI Global. doi:10.4018/978-1-5225-2610-0.ch005

Studdard, N., Dawson, M., Burton, S. L., Jackson, N., Leonard, B., Quisenberry, W., & Rahim, E. (2016). Nurturing Social Entrepreneurship and Building Social Entrepreneurial Self-Efficacy: Focusing on Primary and Secondary Schooling to Develop Future Social Entrepreneurs. In Z. Fields (Ed.), *Incorporating Business Models and Strategies into Social Entrepreneurship* (pp. 154–175). Hershey, PA: IGI Global. doi:10.4018/978-1-4666-8748-6.ch010

Sun, Z. (2016). A Framework for Developing Management Intelligent Systems. *International Journal of Systems and Service-Oriented Engineering*, *6*(1), 37–53. doi:10.4018/IJSSOE.2016010103

Swami, B., & Mphele, G. T. (2016). Problems Preventing Growth of Small Entrepreneurs: A Case Study of a Few Small Entrepreneurs in Botswana Sub-Urban Areas. In N. Baporikar (Ed.), *Handbook of Research on Entrepreneurship in the Contemporary Knowledge-Based Global Economy* (pp. 479–508). Hershey, PA: IGI Global. doi:10.4018/978-1-4666-8798-1.ch020

Tabach, A., & Croteau, A. (2017). Configurations of Information Technology Governance Practices and Business Unit Performance. *International Journal of IT/ Business Alignment and Governance*, *8*(2), 1–27. doi:10.4018/IJITBAG.2017070101

Talaue, G. M., & Iqbal, T. (2017). Assessment of e-Business Mode of Selected Private Universities in the Philippines and Pakistan. *International Journal of Online Marketing*, *7*(4), 63–77. doi:10.4018/IJOM.2017100105

Tam, G. C. (2017). Project Manager Sustainability Competence. In *Managerial Strategies and Green Solutions for Project Sustainability* (pp. 178–207). Hershey, PA: IGI Global. doi:10.4018/978-1-5225-2371-0.ch008

Tambo, T. (2018). Fashion Retail Innovation: About Context, Antecedents, and Outcome in Technological Change Projects. In I. Management Association (Ed.), Fashion and Textiles: Breakthroughs in Research and Practice (pp. 233-260). Hershey, PA: IGI Global. doi:10.4018/978-1-5225-3432-7.ch010

Tambo, T., & Mikkelsen, O. E. (2016). Fashion Supply Chain Optimization: Linking Make-to-Order Purchasing and B2B E-Commerce. In S. Joshi & R. Joshi (Eds.), *Designing and Implementing Global Supply Chain Management* (pp. 1–21). Hershey, PA: IGI Global. doi:10.4018/978-1-4666-9720-1.ch001

Tandon, K. (2016). Innovative Andragogy: The Paradigm Shift to Heutagogy. In S. Tiwari & L. Nafees (Eds.), *Innovative Management Education Pedagogies for Preparing Next-Generation Leaders* (pp. 238–257). Hershey, PA: IGI Global. doi:10.4018/978-1-4666-9691-4.ch014

Tantau, A. D., & Frăţilă, L. C. (2018). Information and Management System for Renewable Energy Business. In *Entrepreneurship and Business Development in the Renewable Energy Sector* (pp. 200–244). Hershey, PA: IGI Global. doi:10.4018/978-1-5225-3625-3.ch006

Teixeira, N., Pardal, P. N., & Rafael, B. G. (2018). Internationalization, Financial Performance, and Organizational Challenges: A Success Case in Portugal. In L. Carvalho (Ed.), *Handbook of Research on Entrepreneurial Ecosystems and Social Dynamics in a Globalized World* (pp. 379–423). Hershey, PA: IGI Global. doi:10.4018/978-1-5225-3525-6.ch017

Trad, A., & Kalpić, D. (2016). The E-Business Transformation Framework for E-Commerce Architecture-Modeling Projects. In I. Lee (Ed.), *Encyclopedia of E-Commerce Development, Implementation, and Management* (pp. 733–753). Hershey, PA: IGI Global. doi:10.4018/978-1-4666-9787-4.ch052

Trad, A., & Kalpić, D. (2016). The E-Business Transformation Framework for E-Commerce Control and Monitoring Pattern. In I. Lee (Ed.), *Encyclopedia of E-Commerce Development, Implementation, and Management* (pp. 754–777). Hershey, PA: IGI Global. doi:10.4018/978-1-4666-9787-4.ch053

Trad, A., & Kalpić, D. (2018). The Business Transformation Framework, Agile Project and Change Management. In M. Khosrow-Pour, D.B.A. (Ed.), Encyclopedia of Information Science and Technology, Fourth Edition (pp. 620-635). Hershey, PA: IGI Global. doi:10.4018/978-1-5225-2255-3.ch054

Trad, A., & Kalpić, D. (2018). The Business Transformation and Enterprise Architecture Framework: The Financial Engineering E-Risk Management and E-Law Integration. In B. Sergi, F. Fidanoski, M. Ziolo, & V. Naumovski (Eds.), *Regaining Global Stability After the Financial Crisis* (pp. 46–65). Hershey, PA: IGI Global. doi:10.4018/978-1-5225-4026-7.ch003

Turulja, L., & Bajgoric, N. (2018). Business Continuity and Information Systems: A Systematic Literature Review. In N. Bajgoric (Ed.), *Always-On Enterprise Information Systems for Modern Organizations* (pp. 60–87). Hershey, PA: IGI Global. doi:10.4018/978-1-5225-3704-5.ch004

van Wessel, R. M., de Vries, H. J., & Ribbers, P. M. (2016). Business Benefits through Company IT Standardization. In K. Jakobs (Ed.), *Effective Standardization Management in Corporate Settings* (pp. 34–53). Hershey, PA: IGI Global. doi:10.4018/978-1-4666-9737-9.ch003

Vargas-Hernández, J. G. (2017). Professional Integrity in Business Management Education. In N. Baporikar (Ed.), *Management Education for Global Leadership* (pp. 70–89). Hershey, PA: IGI Global. doi:10.4018/978-1-5225-1013-0.ch004

Vasista, T. G., & AlAbdullatif, A. M. (2017). Role of Electronic Customer Relationship Management in Demand Chain Management: A Predictive Analytic Approach. *International Journal of Information Systems and Supply Chain Management, 10*(1), 53–67. doi:10.4018/IJISSCM.2017010104

Vergidis, K. (2016). Rediscovering Business Processes: Definitions, Patterns, and Modelling Approaches. In P. Papajorgji, F. Pinet, A. Guimarães, & J. Papathanasiou (Eds.), *Automated Enterprise Systems for Maximizing Business Performance* (pp. 97–122). Hershey, PA: IGI Global. doi:10.4018/978-1-4666-8841-4.ch007

Vieru, D., & Bourdeau, S. (2017). Survival in the Digital Era: A Digital Competence-Based Multi-Case Study in the Canadian SME Clothing Industry. *International Journal of Social and Organizational Dynamics in IT, 6*(1), 17–34. doi:10.4018/IJSODIT.2017010102

Vijayan, G., & Kamarulzaman, N. H. (2017). An Introduction to Sustainable Supply Chain Management and Business Implications. In M. Khan, M. Hussain, & M. Ajmal (Eds.), *Green Supply Chain Management for Sustainable Business Practice* (pp. 27–50). Hershey, PA: IGI Global. doi:10.4018/978-1-5225-0635-5.ch002

Vlachvei, A., & Notta, O. (2017). Firm Competitiveness: Theories, Evidence, and Measurement. In A. Vlachvei, O. Notta, K. Karantininis, & N. Tsounis (Eds.), *Factors Affecting Firm Competitiveness and Performance in the Modern Business World* (pp. 1–42). Hershey, PA: IGI Global. doi:10.4018/978-1-5225-0843-4.ch001

von Rosing, M., Fullington, N., & Walker, J. (2016). Using the Business Ontology and Enterprise Standards to Transform Three Leading Organizations. *International Journal of Conceptual Structures and Smart Applications, 4*(1), 71–99. doi:10.4018/IJCSSA.2016010104

von Rosing, M., & von Scheel, H. (2016). Using the Business Ontology to Develop Enterprise Standards. *International Journal of Conceptual Structures and Smart Applications, 4*(1), 48–70. doi:10.4018/IJCSSA.2016010103

Walczak, S. (2016). Artificial Neural Networks and other AI Applications for Business Management Decision Support. *International Journal of Sociotechnology and Knowledge Development, 8*(4), 1–20. doi:10.4018/IJSKD.2016100101

Wamba, S. F., Akter, S., Kang, H., Bhattacharya, M., & Upal, M. (2016). The Primer of Social Media Analytics. *Journal of Organizational and End User Computing, 28*(2), 1–12. doi:10.4018/JOEUC.2016040101

Wang, C., Schofield, M., Li, X., & Ou, X. (2017). Do Chinese Students in Public and Private Higher Education Institutes Perform at Different Level in One of the Leadership Skills: Critical Thinking?: An Exploratory Comparison. In V. Wang (Ed.), *Encyclopedia of Strategic Leadership and Management* (pp. 160–181). Hershey, PA: IGI Global. doi:10.4018/978-1-5225-1049-9.ch013

Wang, F., Raisinghani, M. S., Mora, M., & Wang, X. (2016). Strategic E-Business Management through a Balanced Scored Card Approach. In I. Lee (Ed.), *Encyclopedia of E-Commerce Development, Implementation, and Management* (pp. 361–386). Hershey, PA: IGI Global. doi:10.4018/978-1-4666-9787-4.ch027

Wang, J. (2017). Multi-Agent based Production Management Decision System Modelling for the Textile Enterprise. *Journal of Global Information Management, 25*(4), 1–15. doi:10.4018/JGIM.2017100101

Wiedemann, A., & Gewald, H. (2017). Examining Cross-Domain Alignment: The Correlation of Business Strategy, IT Management, and IT Business Value. *International Journal of IT/Business Alignment and Governance, 8*(1), 17–31. doi:10.4018/IJITBAG.2017010102

Wolf, R., & Thiel, M. (2018). Advancing Global Business Ethics in China: Reducing Poverty Through Human and Social Welfare. In S. Hipsher (Ed.), *Examining the Private Sector's Role in Wealth Creation and Poverty Reduction* (pp. 67–84). Hershey, PA: IGI Global. doi:10.4018/978-1-5225-3117-3.ch004

Wu, J., Ding, F., Xu, M., Mo, Z., & Jin, A. (2016). Investigating the Determinants of Decision-Making on Adoption of Public Cloud Computing in E-government. *Journal of Global Information Management, 24*(3), 71–89. doi:10.4018/JGIM.2016070104

Xu, L., & de Vrieze, P. (2016). Building Situational Applications for Virtual Enterprises. In I. Lee (Ed.), *Encyclopedia of E-Commerce Development, Implementation, and Management* (pp. 715–724). Hershey, PA: IGI Global. doi:10.4018/978-1-4666-9787-4.ch050

Yablonsky, S. (2018). Innovation Platforms: Data and Analytics Platforms. In *Multi-Sided Platforms (MSPs) and Sharing Strategies in the Digital Economy: Emerging Research and Opportunities* (pp. 72–95). Hershey, PA: IGI Global. doi:10.4018/978-1-5225-5457-8.ch003

Yusoff, A., Ahmad, N. H., & Halim, H. A. (2017). Agropreneurship among Gen Y in Malaysia: The Role of Academic Institutions. In N. Ahmad, T. Ramayah, H. Halim, & S. Rahman (Eds.), *Handbook of Research on Small and Medium Enterprises in Developing Countries* (pp. 23–47). Hershey, PA: IGI Global. doi:10.4018/978-1-5225-2165-5.ch002

Zanin, F., Comuzzi, E., & Costantini, A. (2018). The Effect of Business Strategy and Stock Market Listing on the Use of Risk Assessment Tools. In *Management Control Systems in Complex Settings: Emerging Research and Opportunities* (pp. 145–168). Hershey, PA: IGI Global. doi:10.4018/978-1-5225-3987-2.ch007

Zgheib, P. W. (2017). Corporate Innovation and Intrapreneurship in the Middle East. In P. Zgheib (Ed.), *Entrepreneurship and Business Innovation in the Middle East* (pp. 37–56). Hershey, PA: IGI Global. doi:10.4018/978-1-5225-2066-5.ch003

About the Contributors

Sara Elouadi is a Doctor of the Institute of Administration of Companies of Toulon in France, Sara Elouadi teaches finance and accounting in many establishments in France and Morocco. Currently, a professor and researcher in finance at Hassan II University in Casablanca, she is also the author of several scientific articles on employee shareholding and pluralist governance.

* * *

Nicolas Aubert is a professor at Aix-Marseille University graduate school of management (IAE), director of Aix-Marseille University research center in management (CERGAM) and Faculty fellow and mentor of the Rutgers University Institute for the study of employee ownership and profit sharing. he also serves as a member of the French employee ownership association scientific committee (FAS) and a member of the European Federation for Employee Shareownership (EFES).

Asmaa Boukhima holds a doctorate in legal sciences, specializing in Business Law. She has been a teacher since 2007 at the Faculty of Legal, Economic and Social Sciences Ain Sebaa Casablanca. She is a member of the Management, Information and Governance research laboratory (LARMIG) and head of the corporate law and socio-political environment research team. His research focuses on corporate governance, CSR, corporate difficulties, managerial responsibility, corporate legal culture. Since 2016, she has been responsible for the Master of Business Law.

Remigijus Civinskas is an associate professor in public policy and management at the Department of Public Administration of Vytautas Magnus University (Lithuania). Areas of interests: Employee financial participation, Industrial relations; Public policy studies; Public service management.

Miguel Cordova is an Associate Professor and Internationalization Leader for the Management Department and Management School at Pontificia Universidad Católica del Perú (PUCP). He holds a PhD in Strategic Management program of Consorcio de Universidades in Lima; he has doctoral studies at Copenhagen Business School, and an MBA of Centrum Católica. His research is oriented to Corporate Governance, Power and Influence in Organizations, Sustainable Supply Chain Management, Entrepreneurship, and International Business. He was visiting professor at Inseec Business School in París, Universidad del Desarrollo in Santiago de Chile, ESADE University in Barcelona, and UDEM in Monterrey. He is the coordinator of NEO Research Group at PUCP, Deputy Editor of 360 Journal of Management Sciences (Peru), and member of the editorial boards of CEA Management Journal (Colombia), Alcance Journal (Brazil), and International Journal of Applied Business and International Management (Indonesia). He received five research funds, a teaching innovation award, and a scholarship for teaching of the EFMD. He is Chair for Global and Regional Supply Chains track in the Academy of International Business (AIB) for the Latin America and the Caribbean Chapter, and an executive board member of the AIB Global Teaching & Education SIG.

Jaroslav Dvorak is a professor and head of the Department of Public Administration and Political Sciences at Klaipeda University, Lithuania. He was visiting researcher at Uppsala University (2017), Institute of Russian and Eurasian Studies, Sweden, and visiting professor at Bialystok Technical University (2017), Poland. Jaroslav Dvorak is involved in the editorial board of international scientific journals. He has executive and expert experience in national and international institutions. He was the Klaipeda University representative on the Klaipeda regional development council (2019-2021). He is a member of the Research Board at People Powered. Area of interests: Public policy, industrial relations, employee financial participation.

Hicham El Bouanani, holds a doctorate in Applied Mathematics from the University of Sud Toulon Var in France. Currently Dr. El Bouanani is a research professor at Hassan II University and I teach technical subjects such as: Analysis, Algebra, Statistics, Probability, Financial Mathematics, Multi-criteria Decision. Dr. El Bouanani is interested in the study of linear and nonlinear complementarity problems in different matrix situations and for objective to present more reliable and efficient algorithms.

Meriem El Kerbani is a PhD student at Hassan II University. She is working in her doctoral project on the behavioral repercussions of employee shareholding, especially in the context of Moroccan companies.

Houssam Errommani is a PhD student from Hassan II University and is working on their doctoral project on the financial repercussions of employee shareholding, especially in the context of listed companies.

Paul Katuse is a School of Business faculty member in the area of business administration specializing in Strategy. Mr. Katuse holds a D. in Strategic Management Trained in Business Administration and certified in several areas in Commerce and Business management related area. He has over 15 years as a business school faculty member, began as a graduate teaching assistant. He has cross-cultural and cross-national experience which spans three geographical locations in Asia, Africa and now Middle East. He has served as a faculty member, Institutional administrator, Consultant, Researcher and Quality assurance officer specifically an external examiner. He is Certified in pedagogical approaches, Teaching through Management Simulations, Case Study teaching. Research interests in change management, business impacts on society and globalization.

Tahar Khallouki is a PhD student in private law at the Management, Information and Governance Research Laboratory (L.A.R.M.I.G) - Hassan II-Casablanca University. Tahar is working on the following research problem: An attempt to assess the preventive scope of the procedure for preventing business difficulties instituted by the Moroccan legislator and its capacity to fight effectively against the mortality of SMEs which tends to take on a worrying scale.

ElKhamlichi Mohamed is assistant professor at the Higher Institute of Maritime Studies in Casablanca. He has held several teaching and academic positions with several higher education institutions in Morocco. He is a legal consultant for several national and foreign companies.

Wafae Nada Nejjar is a research professor at Hassan II University in Casablanca. She holds a PhD from the University of Orleans in France on corporate governance and financial communication. In parallel to her teaching career in Morocco and France, Wafae Nada Nejjar has held a position as financial analyst at the AMMC, the Moroccan stock market regulator. Her areas of expertise are corporate governance, management control, financial communication, corporate finance, and market finance.

Joyce Nzulwa is a faculty member in the College of Human Resource Development of the Jomo Kenyatta University of Agriculture & Technology. Her areas of expertise are Human Capital Development and Organizational Behaviour. She is a certified HR Professional, A trained Coach, Mediator and Counselor.

Mohamed Ouiakoub is Lecturer at IAE La Rochelle School of Management. He holds a double PhD in Management Sciences from La Rochelle University (France) and Cadi Ayyad University (Morocco). He teaches at undergraduate and masters level modules including management control, management accounting, quantitative finance, mathematics applied to management, data analysis and corporate strategy at La Rochelle University. His Research interests includes business model innovation, sustainable business model and micro-foundations of family business behavior.

Chibani Siham Doctor in Educational Sciences, currently professor - researcher at the International University of Casablanca. Certified coach in Personal Development and Self-esteem. Specialist in NLP and group dynamics. Expert in work psychology. Professor of Psychosociology, Communication and Personal Development, Work Psychology, Individual and Collective Behavior in a company, Professional Behavior, Applied Psychology, Scientific Work Methodology, Psycholinguistics & Psychopedagogy in various higher institutes, Faculties in Rabat and Casablanca. Consultant in a well-known recruitment firm in Casablanca; she conducts recruitment interviews, psychotechnical tests, reports and assessments. She is an active member of the scientific research network of the Observatoire de la Francophonie Economique of the University of Montreal – Canada.

Index

N

O

P

R

S

www.ingramcontent.com/pod-product-compliance
Lightning Source LLC
LaVergne TN
LVHW081326300926
849161LV00008B/1887